20.50

PHILOSOPHIES OF BEAUTY

PHILOSOPHIES OF BEAUTY

FROM SOCRATES TO ROBERT BRIDGES

BEING THE

SOURCES OF AESTHETIC THEORY

Selected and edited

by

E. F. CARRITT

*Fellow of University College and University
Lecturer, Oxford ; sometime Visiting Professor
in the University of Michigan*
Author of *The Theory of Beauty*

With a Foreword

by

D. W. PRALL

GREENWOOD PRESS, PUBLISHERS
WESTPORT, CONNECTICUT

Library of Congress Cataloging in Publication Data

Carritt, Edgar Frederick, 1876-   ed.
    Philosophies of beauty from Socrates to Robert Bridges.

    Reprint of the 1931 ed. published by Oxford University
Press, New York.
    Includes index.
    1. Aesthetics--Collected works. I. Title.
BH21.C3 1976   111.8'5   76-5885
ISBN 0-8371-8812-1

Originally published in 1931 by Oxford University Press,
Oxford

This reprint has been authorized by The Clarendon Press Oxford

Reprinted in 1976 by Greenwood Press,
a division of Williamhouse-Regency Inc.

Library of Congress Catalog Card Number 76-5885

ISBN 0-8371-8812-1

Printed in the United States of America

PREFACE

A BIBLIOGRAPHY of aesthetic writers up to the time of its publication (1892) can be found in Bosanquet's *History of Aesthetic*. A fuller and more recent one is the historical part of Croce's *Estetica*.[1] One still more complete for the period 1668–1762 is in Professor J. G. Robertson's *Genesis of Romantic Theory*, and one for the succeeding period in English is given by Mr. Hussey in *The Picturesque*.

I should naturally have wished to quote many more passages had I not been prevented by lack of space and, in one or two instances, by difficulties of copyright.

I should hardly have undertaken a selection had I not early been encouraged by Signor Croce's courteous permission to translate and quote him. I have also to thank him for his kindness in revising my translation. I am grateful for the friendly help of my colleague Lieutenant-Colonel Farquharson, who guided me in choosing passages from Marcus Aurelius, and most generously corrected my proofs. I am also indebted to three old friends and pupils: the Master of Balliol, who read my translation of Kant; Mr. Collingwood of Pembroke College, Oxford, who, besides giving me leave to quote him, revised my translations of Hegel and Gentile; and Professor Dodds of Birmingham University, who did the same for my translation of Plotinus and called my attention to an interesting passage. Father D'Arcy of Campion Hall, Oxford, has advised me on St. Thomas. Professor Prall of Harvard, to whom I ventured to introduce myself on the strength of an interest in his book, has allowed me to quote him and has kindly introduced me to an American public which I shall be very glad to meet. The idea of making such a compilation was suggested to me by my host Professor Blanshard of Swarthmore College. Mr. Etty, my brother-in-law, read my translations and suggested several simplifications.

[1] Translation by Douglas Ainslie (2nd edition).

I have generally preferred to attempt my own translations, except from the Russian, and to err on the side of freedom rather than obscurity. But, for different reasons, I did not care to rival Jeremy Collier's racy paraphrase of Marcus Aurelius, Haldane and Kemp's accurate translation of Schopenhauer, or that of Hanslick by Mr. Gustav Cohen. The excellent translation of Professor Bergson's *Le Rire* is exclusively authorized, so that here I had no choice.

It has naturally been difficult to hold the balance between ancients, moderns, and contemporaries, or again between English and foreign languages. If I have given undue space to English among the modern the reason is obvious. An excuse would be that readers of English may be more interested in writers who have directly influenced our own taste. Rather unwillingly, I have prefixed introductory notes to those more important quotations which might present difficulty to a reader unacquainted with their authors' general philosophy. These notes are as short as possible. I wish the whole book were shorter; but past thought is at least a prophylactic against present chatter.

My gratitude for free permission to quote is also due to the authors of the following books (or their representatives), or to the publishers.

ALEXANDER. *Space, Time, and Deity*. Macmillan.

BELL. *Art*. Chatto and Windus.

BERGSON. *Laughter*, transl. Brereton and Rothwell. Macmillan.

BOSANQUET. *A History of Aesthetic*. George Allen and Unwin.

    ,,   *Three Lectures on Aesthetic*. Macmillan.

BRADLEY, A. C. *Oxford Lectures on Poetry*. Macmillan.

DUCASSE. *The Philosophy of Art*. George Allen and Unwin.

FRY. *Vision and Design*. Chatto and Windus.

    ,,   *Transformations*. Chatto and Windus.

HANSLICK. *The Beautiful in Music*, transl. Cohen. Novello & Co.

HULME. *Speculations*. Kegan Paul, Trench, Trubner.

LAIRD. *The Idea of Value*. Cambridge University Press.

LEON. *Aesthetic Knowledge*. The Aristotelian Society.

„ *The Metaphysic of Quality*. The Editor of *Mind*.

LIPPS. *Empathy*. Engelmann.

MITCHELL. *Structure and Growth of the Mind*. Macmillan.

MOORE. *Principia Ethica*. Cambridge University Press.

NETTLESHIP, R. L. *Philosophical Remains*. Macmillan.

PATER. *Appreciations*. Macmillan.

PERRY. *General Theory of Value*. Longmans.

RICHARDS. *Principles of Literary Criticism*. Kegan Paul, Trench, Trubner.

RICHARDS, OGDEN, AND WOOD. *The Foundations of Aesthetics*. George Allen and Unwin.

ROSS. *The Right and the Good*. Oxford University Press.

SCHOPENHAUER. *The World as Will and Idea*, transl. Kemp and Haldane. Kegan Paul, Trench, Trubner.

SPENCER. *Principles of Psychology*, summarized by Collins. Spencer Trustees.

STACE. *The Meaning of Beauty*. Grant Richards and Humphrey Toulmin.

STEVENSON, R. A. M. *Velasquez*. Bell.

TOLSTOY. *What is Art?* transl. Maude. Oxford University Press.

I have also obtained leave from Messrs. Scribner's Sons for quotation from Professor SANTAYANA's *The Sense of Beauty*, from Messrs. George Allen and Unwin for Professor DEWEY's *Experience and Nature*, from Captain V. B. Holland and Messrs. Groves and Michaux of Paris for WILDE's *The Picture of Dorian Gray*, and from Mr. E. W. Titus of Paris for *La Filosofia dell'Arte* of Professor Gentile.

FOREWORD

By D. W. PRALL

THE bland and sometimes condescending ignorance of aesthetic theory among professional students of philosophy; the anxious distrust of it shown by literary scholars; the irresponsible derogation or dismissal of it by moralists; the misunderstanding and abuse of it by artists; the unjustified claims made upon it by critics and young intellectuals—all these are only too well matched by the ignorance, the prejudice, the confusion and the easy arrogance of those who have the dubious reputation of being aestheticians, a term taken roughly to mean those who—paradoxically enough in a scientific age—pretend to know the secrets of beauty and of art. As Mr. Carritt's selections will show, all of these rejections and acceptances of the subject are only too well authenticated in its historical exponents, most of these being philosophers who erred occasionally, or even habitually, by turning their attention away from metaphysics and logic and ethics to what even Santayana refuses to recognize as a 'separable thing called aesthetics'. He adds, for the applause of every teacher of a 'course' in that subject, that 'what has gone by the name of the philosophy of art' seems to him 'sheer verbiage'.

Aesthetics is in fact only a pseudo-science or pseudo-philosophy, a study that no self-respecting member of an academic faculty can safely devote himself to exclusively, or even mainly. Its subject-matter is such wavering and deceptive stuff as dreams are made of; its method is neither logical nor scientific, nor quite whole-heartedly and empirically matter of fact; and its results are an unhappy jargon, no worse than others in its infelicities and incomprehensibility, but without application in practice to test it and without an orthodox terminology to make it into an honest superstition or a thorough-going, soul-satisfying cult. It is neither useful to creative artists nor a help to amateurs in appreciation. It shifts from Hegelian 'moments' to 'empathic responses', from bits of minute critical analysis to irrelevant rhapsodic effusions, from 'the principles of aesthetic form' to the 'materials of beauty', from the media of the arts to the nature of tragedy or the sublime in nature. It uses the terms of all the arts and sciences as well as those of literary study and criticism and history. In an essay on aesthetics, value, for example, may mean one sort of colour variation, or the price of a picture, or 'any object of any interest'. And to make the confusion complete, it has been said that the 'home' of all values is God, and that God is irradiated in all beauty. Aesthetics is thus accurately designated in Spinoza's 'asylum of ignorance'. No wonder it is shunned and a little feared.

But aesthetics will not down, and the reasons are simple enough. They are given negatively in the *Republic*. They are given aristocratically in the *Poetics*. Plotinus knew them, and they were not disregarded by Aquinas. Aesthetic principles and aesthetic criteria were the last appeal of Leibniz in his rationalistic and admirably logical metaphysical system, as they are the last appeal in the mathematical formulation of modern scientific 'laws'. The seventeenth and eighteenth centuries took even the emotions and the passions seriously. Hobbes made them the necessary condition of 'either a great fancy or much judgement', the guiding principles of rational discourse, the very determinants of his 'laws of Nature', and thus the basis of political theory. Hume analysed them, classified them, and defined them, as Spinoza had also done. Burke could discourse—at least in his youth—on the Sublime. Kant could not finish his system, nor Hegel his, without venturing into the turbid shallows of a theory of the beautiful, and Ruskin and Tolstoy, moralists though they were, could not resist the question, What is art? or What is art for?, though their answers, significant as they may be, are not solely aesthetic theory.

We moderns are more enlightened. What science in the

Authorized Version cannot tell us we refuse to know. And science cannot yet say how we came to have eyes to see with, nor just how, having eyes, we do see colours and shapes through them, nor how our ears manage to hear the chords of music. How then can we respect a study the very data of which must be found in intuition—intuition which is itself only the word for the fact that we do so find data—a science the method of which is utterly unsettled and all of its results so indeterminately stated that we cannot be quite sure of their meaning, much less of their general bearing?

It is not, however, a question of respect, but one of necessity. The bearing of aesthetics upon the most abstract intellectual theories has become plain enough in modern relational logic. The questions of epistemology cannot even be formulated without disposing of the given, and the given, provided only that we have an actual meaning for this abused word, is the very subject-matter of aesthetic analysis. If there is properly such a thing as metaphysics, then the qualitative aspects of experience are its primary concern and its ultimate criteria. And the classification of sensory qualities as felt is the first business of aesthetics. The symbolic nature of discourse in linguistic form is only too obviously fundamental in any adequate critical estimate of any philosophical theory of anything; and the direct attack on language as the medium of communication and expression for discourse is neither philology nor literary history, nor yet investigations into the origin of speech, but the analysis of the medium as used. Since language is both a useful and a fine art, its nature and medium as of one art among the many others are the chief subject-matter of aesthetics.

Until we admit that aesthetic theory is one of our fundamental theoretical needs, and until, in spite of our glaring and childishly stubborn ignorance of it, and our lack of method, we turn to it with vigour and seriousness, we shall no doubt continue to think that all values are intrinsically and ultimately moral or religious, and that the language in which we confidently pursue our studies is somehow transparent and directly intelligible. But these things can hardly be so, as even the despised aestheticians have already made fairly clear. The sense in which knowledge itself is an artistic creation has been suggested by Alexander, and Ogden and Richards have at least indicated some of the opacity inherent in the most perspicuous and supposedly exact linguistic discourse. Although current aesthetics is not limited to this Socratic programme, it does exhibit the genuineness of our ignorance upon matters about which we discourse only too fluently, and thus it does offer us a modicum of philosophical wisdom.

Moreover, any slightest grasp of the subject will show us that we neither hear the music that is played to us nor see the beauties we pretend to admire in pictures and buildings. The aesthetician is not so much concerned to fight bad taste as to fight good taste. He would show the emptiness it relies on in essentials. He would point out the elementary discriminations that it fails to make, discriminations without which works of art cannot be apprehended as those coherent unities that we all judge verbally, our ease in judgement varying inversely with the fullness of our actual appreciative apprehension. The aesthetician would remind us that, with relation to art, judging of relative merit is for the most part irrelevant. In fact it is all sheer irrelevance unless certain of these primary discriminations have been almost automatically made, though most of us are so innocent here that only years of perceptual training would reveal to us this innocence for the sheer ignorance that it is, the blank unawareness of most of the ways in which our world impinges upon acute and co-ordinated senses in the infinite variegations of its appearance. The aesthetician would first of all have nature and works of art apprehended as they are and thus appreciated. Judging them he would leave to others, less interested, perhaps, in direct valuing than in sophisticated and largely verbal evaluations.

But if all this is so, it is clear enough that what we lack is systematic aesthetic theory or some beginnings of such theory and not historical 'Selections in Aesthetics'; for there is surely some truth in Mr. Whitehead's dictum that 'a science which hesitates to forget its founders is lost'. Since aesthetics has scarcely been found, remembering its founders at the present juncture would seem plain abortion.

But perhaps one need not share this fear of memory. Perhaps the dictum does not quite apply to what is not yet a science or is destined never to become one. At any rate another of Mr. Whitehead's theses is altogether to the point. One can make theories neat, he tells us, in proportion as one's data are confined, and the easiest confines to draw are those of one's own time. Since we are only at the point of essaying aesthetic theory, we must beware of an unhistorical view.

One illustration of the dangerous benefits of the history of theory will suffice. Modernistic art likes to call itself abstract. But that for some centuries art has been characteristically expressive we are likely to take as authenticated fact. And it is only one step further to the generalization that art as such is expressive, that its defining function is the objective specification of feelings and emotions in a given medium. There is not much doubt that in some just sense this is so, a sense which has still to be made fully determinate, however, in the face of the current claim to abstractness of pattern as the prime criterion of strictly artistic achievement. We need then to notice what Bosanquet has pointed out: that this principle of expression, what he calls 'the characteristic', is the 'central idea of modern aesthetic', first fully and explicitly enunciated by Goethe and Schiller and the contributors to their *Horen*. But there was art, and there were aesthetic theories, centuries before Goethe and Schiller discussed these matters. If Bosanquet is right, what now seems to us so obvious as to the expressive character of art was not even explicitly understood by Plato or Aristotle; and the significant obverse of this is that what *was* explicitly understood by them and what was explicitly understood by a multitude of theorists down to 1800, is no doubt less obvious to us on the basis of our current data in the arts than it was on the basis of theirs. Hence the illumination their theories may offer beyond those provincial confines that our own temporal perspective might so easily mistake for the boundaries of the universe.

But there can after all be no real need for defending a minimum of attention to the famous historical contributions to aesthetic theory, and if Mr. Carritt's selections and omissions in the case of his contemporaries raise objections in their minds, that is no doubt unavoidable. Contemporary books on aesthetics are in any case easily available. At any rate there is not the least reason for apology or excuse for this volume; the obviously appropriate feeling for it is gratitude. The table of contents indicates the extremely wide reading from which the selections have been made. The judgement and learning at Mr. Carritt's disposal in making them, all readers of his *Theory of Beauty* are familiar with. The actual labour of translation in some cases, as well as the editing, we take too easily for granted, of course; but if such labour was ever needed, surely it was needed here. And to beginners, as well as to any student less widely read than the editor, his selections are a fairly priceless offering, the value of which must be patent to a much larger class of readers than those college teachers of aesthetics who will realize it in the practical convenience of a wanted text.

We may hope that if the volume does nothing else, it will acquaint us a little more fully with some of the questions of aesthetics as made out and sometimes answered by the philosophers of the centuries, so that we may now despise the subject intelligently and with information, as becomes modern scholars. Those of us who are weak enough to be seduced by an interest in the questions themselves may even feel that the volume exhibits high precedent for our weakness, and we may hope that in time—though this is perhaps chimerical—more competent, more learned, and more scientifically expert minds may see its fundamental bearing and the necessity for solving its problems, if we are not to go on building up philosophical theories of symbolism and of knowledge and of value, scientific theories of perception and of language, and critical theories of prose and poetry and painting and sculpture and music over the hollow chasm of an aesthetic ignorance into which they might at any moment so easily collapse.

CONTENTS

INTRODUCTION

IN choosing these extracts I gave some weight to their literary merit, more to their historical interest, and most to their philosophical importance. How literary merit should be defined I must leave those to judge who have digested the book; but I mean that when the same view has been expressed by two writers I preferred the clearer, shorter, and more lively expression unless the other were more interesting for historical reasons. Historical interest is complex. It allows some credit to an author for originality, some for his reputation in other fields—as that he was a good poet or painter as well as a thinker—and much for the influence of his work upon posterity. Our judgement of philosophical importance must depend upon what we think the aim of philosophy to be. One of my reasons for giving so large a proportion of my space to Plato was that he helps us more than later writers to make up our minds on this question. In the time of Socrates people were evidently used to discussing whether particular works of art and nature were beautiful, but the question which he is represented as asking about the nature of beauty seems to have been new. And what he meant by it is fairly clear. He was convinced that it is by no linguistic accident that we call various things beautiful. We really recognize in them one common character, and this character, he thought, must be capable of definition. That is, we must be able to say what other common and peculiar quality or relation, or combination of qualities or relations, beautiful things have, in virtue of which they are all beautiful. Plato appears to have carried on the inquiry accepting the same presuppositions. On another topic he seems to represent Socrates as suggesting that, if a number of things have one common quality or relation, we cannot assume that they have any other.[1] But about beauty he perhaps assumed this without scruple.

[1] *Philebus*, 12–13.

If I had to choose the two authors who might give most insight into what is meant by aesthetic, I should choose one from each end of the series, Plato and Croce. If I had to choose one it would be Plato. For while there is hardly any notable progenitor who has not left his mark among the features of the modern theory, the ancient contained the seed of all within its loins. And here it seems easier to understand the earlier than the developed stage. For through the skill of Socrates the Platonic philosophy was born fully formed.

Plato makes it pretty clear that beauty is not just truth nor edification. So long as people go to artists for their politics, their science, or their religion because the artists' work is beautiful or witty, so long censorship has a good case. For the Homeric poems are very beautiful and very poor guides. And yet beauty does, as Plato says, 'imitate' or correspond to states of mind as well as to physical objects; for it is no physical thing like gold, but rather some relation of things to our minds, perhaps to our purposes. Yet to identify beauty with usefulness, he thought, would degrade it; it must at least be what is useful for the highest purpose—truly profitable—and have its own intrinsic charm or pleasantness as well. There is nothing more obviously delightful than the beauties of nature and of art, and Plato thinks that what distinguishes them from other delightful things, is that they are also profitable, or at least harmless. Art is only to be condemned outright when it forsakes beauty and aims at an imitation of what is bad. So it might seem that Plato has fallen back into the moralistic heresy against which he had protested, and that, after all, we cannot accompany him far. But if this be an error in him, it is an error which more grievously beset his successors, and from which the escape was slow and difficult, only fully achieved by Croce, and still maintained by Croce's critics to be no error but the truth.[1]

Aristotle would seem to make little advance. He is not

---

[1] But see Postscript to this Introduction.

satisfied with the Platonic view, but his efforts to amend it are seldom improvements, though they have been more widely accepted. Seeing that the bad effect of drama upon us had been exaggerated, he suggested that its bad effect is slight and momentary and in the end beneficial like that of a purge. Seeing that the degree to which artists copy nature had been exaggerated, he suggested that they copy not particular things but universals. About the universal character of beauty itself he has only to repeat that it depends upon a certain size and an order of parts. Drama arises from a combination of our instinctive love of such order, here manifested as rhythm, with our love of imitation.

Aristotle dominated such aesthetic theory as existed in the Middle Ages and the Renaissance. The 'romantic revival' was a conflict fought out through the eighteenth century, in which the two parties ranged themselves one with Aristotle and the other with 'Longinus', whose treatise on sublimity, having been popularized by Boileau, at first ran in double harness with the *Poetics*, till the yokefellows proved unequal.

The author of the essay *De Sublimitate* brought into relief elements of Plato's thought which Aristotle's implied criticism had shown to need elucidation. And he has an advantage over them both in being able to survey two languages and a period, however brief, of artistic development and of change in taste. This leads him to think that there may be two types of beauty in both art and nature, one of which has unaccountably usurped the generic name, while the other is called lofty, elevated, great. The latter appeals to a corresponding character or capacity of our own, which we recognize as embodied in it, while the character of beauty in the narrow sense is mere inoffensiveness. The historical influence of this distinction has been very great; it shows itself whenever, owing to new fashions in art, or new discoveries in archaeology, men become acutely conscious of discrepancy among their own tastes or between the tastes of themselves and their fathers. Addison, Burke, Kant, the upholders of Shakespeare against Jonson in this country and against Racine on the Continent, were in this tradition. But in England the very number of the aesthetic species which were suggested discredited the tendency. After Burke we get two sublimities, one of size and one of fear, and we also get several species of beauty proper, suggested chiefly by the national arts of landscape painting and gardening. Uvedale Price distinguishes the Picturesque, and others the Romantic, and the Strange.

Hegel, though retaining and narrowing the sublime, transferred its wider meaning to Symbolical or primitive and to Romantic art in contrast with the Classical. He thus substituted for two species of beauty three, and identified these with periods of development, though he also suggested that the typically classical or beautiful art is sculpture, while the typically symbolical is architecture and the typically romantic are painting, poetry, and music. Schopenhauer similarly, though he retained the term sublime with a narrow meaning, discovered its more profound implications only in music. All other beautiful things embodied the Will in Forms which disguised it; music revealed in stark nakedness the infinite force which has begotten and will destroy us. Nietzsche, combining Hegel with Schopenhauer, as one might oil with vinegar, developed the contrast between musical and other beauties into one between two types of art, that in which crude passion and that in which formal beauty predominated. Typical of the first was the savage dance, and of the second Homer's epic, which were to find their synthesis in Greek tragedy. But beauty's lute once riven could not be patched up. Some modern writers distinguish two kinds of art, which either alternate in recurring cycles or satisfy different types of mind. One is the optimistic naturalism of Greece, of the Renaissance, of the romantics, which sympathizes with the joy of life; the other is the sombre genius of Egypt, Byzantium, and per-

haps of our own day, which turns away from life to the
rigidity of formal patterns. Only Croce, unfolding
Hegel's implication, points out that these distinctions
are not between 'kinds' but between elements of beauty.
Every beautiful thing must have a 'matter,' which
he holds to be feeling or will, and a sensible 'form'
which expresses it. Neither could be beautiful alone.

The great merit of Croce's theory is that, more clearly
than any writer since Plato, he emphasizes the unity of
beauty. And his strongest argument is his appeal to the
history of aesthetics, his contention that all theories
opposed to his own have only gained plausibility by
admitting two or more realms of beauty, to but one of
which their explanations properly apply. Still, it may
be possible to accept his Platonic assertion that beauty
is a real universal and yet to doubt whether he has
answered the Platonic question—What is that which
by its presence in all beautiful things renders them
beautiful?

Followers of Croce have mainly contented themselves
with emphasizing one side of his theory at the expense of
the other: either that beauty is expression or that it is
apprehension of the individual. His critics may be very
roughly labelled as going either 'back to Kant' and to
beauty's purely formal character, or 'back to Hegel' and
its sensuous revelation of truth. More original, if confused, work has perhaps been done from the starting
point of psychology. Psychological writers on aesthetics
fall into two main schools. Herbart and his followers
maintain the Kantian tradition that beauty consists in a
certain form or relation of parts in what is apprehended.
The followers of Lipps accept his development of the neo-
Platonic view, as later modified by the associationists,
and believe that we ascribe beauty to all things into
which we can read a spirit analogous to our own.
These two theories nearly correspond to the two impulses which Aristotle found satisfied by drama, the
instinct for rhythm and the instinct for imitation;

especially if we remember the Platonic suggestion that what music imitates is a state of mind.[1]

This controversy between the aesthetics of form and of expression, which has run through the whole history of philosophy, and is still a crux of the subject, is closely connected, though not identical, with another question, even more burning in modern times, the question whether beauty is on the one hand a quality of things or on the other only a relation to ourselves (like novelty) which arouses in us a certain emotion—an attitude of ours to things. The questions are connected, because if beauty is expressiveness it would seem to be a relation to us; if it is a relation between the parts of things it is a character of the things. They are not identical, because, if beauty is a relation to us, it need not be the relation of expressiveness; if it is a character of the things, that character need not be the interrelation of their parts.

The problem whether beauty is a quality of things or a relation to us is complicated by the use of the terms objective and subjective. It is perhaps this usage which since Berkeley has entangled the question with the general philosophical issue between idealists and realists. Idealists have hesitated to allow that beauty could be 'objective' and like Croce, have tended to make it expressive. Realists, like Reid and Professor Moore, have thought to grind their axe by making it a real quality of things. Neither prejudice was justified. For, since all idealists admit degrees of 'objectivity' in our experience, beauty might conceivably have the maximum degree. Hegel, not only an idealist but an expressionist, gave beauty 'objectivity' as the self-expression of objective or universal reason. And since all realists allow some 'subjectivity' to novelty and pleasantness, they have perhaps only discredited their cause by denying this of beauty.

Among contemporaries Mr. Richards and Professor

[1] It would be out of place here to argue for my acceptance of the usual interpretation of the passage in the *Poetics* quoted below, as against the great authority of Professor Bywater. See R. P. Hardie in *Mind*, 1895.

Dewey hold that beauty is a relation, but a relation among our own feelings or 'attitudes'. The relation, being a kind of harmony, seems more akin to Croce's emotionally coherent imagination than its upholders might be prepared to grant. The chief difference between the supporters of this view and the expressionists seems to be that the former are more or less frankly hedonistic or pragmatist or moral in their account of art. The wheel has come full circle; we seem back with Plato, or perhaps only with Tolstoy.

If beauty be a relation to us, it remains to determine what that relation is, and further, if the relation be one of expression, whether what is expressed is reason or will and desire. If beauty be a quality of things it remains to determine what that quality is, and further, if the quality be an interrelation of parts, what interrelation. To this last question no very clear answer appears. The suggestion that it is an interrelation analogous to the interrelation of the parts of the universe gives more warmth than light. The essential task for either formalism or expressionism is to show that it covers the whole field of beauty. Expressionists have generally faced this task with more courage. Formalists have sometimes tried to shirk it by denying beauty where it seems most unquestionably present, as in lyric poetry and organic life. Plato, in the *Hippias Major*, had already refuted such devices.

PS.—Professor Gentile's book appeared while my own was in the press, but, with his permission, I have been able to include some extracts from it. His criticisms of Croce speak for themselves. On his own view, as I understand it, everything must *have* beauty since everything is the creation of spirit, and must therefore contain the subjective form of feeling as well as the objective matter of what is thought. By a subsequent act of thinking (and only in act is the spirit real) we may analyse the dead thought and detect within it the subjective element which we *call* beauty.

XENOPHON
About 430–350 B.C.

The teachings of Socrates (about 469–399 B.C.) are presented much more simply by Xenophon than by Plato. There was probably much in them that he did not understand and he surely added nothing profound of his own as Plato did. We can only conjecture which gives the truer account. Socrates tried to define universals such as beauty and justice, and he tested the definitions by acknowledged instances.

Memorabilia [1]

Bk. III, Ch. viii, §§ 4–7. When Aristippus asked Socrates if he recognized anything as beautiful, he replied, 'Yes, many things.'

A. Are they all alike?

S. No, some of them as different as possible.

A. But how can a thing unlike what is beautiful be beautiful?

S. Why, because a man who is a beautiful runner is unlike another who is a beautiful wrestler, and a shield which is a beauty for defence is as different as possible from a javelin which is a beauty for speed and power.

A. You answer me just as you did when I asked whether you recognized anything as good.

S. Then do you think that good and beautiful are two different things? Don't you know that whatever is beautiful is also good from the same point of view? For instance, virtue is not good from one point of view and beautiful from another; and again of men we say handsome is that handsome does.[2] So too with our bodies; and in short everything which we use is considered both good and beautiful from the same point of view, namely its use.

A. Why then, is a dung-basket a beautiful thing?

S. Of course it is, and a golden shield is ugly, if the one be beautifully fitted to its purpose and the other ill.

---

[1] There is a translation by Marchant (Loeb Classics).

[2] τὸ αὐτό τε καὶ πρὸς τὰ αὐτὰ καλοὶ κἀγαθοὶ λέγονται.

A. Do you mean then that the same things are both beautiful and ugly?

S. Of course I do, and good and bad too.[1] For what is good for hunger is often bad for a fever and what is beautiful in running is ugly in wrestling, and conversely. For everything is good and beautiful for whatever purpose it serves well, but bad and ugly for what it does not.

PLATO

428–348 B.C.

The central doctrine of Plato's philosophy is that a particular thing is essentially incapable of being known with scientific certainty. Science always deals with universals, the 'forms' or essential characters of things, and the relations of these to one another. A universal, such as equality or beauty, is always what it is and may be understood. A particular thing is constantly changing and has many different aspects; it is equal to one thing but unequal to another, and every moment it is growing or decreasing in size. In its particularity it can never be understood, it is only perceived with the senses, and the senses are notoriously misleading; their evidence is corrupted by time, by distance, by contrast, and, above all, by the passions.

It is true that as practical men we have to deal with particular things. But here we are in the sphere of guess-work and rules-of-thumb, very different from the serene certainties of science. Yet Plato thinks that the man of science who knows the universal characters and relations of things is best fitted to form true opinions about particular instances. This doctrine affects Plato's aesthetic doctrine in several ways. First, it will obviously be incumbent upon him to discover the intelligible universal character of beautiful things, instead of resting content in the sensuous apprehension of them as instances of beauty. Next, since truth is only to be got about universals, and artists are only concerned with particular things, it will be vitally necessary for him to warn us against the error of mistaking art for truth, of accepting its guidance, instead of that of reason, in morals or politics or religion. The merely practical man, intent upon the perishable things which he can see or taste or handle, is living,

[1] Cf. Moore, p. 250; Ross, p. 319.

according to Plato, in a world of illusion; but the man intent upon pictures, poetry, and music is mocked by the shadow of an illusion. He takes the image of an image for the reality. As a legislator especially, Plato mistrusts art, which stirs up the passions and hurries men into sentimental, vainglorious, or revengeful action when they should wait upon the calm voice of reason.

Hippias Major[1]

[Socrates consults Hippias how to answer an imaginary inquiry what beauty is.]

287 c. *Socrates.* Is it not by having wisdom that wise men are wise and by having goodness that all good things are good?

Hippias. Of course.

S. Then wisdom and goodness must be real, for unrealities would not have served the purpose.

H. Certainly they are real.

S. And are not all beautiful things then beautiful by having beauty?

H. That is the way of it.

S. Then beauty too is something real?

H. Real. Why ask?

S. 'Tell me then,' my questioner will say, 'what this beauty is.'

H. Does not this inquirer really want to learn what is beautiful, Socrates?

S. I think not, Hippias, but rather what beauty is.

H. What is the difference?

S. Don't you see any?

H. No, for there is none.

S. Of course you know best. All the same, my friend, consider: he does not ask you what is beautiful but what is beauty.

H. I understand, my friend. And I will give him an answer that cannot be refuted. For, Socrates, to tell the truth, a beautiful girl is surely a beauty.

---

[1] There is a scarce and mediocre eighteenth-century translation by Floyer Sydenham. The ascription to Plato has been questioned.

S. A good answer, Hippias, and plausible indeed. If I give that answer shall I really have answered [288] the question rightly and be safe from refutation?

H. Why, how could you be refuted, Socrates, where all men agree with you, and every one that hears will bear witness to the truth?

S. Well, so be it. But let me take up your reply for myself, Hippias. My questioner will ask me something of this sort: 'Come, Socrates, tell me: what must the nature of beauty be to make all the things beautiful which you call so?' Shall I then say that the beauty that can make them all beautiful is a beautiful girl?

H. Why, do you think he will try to maintain that what you mention is not a beauty? Or if he does try will he not make himself ridiculous?

S. I am sure enough that he will try, my good sir; but whether he will make himself ridiculous we shall see. But I should like to tell you what he will say.

H. Tell me then.

[Beauty is a single Universal existing only in differences.]

S. 'You are delicious, Socrates,' he will say. 'Is not a beautiful mare beautiful, such as the holy oracle praised?' Can we help admitting that a mare is a beauty, if it be a beautiful one? For how could we venture to deny that beauty is beautiful?

H. True enough, Socrates. For the inspired saying was right. We have lovely mares in my country.

S. 'Well,' he will go on, 'what about a beautiful lyre? Is there not beauty there?' Shall we agree, Hippias?

H. Yes.

S. And after that he will say, as I can pretty well guess from his character, 'But, my good man, what about a beautiful porridge-pot? Has that no beauty then?'

H. Oh, Socrates, who is he? A philistine, I feel sure, to name things so inappropriate to the dignity of our subject.

S. Just what he is, Hippias, grossly unimaginative, thinking of nothing but the facts. Still he must be answered, and I will sketch the answer. If the porridge-pot is turned out by a good potter, smooth and round and well baked, like some of those beautiful two-handled porridge-pots, the lovely six-pint size—if that is the kind of porridge-pot in question, we must allow it to be beautiful. For how could we say there is not beauty when there is?

H. We must not do that, Socrates.

S. 'Then,' he will say, 'a beautiful porridge-pot is a thing of beauty? Answer me.'

H. Why, Socrates, I believe it is. Even a thing like that is beautiful if it is beautifully made. But no goods like that deserve to be put in the same class of beauty as a beautiful horse or girl or other real beauty.

289. *S.* Very good. Then I understand, Hippias, that this is what I must reply to our questioner: 'My dear man, do you not see that Heracleitus was right, when he said that of course the most beautiful ape is ugly compared with the human species? And so, our sage Hippias says, the most beautiful porridge-pot is ugly compared with the fair sex.' Is that right, Hippias?

H. That is just the right answer, Socrates.

S. Listen then, for I know well enough what he will say next:—'But what follows, Socrates? If we compare the class of girls with the class of gods, will it not suffer the fate of the porridge-pots compared with the girls? Will not the most beautiful girl seem ugly? Does not Heracleitus, whose evidence you cite, actually say that the wisest man would seem an ape beside the gods for wisdom and beauty and everything else?' Must we agree, Hippias, that the most beautiful girl is ugly if classed among gods?

H. Nobody could deny that, Socrates.

S. But if we grant it, he will laugh and say: 'Do you remember, then, what I asked you, Socrates?' 'Yes,' I shall answer, 'what beauty is in itself.' 'And then,' he will reply, 'though you were asked about beauty, do you name in your answer something which, as you confess yourself, may just as well be called ugly as beautiful?'

'It looks like it,' I shall have to say; or what do you advise me to say?

H. Just that. For in fact he will be right in saying that the human species is not beautiful, when compared with gods.

S. 'But,' he will say, 'if I had begun by asking you what is both beautiful and ugly, would not the answer you have just given me have been a very good one? And do you still think that the true beauty, to which all things owe their charm, so that they look beautiful when they have this essential character,[1] can be a girl or a horse or a lyre?'

[Things are not beautiful absolutely, but only in certain contexts.]

H. Why, Socrates, if all he wants is to be told what the beauty is to which all things owe their charm so that they look beautiful when it is added to them, nothing could be easier. He must be a very simple and inartistic person. For if you answer him that the beauty he is asking about is nothing but gold, he will be silenced and will not try to refute you. For I suppose we all know that when a thing is gilded, even if it were ugly before, it will look beautiful through the addition of gold.

S. You do not know what a brute the man is, Hippias, and how hard to please.

H. What of that, Socrates? For if he is not pleased when he is told the truth, he will make himself ridiculous. [290]

S. And yet he will be so far from accepting this answer that he will be quite sarcastic with me and will say: 'Is your head so swollen then, that you think Pheidias a bad artist?' to which I suppose I must say, No.

H. That would be right, Socrates.

S. Of course. Yet as soon as I have admitted that Pheidias was a good artist, he will say: 'Do you suppose that Pheidias was unaware of this beauty you speak of?' 'Why?' I shall ask. And he will reply: 'Because he did

---

[1] εἶδος.

not make his Athene's eyes of gold, nor the rest of her face, nor the hands and feet, but of ivory, though gold would have made her look more beautiful. And this mistake must have been due to his ignorance of the fact that, as you say, it is gold which gives beauty to everything.' What are we to say to that, Hippias?

H. Nothing very difficult. We shall say that Pheidias was quite right. For I suppose ivory is beautiful too.

S. 'But why,' he will ask, 'did he work the eyeballs not in ivory but in stone, exquisitely matching the stone to the ivory. Or is beautiful stone beauty too?

H. In its right place, we must agree that it is.

S. And if he asks whether it is ugly when out of place, shall I agree or not?

H. You must agree.

S. 'Then,' he will say, 'does your wisdom come to this, that ivory and gold make things look beautiful when they are appropriate, but, otherwise, ugly?' Must we retract, or confess that he has the right of it?[1]

. . . . . .

293 D. *H.* Explain, Socrates.

S. 'My dear Socrates', my friend will say, 'stop giving this sort of answer, for it is too simple and easy to refute; and see whether you think beauty is something of the kind we touched on just now in our discussion, when we said that gold is beautiful where it is becoming but not otherwise, and the same with other materials to which this can be applied. See if it does not turn out that beauty can be identified with what is becoming and with the character of comeliness itself.' For my part, I have got into a way of agreeing whenever he says things like this, for I see no escape; but do you think that what is becoming is beautiful?

H. Absolutely so, Socrates.

S. Let us consider it, for fear we might be mistaken.

H. Go on, then.

[1] Cf. Hegel, p. 162.

[If the beauty of things depends on their context, does it arise from their own nature or from our way of regarding them?]

S. Then look at it in this way. Do we mean by [294] *becomingness* what makes everything that has it really beautiful or only apparently so, or neither of the two?

H. I think it is what makes things seem beautiful. For instance, if even a clumsy man put on clothes and shoes that fit him he looks handsomer.

S. Then if becomingness makes things appear more beautiful than they are, it would be a kind of illusion of beauty, and not what we are looking for, Hippias. For I imagine we are asking what it is in virtue of which all beautiful things are beautiful; just as we might ask in virtue of what great things are great and reply that it is in virtue of outmeasuring others; for that makes anything great, and, whatever size things look, if they outmeasure others, great they must be. And so we speak of beauty: what can it be in virtue of which all beautiful things are so, whether they seem so or not? It cannot be becomingness, for that makes things look more beautiful than they are, as you say, and conceals the facts. Our business, however, is to try to tell what makes things beautiful, as I said just now, whether they seem so or not. That is what we are looking for if we are looking for beauty.

H. But becomingness, Socrates, makes everything which has it both really and apparently beautiful.

S. Then it is impossible for things really beautiful not to appear so, since they must have what makes them appear so.'

H. It is.

S. Are we to agree then, Hippias, that all things which are really beautiful, including customs and ways of life, are also thought beautiful and always seem so to all men? Or is it just the opposite—that men fail to recognize them and there is more dispute and contention about them than about anything, both privately between individuals and publicly between states?

H. It would be truer that men fail to recognize what is beautiful, Socrates.

S. But it would not have been so, I suppose, if things had the appearance as well as the reality. And they would have had, if becomingness were beauty and made things apparently as well as really beautiful. So becomingness, if that is what makes things beautiful, would be beauty, which is what we are looking for, but would not be what makes things look beautiful. But if it is what makes them look beautiful, it would not be beauty, nor what we want. For beauty makes things really beautiful, but the same cause could never give things both the reality and the appearance of beauty or of any other quality. So let us make up our minds whether we think becomingness makes things really or only apparently beautiful.[1]

H. Apparently, in my view, Socrates.

S. Upon my word, Hippias, beauty has given us the slip, and every chance of knowing what in the world it is has vanished. For, anyhow, what is becoming has turned out quite other than beautiful.

H. So it has, Socrates, and I swear it was the last thing I expected.

295. *S.* Still, let us stick to it a little together. I still have hopes that the mysterious nature of beauty will be revealed.

. . . . . .

[Are beautiful things those which are useful?]

295 B. Now then, reflect on what you think beauty really is. I offer as a definition—and examine it carefully for fear I should be saying something silly—that we should say whatever is useful is beautiful. This was what gave me the idea; we do not call eyes beautiful if they look blind, do we? but only if they look useful and able to see.

H. If they look useful.

S. And we speak of the beauty of the whole body in the same way, whether for running or wrestling; and so too among beasts, we speak of a beautiful horse, or cock, or

[1] Cf. Hegel, p. 160.

quail; and chattels of all kinds and land-carriages and sea-going vessels such as triremes, and instruments of music and of other crafts? Add, if you like, institutions and ways of life. We call all these beautiful in much the same sense. We consider the origin and fashion and place of each thing, and if it be useful, so far as it is useful and when and where it is useful we call it beautiful, but what is quite useless, ugly. Do you agree, Hippias?

H. Yes.

S. Then now we are right in saying that what is useful is unquestionably beautiful?

H. Quite right.

S. And what can effect anything is useful for what it can effect, but the ineffective is useless?

H. Certainly.

S. Efficiency, then, is beauty and inefficiency ugliness?

H. Absolutely. All the evidence shows we are right, and [296] especially that of politics. For in political life, and in the service of a man's country, power is what is most admired,[1] but nobody has a taste for inefficiency.

S. True enough, Hippias, and, in heaven's name, does not that make wisdom the most beautiful of all things and ignorance the ugliest?

H. Why, what do you suppose, Socrates?

S. Still, take care where we are going together, for once more I am frightened at what we may be saying.

H. But what are you afraid of now, Socrates? For this time at any rate your argument has come on beautifully.

[But beautiful things cannot be those which are useful for bad ends; are they then those which are profitable or edifying?]

S. I hope it may be so, but help me to consider this. Could a man do anything for which he had neither the knowledge nor any kind of ability?

H. Impossible. How could he do what he was not able to do?

S. And is it not true that people who go wrong and

---

[1] καλλιστον . . . αἴσχιστον.

behave badly or produce bad work in spite of all their efforts, would never have gone wrong had they been unable?

H. Clearly.

S. But people are able to do things by ability—or, anyhow, surely not by inability.

H. No, not that.

S. But anybody who does anything must be able?

H. Yes.

S. But all men from their childhood do much more evil than good, and go wrong for all their efforts.

H. True.

S. Well then, are we to call beautiful this ability to go wrong and these things which are useful but only for wrong ends? Or are they just the opposite?

H. Just the opposite, I think, Socrates.

S. Then what is efficient and useful does not seem to be our beautiful, Hippias.

H. Only if it effects good and is useful for that.

S. That idea is done for, then, that to be beautiful it is enough for a thing to be efficient and useful. But what we meant in our hearts to say was really this, that what is useful and efficient for some good purpose is beautiful?

H. I think so.

S. And that is what is profitable, is it not?

H. Certainly.

S. And so beautiful bodies and beautiful ways and wisdom and all the things we mentioned just now are beautiful because they are profitable.

H. Clearly.

S. So we agree that profitableness and beauty are identical?

H. Certainly.

S. But what is profitable is what produces something good.

H. Yes.

.   .   .   .

297 B. *S.* Then if beauty is the cause of goodness, goodness would be produced by beauty; and that, it

seems, is why we value right-mindedness[1] and all other beautiful qualities, because their result and offspring, which is the good, is valuable. And our conclusions seem to show that what is beautiful is a kind of father to what is good.

H. Excellent. You speak truly, Socrates.

S. Then is this true, too, that neither is the father the son nor the son the father?

H. Excellently true.

S. Nor is the cause its product nor yet the product its cause.

H. Quite right.

[Or are beautiful things rather those which are intrinsically good —as some pleasures seem to be?]

S. Then upon my word, my dear man, what is beautiful cannot be good nor what is good beautiful. Or do you think it possible after what we have said?

H. Upon my word, I think not.

S. Then is it our good will and pleasure to vote that what is beautiful is not good nor what is good beautiful?

H. Upon my word, it is not my pleasure at all.

S. Hear, hear. And it pleases me less than anything we have said yet.

H. So I see.

S. I am afraid, then, our theory that the profitable, or the useful, or the efficient cause of good is beautiful is not, as we supposed just now, the best of all; but, if possible, it is more absurd than our first theories when we said that a girl was beauty, or any of the other things we mentioned at first.

H. So it seems.

S. And for my part, Hippias, I do not know what to do about it. I am puzzled. Have you anything to say?

H. Not off-hand. But, as I said before, I am sure I shall find something with thought.

S. But I feel so eager to know the answer that I cannot

_____
[1] φρόνησιν

wait while you think. Why, indeed, I do believe I have just found a sort of clue. Look here. Suppose we said that whatever gives us pleasure, not any sort of pleasure, but pleasure of the eye or ear, is beautiful; could we [298] find any arguments against that? For surely, Hippias, beautiful men and colour-patterns and pictures and statues please us when we see them; and beautiful voices and all music and poetry and prose and legendary stories have the same effect. Do you think if we answered our persistent friend, 'We submit that what pleases through ear and eye is beautiful,' his persistence would be ended?

H. Now at last, Socrates, I am satisfied that beauty is well defined.

[But there is one same beauty in pleasant sights and sounds. This is not pleasantness, for some pleasant things are ugly. What else is common to pleasant sights and sounds, and to them only, which makes them beautiful?]

298 D. *S.* But suppose the man I am talking of, or anybody else, should ask us 'Pray, Hippias and Socrates, why have you distinguished from other pleasures that species which you identify with beauty, while you deny the name of beautiful to the pleasures of other senses, which come from food and drink and sex and so on? Do you deny that there is any pleasure or pleasantness at all in such things or in anything except seeing and hearing? What should we answer, Hippias?

H. Surely we must by all means allow, Socrates, that there are very great pleasures in these other things too.

S. 'Why then,' he will say, 'if these are just as much pleasures as the others, do you deprive them of this [299] title and deny that they are beautiful?' And we shall answer that it is because there is nobody who would not laugh at us if we called food and sweet smells beautiful instead of pleasant. And I suppose everybody would maintain that, though the sexual pleasure is very great, it should only be indulged privately and is most uncomely in public. If that is our reply, Hippias, I fear he may say: 'I quite see that all this time you have not dared to call all these pleasures beautiful for fear of differing from the majority. But I was not asking what is conventionally thought beautiful, but what really is.' And our answer can only be what we suggested just now: 'We call that class of pleasure which comes to us through sight and hearing beautiful.' Can you maintain the argument, Hippias, or shall we amend our answer?

H. That is the only answer we can make, Socrates.

S. 'Good,' he will say; 'then, since what is pleasant to sight and hearing is beautiful, whatever is not in this class of pleasant things clearly cannot be beautiful.' Shall we agree?

H. Yes.

S. 'Then,' he will say, 'is a pleasure that comes to us through sight one of the class that come to us through sight *and* hearing, or is one that comes to us through hearing a member of that class?' And we shall reply that what is pleasant through one of these senses certainly could not be pleasant through both, if that is his meaning, but we mean that each of these pleasures taken by itself is beautiful and so both are beautiful. Is that right?

H. Of course.

S. 'Well then,' he will say, 'does any class of pleasure differ from any other in the fact of its pleasantness? I am not asking if one is stronger or weaker or more or less pleasant than another, but if they can ever differ in being one of them a pleasure and the other not?' We do not think it possible, do we?

H. No.

S. 'Then,' he will say, 'it was not because they are pleasures that you picked these two out of all the others. Was it not because of something you had noticed in them to distinguish them from all the rest, that you called them beautiful? It goes without saying that the pleasure of sight is not beautiful merely because it comes through sight; for if that were what made a pleasure beautiful, the other pleasure, which comes through hearing, would not have been beautiful, since it certainly does not come through sight.' I suppose we shall have to agree?

300. *H.* We shall.

S. 'Nor again is the pleasure of hearing beautiful because it happens to come through hearing; for, once more, if that were so, the pleasure of sight would not have been beautiful, since it certainly does not come through hearing.' Shall we grant he is right here, Hippias?

H. Quite right.

S. 'Yet you say they are both beautiful?' And I think we do?

H. Yes.

S. 'Then they share some common character which makes them beautiful, which belongs to them both and to each separately. Otherwise they would not both have been beautiful and each separately.' Answer to me as if I were the man.

H. My answer is that I think you are right.

.   .   .   .   .   .

[The character common to pleasures of sight and hearing, which differentiates them from others, is their profitableness. So beautiful things are those which are both intrinsically pleasant and also profitable. Neither pleasantness nor profitableness alone would make them beautiful.]

303 D. *S.* 'Start afresh then,' he will say, 'since you have made a bad shot. How do you define the beauty which is in both these pleasures, which made you distinguish them from all others with the title of beautiful?' I think we must say, Hippias, that they are the most harmless and the best of pleasures, and this is true not only of both taken together but of each.[1] Do you know of anything else which distinguishes them?

H. Nothing. They really are the best.

S. 'Is this, then, the definition you now give of beauty,' he will say, '*profitable pleasure*?' I shall say that I think it is. Do you agree?

---

[1] Cf. St. Thomas Aquinas, p. 51; Schopenhauer, p. 144.

H. I agree.

S. 'And did we not prove,' he will say, 'that the profitable is what causes good, and that cause and effect are different? So that your argument brings you back to the old position. For beauty cannot be good nor good beautiful [304], since each of them is different from the other.' And we shall heartily agree, Hippias, if we are impartial. For it is an unpardonable sin not to yield to sound argument.

Phaedrus[1]

[The essence of beauty is better manifested in things than is any other essence.]

250 c. And the essence of beauty, as I have explained, was revealed to us along with the other essences, but in this world it is beauty that we apprehend the most clearly, shining through the clearest of our senses. For sight is the sharpest of all our bodily senses. Wisdom cannot be seen; for if wisdom could have afforded any such lively and visible image of herself, we should have been mad with love of her, or any other of the essences that are lovely. But, as it is, beauty alone has this privilege, so that it is the most manifest and lovable of all things.

Symposium[2]

[Beautiful things point to absolute beauty.]

210 E. When a man has gone deep enough in the lore of love, and turned his attention to things of beauty in their due order, and has at last become a master in that school, there shall dawn upon his eyes a vision of surpassing beauty, for whose sake he endured all his former toils; a beauty which, in the first place, is eternal, without beginning and without end, unbegotten and without decay; and, secondly, is not beautiful in one way and ugly in another, nor beautiful at one time or place or

---

[1] There is a translation by Jowett.
[2] There are translations by Shelley and Jowett.

from one point of view and then again ugly, as if its beauty depended upon the beholders. Nor again will that beauty to his eyes take on the likeness of a face or hands or any other fleshly part, nor of speech or learning, nor will it have its being in any living thing, or in earth or in the heavens or in any other creature, but will have its simple and essential being ever one within itself. And of it other beautiful things in such wise partake that, while they all are born and then again decay, it neither wanes nor waxes nor suffers any change. So when any one climbs the ladder of true love in this world till he catch a glimpse of that other beauty, he has almost attained his goal. And this is the true discipline of loving or being loved: that a man begin with the beauties of this world and use them as stepping-stones for an unceasing journey to that other beauty, going from one to two and from two to all, and from beautiful creatures to beautiful lives, and from beautiful lives to beautiful truths, and from beautiful truths attaining finally to nothing less than the true knowledge of Beauty itself, and so know at last what Beauty is. This, my dear Socrates, said the wise woman from Mantineia, is man's true home, with its vision of absolute beauty, if he have in this life any home at all.

Republic [1]

[Formal beauty expresses virtuous character.]

400 D. *Socrates.* Then good style and harmony and grace and rhythm spring naturally from goodness of nature,— not the good-nature we politely speak of when we really mean weakness—but from a truly good and beautiful character of mind.

Glaucon. Certainly.

S. Then must they not always be the aim of young men who are to fulfil their calling?

G. Yes, they must.

[1] There are translations by Jowett, Davies and Vaughan, Lindsay.

401. *S.* And, I suppose, the art of design is full of such qualities; and so are all similar crafts, weaving, embroidery, and architecture, and the fashioning of other useful things, and, not least, human bodies and other creatures. For all these are graceful or clumsy. And clumsiness and harshness and discord are akin to a vulgar style and a vulgar temper, while their opposites are akin to the opposite, to a steady and noble temper—indeed they are its very image.

G. Absolutely true.

S. Then is it only our poets whom we must order and compel to print the images of noble character in their poems, if we allow them to write at all, or must we not instruct the other craftsmen too, and prevent them from expressing the debauchery and meanness and vulgarity of an evil nature either in figures or in buildings or in any other work of art? And if any cannot comply, he must be forbidden to work among us. For otherwise our young rulers, nourished on images of vice, as on some poisonous pasture, nibbling and browsing their fill, little by little, every day from so many sources, before they know it will suffer a malignant growth to gather in their own souls. Rather we must seek out another kind of artists, who by their own virtuous nature can divine the true nature of beauty and grace, so that our young men, dwelling in a wholesome region, may profit every way, if every way there strike upon their eyes and ears from works of beauty a breeze, as it were, bringing health from kindly places, and from earliest childhood leading them quietly into likeness and fellowship and harmony with the beauty of reasonableness. . . . [402] Surely one so nurtured would, beyond others, welcome reason, when it came to him, and know it for his own? . . .

[Particular things imply an essence of their kind.]

596. *S.* Shall we begin our discussion on our usual lines? —I think we always allow that all the particular things

which we call by a single name have one single essence,[1] if you understand what I mean.

G. I understand.

S. Take for our present instance any such class you like. For example, if you accept it, I suppose there are many beds and tables.

G. Of course there are.

S. But there are only two essences of these products, the essential character of a bed and the essential character of a table.

G. Yes.

S. And should we not generally say that the maker of these useful products, makes his beds or his tables, as it may be, and suchlike things, keeping the essence before his mind's eye? For I suppose no workman creates the essence itself—how could he?

G. That is impossible.

[The Artist imitates particular things.]

S. Think now, how will you name *this* kind of workman?

G. What kind?

S. One who makes everything that any artisan ever makes.

G. You seem to be describing a highly skilled personage.

S. You will have better reason to say so presently; for with his own hands this artisan can make not only every kind of product but everything that grows on the earth, and all beasts, including himself, and heaven and earth into the bargain, and he fashions the gods and everything in heaven above and in hell beneath too.

G. Quite an encyclopaedia of the arts and sciences!

S. Do you doubt it? Tell me, do you think it quite impossible for there to be such a workman, or that, in one sense, a man might easily become such a universal

---

[1] The terms εἶδος and ἰδέα in Plato are not usually distinguished. The translation Idea is very misleading, as suggesting something mental. The translation Form has little but philology to recommend it. The word Universal would represent, perhaps, the chief element in what Plato means, but it may be less question-begging to use the vaguer word Essence.

producer but, in another sense, never? Don't you see that, in one way, you could easily do it all yourself?

G. What way do you mean?

S. Quite an easy way. In fact the job is a quick one and there are several ways of doing it. But the quickest, I think, is if you would take a mirror and swing it about. You would soon produce a sun and stars and the earth too, and yourself and the other animals and products and vegetables, and everything I mentioned.

G. Yes, the appearance of them, but surely not their true realities.

S. Good; that is exactly my point. For I suppose that the painter is a producer of that sort, don't you think so?

G. Certainly.

S. And I suppose you will admit that what he produces is not reality, though in a certain sense he produces a bed by painting a picture of it?

G. Yes, at least he, too, produces an appearance of one.

[Even a particular material bed is not ultimate reality.]

597. *S.* But what about the manufacturer? Didn't you say just now that he does not make the essence, what we call the nature of beds, but only a given bed?

G. I did.

S. Then if he does not make the nature of beds, he does not make the reality of bed; something like the reality, no doubt, but not the reality. And if anybody were to say that the manufactured product of any craftsman were the absolute reality, he must be mistaken?

G. That is what the authorities on such matters would hold.

S. Then we must not be surprised to find that even the product is only a sort of shadow of the truth.

G. No.

S. Shall we use these instances for discussing the nature of an imitator?

G. If you please.

S. Then we have got three beds: one, the bed as it is in

Reality, which is made, I suppose, by God; or do you think by any one else?

G. Not by any one else, I think.

S. And one made by the carpenter?

G. Yes.

S. And one by the painter. Is that right?

G. Very well.

S. Then the painter, the carpenter, and God are the three masters of the three kinds of bed?

G. Three it is.

. . . . . .

597 D. *S.* Shall we then call God the creator of the bed, or by some such name?

G. That is right, for he has created this and every other nature.

S. What about the carpenter? Would you not call him the manufacturer of the bed?

G. Yes.

S. And is the artist, then, a manufacturer and maker of it?

G. Certainly not.

S. What, then, would you say he does to the bed?

G. I think the fairest thing to say about him is that he imitates what the other makes.

S. Very well; then do you call the author of what is twice[1] removed from the nature of things an imitator?

G. Certainly.

S. Then that is what the writer of tragedies will be, since he is an imitator—two grades below the supreme character and below truth, like all other imitators.

G. It looks like it.

[The artist does not even copy particular things accurately.]

S. Then we are agreed about the imitator. But tell me this about [598] the artist. Do you think he tries to imitate the real nature of each thing or only manufactured things?[2]

---

[1] In Greek 'thrice'.   [2] Cf. Aristotle p. 32, Plotinus p. 48.

G. Manufactured things.

S. But we must make a further distinction; does he imitate them as they are or as they look?

G. What do you mean?

S. This. Whether you look at a bed straight in front of you or from one side, or anywhere else, is it altered at all itself, or does it remain just the same and only look different, and similarly with other things?

G. Why, it looks different but is not.

S. Now this is the point for you to consider: To what is the painter's art directed in any particular thing; to its reality as it is, to imitate that, or to its appearance, as it looks? Is it an imitation of appearance or fact?

G. Of appearance.

[Art does not instruct or edify.]

S. Then imitative art must be a long way from truth. And it looks as if the reason why it can present everything is that it neglects the whole of everything but its shadow. For instance, we say that a painter can paint us a carpenter or a saddler or other tradesman, though he know none of their trades; and yet, if he were a clever painter, and showed his picture of a carpenter a long way off, he could deceive children or simple people through their thinking that it really was a carpenter.

G. Of course.

S. But when anybody tells us that he has met with some man who understood all the arts and everything else that anybody can know, and understood them all better than anybody else could, we must tell him that he is too credulous, and seems to have met with some conjuror or mimic who deceived him and passed himself off as a universal genius, because our friend was unable to distinguish knowledge from ignorance and imitation. For that is the right attitude to the whole business.

G. Quite true.

S. Next, then, we must consider tragedy and its prophet, Homer. For we hear people talking as if the poets were

masters in every faculty, and in all morals, and in
theology too—assuming that a good poet, if he is to write
well of his subject, must write with knowledge or not at
all. Now we must ask whether these people have come
across mere charlatans and been deceived by [599] seeing
their work and not noticing that it is two grades below
reality, and quite easy to produce without any knowledge
of the truth—for it is mere semblance and not reality;
or whether there is something in what they say, and
good poets really do understand what they talk about
with so much applause.

G. I should like to discuss that.

S. Do you think, then, that if anybody were equally
able to produce either the reality or a shadow of it, he
would be ambitious to devote himself to producing the
shadow, and would give up his whole life to this, and
think he had made a good bargain?

G. I doubt it.

S. But if he had real knowledge of what he represents,
too, I suppose he would pride himself much more on
doing something than on representing the deeds of others,
and would try to leave behind him many noble achievements of his own as his monument, and would rather be
celebrated than celebrate others.

G. Surely; the two things are not comparable either for
honour or utility.

S. Then on other points we may forgo a cross-examina-
tion of Homer or any other poet. We need not ask how it
was that, if they were qualified to practise as well as to
talk about medicine, neither he nor any other poet, ancient
or modern, ever cured a patient, as Asclepius did; nor
why they left no school of medicine, as Asclepius did
among his children. And all other special arts we can
likewise pass over without question. But surely it is fair
to question him on the really great and exalted subjects
with which he claims to deal: wars and strategy and con-
stitutions and education. 'Tell us,' one might fairly beg,
'dear Homer,—since you claim to be put not in the third

class for truth about virtue, as a copyist, or imitator as we called it, but rather in the second, as knowing how to train men for good or evil in public or private life,— tell us what city you ever reformed as Lycurgus reformed Lacedaemon, and others other states great and small. What city claims you as its wise law-giver and benefactor, as we do Solon or Italy and Sicily Charondas?' Do you think he could tell us one?

G. I think not. No such claim is made even by his school.

. . . . . .

600 E. *S.* Then shall we set down all the artists, beginning with Homer, as mimics of a copy of virtue, or of whatever else they represent, who never get in touch with the truth? So that, as we said just now, the painter, though he know nothing of saddlery, will produce what looks like [601] a saddler to those who know no more about it than he does and who judge by colours and forms?

G. Certainly.

S. So, too, I suppose we may say that an artist, without any further knowledge of them, can give a colourable imitation of all the sciences, using words and phrases for pigment, so that a person like himself, who is content with mere talk, will admire his sayings about saddlery or strategy or anything else if only they be in musical and rhythmic numbers? Such is the natural magic of just those qualities. For I suppose you know what a poem sounds like when you are told its mere meaning stripped of this musical colouring? You must often have seen it done.

G. I have indeed.

S. Isn't it like a face, which has never been really beautiful, when it loses the bloom of youth?

G. Exactly.

S. Come then, consider this. We say the maker of the artistic image, the imitator, understands nothing about the reality but only about its appearance?

[Beauty consists in the performance of function.]

G. Yes.

S. Don't let us be content with half-truths then, but let us get to the bottom of the matter.

G. Go on.

S. A painter, we say, may paint reins and bit?

G. Yes.

S. But it is the saddler and smith who will make them?

G. Certainly.

S. Then does the painter understand what reins and bit ought to be? Or does even the maker, the saddler or smith, not understand this, but only the rider, the man who knows how to use them?

G. Quite true.

S. And is not that always so?

G. How?

S. That there are always three arts: the art of using a thing, the art of making it, and the art of imitating it?

G. Yes.

S. Now does not the virtue and beauty and excellence of every product or living thing or action depend upon the purpose for which it was made or developed?

G. Yes.

.   .   .   .   .   .

602 B. *S.* And yet the artist will still be imitating everything, though perfectly ignorant in what ways it is good or bad. Probably he will imitate it as it seems beautiful to the ignorant vulgar.

G. Surely.

S. Then it seems a fair conclusion we agreed upon, that the imitator knows next to nothing of what he imitates, but that his imitation is a sort of game and not earnest, and that those who attempt tragic poetry, whether in iambic or in heroic verse, are typical imitators. . . .

[Artists prefer to imitate men performing their functions badly.]

605 C. *S.* But we have not yet brought our chief count

against poetry. Surely its power to degrade even the good, with very few exceptions, is a grievous thing?

G. Yes. But does it do that?

S. Tell me what you think of this. I suppose the best of us are pleased when we hear Homer, or any of the tragic poets, imitating some hero who is in grief and who spins out a long speech of lamentation;—they even imitate people wailing and beating their breasts. We give ourselves up to uncritical sympathy, and quite seriously praise as a good poet the man who affects us most in this way.

G. I know. I could not deny it.

S. Yet when we have some sorrow of our own to bear, you know that we pride ourselves on the very opposite— if we can keep calm and endure it like men instead of in the way we then applauded, like women.

G. I agree.

S. And is that an honourable kind of praise—when we see a character which we could not accept for our own without shame, and instead of being sickened, are pleased, and praise it?

G. That hardly seems reasonable.

606 *S.* Not if you look at it in this way.

G. Which?

S. If you consider that this appetite to be sated with unrestrained tears and lamentings which we forcibly repressed in our own misfortunes, though by its very nature it lusted after such satisfaction, is exactly what is satisfied and pleased by the poets. But our better nature, being insufficiently trained by reason and habit, loosens its hold over this sentimental tendency when we regard the misfortunes of other people. For we think it can be no disgrace for us to pity and praise another who professes to be a good man and yet pities himself beyond measure. We think the mere pleasure of it is so much gain, which we would not lose by condemning the whole poem. For I suppose few of us are able to reflect that evil communications corrupt good manners, since if we nourish our pity for such people it will not be easy to restrain it when we suffer ourselves.[1]

G. Very true.

S. And is it not the same with the things we laugh at? Whenever you are delighted at a joke which you hear in comic imitations, or in conversation, and are not disgusted at its vulgarity, though you would be ashamed to make it yourself, is not this just like your tragic pity? For here again you are indulging something which, when you yourself were tempted to facetiousness, reflection had restrained for fear you might be thought a buffoon. And the consequence of indulging it at such times is that it grows wanton before you are aware, and you may often be carried away and become a comedian in your own person.

G. Very true.

S. And poetical imitation has the same effect on lust and anger and all those experiences of desire and pleasure or pain which, as we believe, accompany all our actions. For it waters them and makes them grow when they ought to starve with drought; and it gives them power over us when we ought to subject them, and so to make ourselves better and happier instead of falling into misery and wickedness.

G. I cannot deny it. . . .

[To be truly beautiful, poetry must be profitable as well as pleasant.]

607 D. *S.* But I suppose we might allow the lovers and advocates of poetry, even if they are not poets themselves, to make what defence of her they can in plain prose, and to show, if they can, that she is not only pleasant but profitable to nations and to mankind. And we shall hear them gladly. For it will certainly be no little gain to us if poetry can be shown to be profitable as well as pleasant.

G. It would be a gain indeed.

S. But if they fail, my dear Glaucon, then we shall behave

---

[1] Cf. Aristotle, p. 33, Lipps p. 254.

like people who have fallen in love with some one, but do not think their love can come to any good; we shall give her up, however hard we find it. And because of the passion for this poetry which has been bred in us by our national culture, we shall be willing [608] that she should be vindicated as perfectly true and good. But until she can establish her innocence, while we listen to her we shall repeat to ourselves this argument, like a charm, for fear of falling back into our boyish and vulgar passion. We shall whisper to ourselves that we must not take the attractions of such poetry too seriously, as if they had anything to do with truth or goodness; and that her hearer must always mistrust her as an enemy of his soul's peace,[1] and believe the character we have given her.

G. I quite agree.

S. And the stake we are playing for, my dear Glaucon, is heavy, heavier than men always see:—whether we are to be good men or bad. So what can it profit a man to be incited by riches or power or honour, or poetry herself, that he should trifle with justice or anything that is right?

Timaeus[2]

[The beauty of sights and sounds is expressive of spiritual states.]

47 B. God devised the gift of sight for us so that we might observe the movements which have been described by reason in the heavens, and apply them to the motions of our own mind, which are akin to them, so far as what is troubled can claim kinship with what is serene. For so we might learn a lesson, and by entering into the ideal nature of that design and imitating the perfect pattern set by God might adjust thereto our own random motions. And the same holds good of voice and hearing; the gods bestowed them on us for the same end and purpose. For that is the end of speech, which it serves more than any other faculty. And so far as vocal music goes, it is given us to be heard for the sake of melody. And melody, since its

---

[1] Cf. Richards, p. 282.   [2] There are translations by Jowett and Taylor.

movements are related to the changes of our own souls, is to be valued, if a man use his mind in art, not for irrational pleasure, as is the fashion now; rather it is given us to help us in ordering and assimilating to it the discordant motions of our souls. And rhythm again was given us from the same source and for the same purpose, to help us in dealing with what is unmeasured and chaotic in the minds of most of us.

Philebus[1]

[Some pleasures and pains are mixed. Comedy gives a mixture of pleasure and pain at the folly of others.]

48. *Socrates*. Do you recall how at tragic spectacles people enjoy a good cry?

Protarchus. Naturally.

S. Then do you see what our frame of mind is at a comedy; that, there too, there is a mixture of pleasure and pain?

P. I don't quite see that. . . .

S. Would you call spite a mental pain?

P. Yes.

S. Yet a spiteful man evidently will find pleasure in the misfortunes of his neighbours.

P. Very much.

S. Now to be ignorant is a misfortune, and so it is to be the sort of man we call fatuous.

P. Certainly.

S. From this you may see the nature of the ridiculous.

P. Explain.

S. It is, in sum, a kind of defect which has been given a specific name. And of defects in general it is that species which is the contrary of the character described in the Delphic inscription.

P. I suppose, Socrates, you mean Know Thyself? . . .

49 c. *S*. Yes. . . . And vain self-conceit in the strong is feared and loathed. For it is dangerous to those who have

---

[1] There is a translation by Jowett.

to do with it either in fact or fiction. But when it is weak it comes into the sphere and character of the ridiculous. . . . Shall we then conclude that our friends who have a vain conceit of wisdom or beauty, if this is harmless to others, are ridiculous?[1] . . .

[Formal beauty is not relative to our purposes.]

51 B. *S.* True pleasures are those which arise from the colours we call beautiful and from shapes; and most of the pleasures of smell and sound. True pleasures arise from all those things the want of which is not felt as painful but the satisfaction from which is consciously pleasant and unconditioned by pain.

P. But again, Socrates, what do we mean by these?

S. Certainly what I mean is not quite clear, but I must try to make it so. I do not now intend by beauty of shapes what most people would expect, such as that of living creatures or pictures, but, for the purpose of my argument, I mean straight lines and curves and the surfaces or solid forms produced out of these by lathes and rulers and squares, if you understand me. For I mean that these are not beautiful relatively, like other things, but always and naturally and absolutely; and they have their proper pleasures, no way depending on the itch of desire. And I mean colours of the same kind, with the same kind of beauty and pleasures. Is that clear or not?[2]

P. I am doing my best, Socrates, but do your best to make it clearer.

S. Well, I mean that such sounds as are pure and smooth and yield a single pure tone are not beautiful relatively to anything else but in their own proper nature, and produce their proper pleasures.[3]

---

[1] Cf. Aristotle, p. 32.
[2] Cf. Kant, p. 121, Bell, p. 264.
[3] Cf. Herbart, p. 155.

ARISTOTLE
about 384–322 B.C.

Poetics[1]

[The 'formal' and 'characteristic' elements in beauty correspond to two primary impulses.]

iv. The birth of poetry in general seems due to two tendencies innate in man. From earliest childhood the instinct for imitation is natural to us, as is the universal pleasure in imitations. Man is superior to the other animals in being more imitative, and his first lessons are learned by imitation. The proof that imitation pleases is in the effect which its products have upon us. We take pleasure in looking at the most realistic representations of things which we should view with horror in their reality, such as the bodies of vermin, and corpses. The reason for this again is that learning is a very great pleasure, to others quite as much as to philosophers, however little gift they have for it. So the reason why they are pleased by seeing representations is that, in looking at them, they learn and come to conclusions what each thing is, as when they identify a portrait. For if they happen not to have seen the original, they will get no pleasure from the work as an imitation but only from the technique or colour or some such cause.

Now not only is imitation instinctive, but also harmony and rhythm,[2] and metre is obviously a kind of rhythm. So people starting with such original predispositions developed these elements in their improvisations, for the most part gradually, until they produced poetry.[3]

[Tragedy and Comedy.]

But poetry became divided into two kinds, according to the idiosyncrasies of poets. The serious-minded imitated noble actions and the actions of noble men, while the

[1] There are translations by Butcher and Bywater.
[2] Cf. *Problems*, xix. 38, p. 35. See p. xx.
[3] Cf. Schiller, p. 125, Fry, p. 267.

trivial-minded imitated the actions of the vulgar and at
first wrote satire, as the others wrote hymns and eulogies.
. . . .

v. Comedy, as we have said, is an imitation of inferior
people, not, however, of people inferior in every way;
rather the ludicrous is only one species of the ugly. For
the ludicrous is a fault or deformity which is not painful
or a cause of pain in others.[1]

[Formal character of beauty.]

vii. For an animal or anything else made up of parts to
be beautiful, it must not only have these parts ordered,
but must have a certain magnitude. For beauty consists
in proper order and size. So neither could very small
creatures be beautiful, since our perception of them
becomes confused as it approaches instantaneousness, nor
again could a very large one, say a thousand miles long.
For here we do not see it all at once, but its unity and
wholeness escape our eyes. Just as a beautiful physical
body or living thing, then, must have a certain size,
namely one that can be easily comprehended by a glance,
so a plot must have a certain length, namely one that can
easily be remembered. . . .

[Poetry creates an imagined unity or consistency.]

ix. It is not the function of the poet to tell what has
happened, but the kind of thing that might happen,—
what is possible, by which I mean either probable or
necessary. The historian and the poet do not differ by
the one writing in verse and the other in prose. The
works of Herodotus might be put into verse and would
still be a sort of history in spite of the versification. The
difference is that the one tells what has happened, the
other what might happen. That is why poetry is a more
philosophical and important thing than history; for
poetry tells us rather the universals,[2] history the particu-

[1] Cf. Plato, pp. 29, 30.
[2] Cf. Butcher, *Aristotle's Theory of Poetry and Fine Art*, and Bywater, *Aristotle on the Art of Poetry*. I have discussed the question in my *Theory of Beauty*, iv, §§ 205. Cf. Plato, p. 21, Plotinus, p. 48, Bergson, p. 205.

lars. The universal is the kind of thing which a person of certain character would necessarily or probably say or do. And this is what poetry aims at, though it gives proper names to the persons. The particular is what Alcibiades did or suffered. . . .

[Two kinds of poetry.]

xvii. A poet must be a man either of sensibility or of inspiration. The first has ready sympathies, the second is possessed.

[Tragedy does not make us emotional; it purges our emotions.]

vi. Tragedy is an imitation of an important action which is rounded off and has a certain size, the language being beautified in the different styles in the different parts. It imitates actual deeds, not by means of narrative; and by pity and fear effects the purgation [1] of such emotions.

Politics [2]

[Sounds and sights can not only give pleasure and recreation but can express and influence mental characters.]

v (viii) 5. That our characters are affected by music is evident from many instances and especially from the music written by Olympus. For that admittedly fills our souls with devotional feeling, [3] and devotion is a passion which affects the disposition of the soul. Further, when we hear imitations, apart from the actual rhythms and melodies, we all experience sympathetic feelings. And as music is incidentally pleasant, and virtue is concerned with feeling pleasure and with liking and disliking rightly, it is plainly necessary to study and practise nothing so much as right judgement and delight in good

[1] κάθαρσις. Bywater in the Appendix to his *Aristotle on the Art of Poetry* gives about sixty versions and paraphrases of this famous saying. Cf. his note on the passage in the same book. Butcher quotes other explanations in his essay on 'The Function of Tragedy' in *Aristotle's Theory of Poetry and Fine Art*. I have added a few in my *Theory of Beauty*, iii, § 16. Cf. Plato, p. 26, Hegel, p. 163, Bradley, p. 211.

[2] There are translations by Welldon and Jowett.

[3] ποιεῖ τὰς ψυχὰς ἐνθουσιαστικάς.

dispositions and noble deeds. And in rhythms and melodies we have the most realistic representations of actual anger and benevolence, and, moreover, of courage and temperance, and the opposites of all these, and the other dispositions. Experience proves this. For we experience the effect upon our soul of hearing them. But to acquire the habit of being pleased or pained at representations goes a long way towards acquiring the same dispositions towards the originals.[1] For instance, if we take pleasure in looking at a portrait-statue merely for its figure, we must enjoy looking at the original himself. But other senses, such as touch and taste, in fact perceive no representation of dispositions, and sight only to a low degree. Shapes, indeed, have this quality, however slightly, which all can perceive. Yet they are not so much representations of dispositions;—rather the shapes, and colours too, are symptoms of the dispositions from which they result; as our bodies show symptoms of our passions. Nevertheless, so far as looking at pictures goes, the young should not study Pauson so much as Polygnotus and other painters and sculptors who portray character. But melodies have the power of representing character in themselves.[2] This is indisputable, for the different nature of the different 'harmonies' is obvious, so that the hearers are differently moved and disposed towards them. Some, like the so-called Mixed Lydian, dispose us to melancholy and gravity; others, such as the Relaxed 'harmonies', to a more melting mood; one other, the Dorian alone, seems to affect us in a more normal way, between the two; and the Phrygian arouses devotional feelings. . . . And the same is true of rhythms; some have a more stately character, others are exciting, and the excitement may be more vulgar or more generous. . . . And there seems to be a sort of kinship of harmonies and rhythms to our souls. . . .

6. The flute is an instrument which does not express character so much as passion; so it is to be used in

[1] Contrast pp. 33, 35.   [2] Cf. Longinus, p. 39.

those performances which achieve purgation rather than
education. . . .

7. Clearly all the 'harmonies' should be used, but not
all in the same way, for we should use those which are
most expressive of character for educational purposes,
but also those which are exciting and devotional when
listening to professionals. What affects some minds
violently is present in all to a greater or less degree, as,
for instance, pity and fear, or devotional excitement.
For some are much subject to this excitement. And when
they listen to religious music which indulges their ecstasy,
we see that they are cured, like people who have been
purged by some drug. And the same must happen to
those who are excessively compassionate or timid, and
in general to all emotional persons, and to everybody in
proportion as he is affected by emotions; all must be as
it were purged and feel a pleasant relief. In the same
way melodies which have this effect afford men a harmless pleasure. . . .

Problems[1]

[Music is more obviously than other arts both expressive and
formal.]

xix. 29. Why do rhythms and melodies, which are mere
sounds, resemble dispositions, while tastes do not, nor
yet colours [2] or smells? Is it because they are movements,
as actions also are? And activity immediately indicates
disposition and determines it further, but tastes and
colours do not so.

38. Why do all men delight in rhythm and melody and
concords generally? Is it because we naturally delight
in natural movements? This is suggested by the fact that
children delight in these sounds as soon as born. We
delight in the various kinds of melody because they
express dispositions, but in rhythm because it contains

[1] There is a translation by Forster (Oxford Aristotle Translations).
[2] Cf. Kant, p. 121, Schopenhauer, p. 146, Herbart, p. 155, Hegel, p. 174.

a recognizable and regular number and moves us in a regular way. For regular motion is naturally more akin to us than irregular, and so more natural.

Metaphysics[1]

[Formal character of beauty.]

xii. 3. Goodness and beauty are different, for the former is found only in conduct, but the latter also in things that are not moved. . . . The essential characters composing beauty are order, symmetry, and definiteness.

MARCUS TULLIUS CICERO

106–43 B.C.

Tusculan Discussions

[The orthodox Stoic view of beauty.]

IV. xiii. 31. There is a certain apt disposition of bodily parts which, when combined with a certain agreeable colour, is called beauty.[2]

The Orator

[Imagination.][3]

(*To Marcus Brutus*). ii. 9. When Pheidias was carving a Zeus or an Athene he did not study a model which he should imitate. Rather, there was an exalted type of beauty residing in his own mind; and, fixing his whole attention upon this, he used all his skill and dexterity to reproduce it.

---

[1] There is a translation by Ross (Oxford Aristotle Translations).

[2] This definition is repeated almost verbally by Augustine (A.D. 354–430) *On the Kingdom of God*, XXII, xix.

[3] A more imaginative account of art than the Stoic definition of beauty would afford is perhaps preserved in the fragments of the Epicurean Philodemus *On Poems* (about 50 B.C.). The fragmentary text of Book V has been restored and edited with a German translation by Jensen (Berlin, Weidmann, 1923). Questions are raised whether the poet need instruct or imitate, whether he need have knowledge, what is the relation of subject-matter to style. The argument is too fragmentary for quotation here.

'LONGINUS'[1]

On the Sublime

vii. The soul seems to be naturally uplifted by true sublimity and, rising on loftier pinions, to be filled with joy and pride, as having itself brought forth what it has heard. . . .

viii. This I know, that nothing is so eloquent in due season as real passion, for it seems to be the prophetic utterance of some possessing spirit, and to inspire every word. . . .

ix. Sublimity is the echo of a great soul. So sometimes a bare thought, not in so many words expressed, is marvellous just for its greatness; as the silence of Ajax in *The Wraiths*[2] is inexpressibly great. . . . Homer can magnify even what is divine: 'As far as man's eye may pierce the haze, who sitteth on a cliff-top gazing over the wine-dark sea, such the resounding leap of the horses of the gods.' He measures their leap by the standard of the universe.[3] . . .

The Jewish lawgiver, no mean writer since he worthily conceived and expressed omnipotence, in the very outset of his laws begins: 'God said—' and how think you he continues? 'Let there be light, and there was light; let the earth be, and it was so.' . . .

Homer often seems himself to live the great lives of his heroes. When he has made a sudden darkness and a great night come down upon the Greek battle, Ajax is at his wits' end and cries: 'O Father Zeus, deliver yet the sons of the Achaians from this darkness; give us day

---

[1] This was the traditional third-century author of the treatise Περὶ Ὕψους (*De Sublimitate*) now usually ascribed to an unknown author of the first century A.D. The first edition was by Robortelli (Basle, 1554), the first English edition by Langbaine (Oxford, 1636); the first English translation by Pulteney, 1680; Boileau paraphrased it in 1674. There is a translation by Rhys Roberts.

[2] *Odyssey* xi. 543–64, 'But to all my questioning he answered never a word, and went after the other wraiths.'

[3] *Iliad* v. 770. Cf. Addison, *Spectator*, 420, p. 69, Kant, § 25, p. 119.

and vouchsafe sight to our eyes. If so be that we must die, let us die in the light.'[1] . . .

xxx. In literature the thought and the diction generally modify each other's development. . . . For in fact the beauty of language is the proper light of the mind.

[Size and strangeness contribute to aesthetic effect.]

xxxv. What then could have been in the minds of those inspired writers who aimed at perfection of style, and yet thought little of minute correctness? Surely this, among other things, that nature has set our human family apart from the humble herd of brutes, and has bidden us to the pageant of life and of the whole universe, that we might both be spectators of the mighty drama and acquit ourselves as worthy actors there. And she has breathed into our souls an unquenchable love of whatever is great and more divine than we. Wherefore not even the whole universe can suffice the reaches of man's thought and contemplation, but oftentimes his imagination oversteps the bounds of space, so that if we survey our life on every side, how greatness and beauty and eminence have everywhere the prerogative, we shall straightway perceive the end for which we were created. Hence it is that we are led by nature to admire, not our little rivers, for all their purity and homely uses, so much as Nile and Rhine and Danube, and, beyond all, the sea. Nor do we reverence that little fire of our own kindling, because it is kept ever brightly burning, as we do the heavenly fires that are often veiled in darkness; nor is it so marvellous in our eyes as the gulfs of Etna, whose outbursts bring up from their depth rocks and whole mountain-sides and again pour forth rivers of subterranean, elemental fire. Always we should say that what is useful or needful seems homely, but what is strange is a marvel.

[Formal beauty is expressive.]

xxxix. Rhythmical style is a device not only naturally apt to please and to persuade but admirably fitted for

[1] *Iliad* xvii. 645–7.

the lofty utterance of passion. All men grant that the flute can communicate passion to its hearers and make them almost frenzied with emotion, and by setting a rhythmical movement can compel the hearer to move in a corresponding rhythm, and to identify himself with the melody, however unmusical he be. The sound of the harp too, though literally it has no meaning, yet by the variety of the notes and their contrast and blending with one another in the harmony, often lays a surprising spell upon us. Yet all these are but symbols and bastard artifices for influencing others, not, as I said, the right issue of the human spirit. And shall we, then, deny that style, being a harmony not of mere sounds but of words, which are natural to man and touch his soul more nearly than his sense, can rain influence upon us, and, moreover, by completely subduing our minds, can always dispose us to honourable, lofty, and sublime feelings and to any others that itself contains? For, to do this, style can bring into play the most varying forms of words, of thoughts, of deeds, of beauty, of melody, all which things are our natural birthright; and at the same time, by the contrast and blending of its mere sounds, can insinuate the speaker's passion to his hearers' souls and put them in communion with himself, building out of words an edifice of sublime proportions.

MARCUS AURELIUS ANTONINUS, EMPEROR
(A.D. 121–180)

Meditations

Translated by Jeremy Collier, 1701[1]

[Though some things in nature show no design, all show some beauty when viewed as part of nature. A development of Stoic doctrine.]

III. ii. 'Tis worth one's while to observe that the least design'd and almost unbespoken Effects of Nature are not without their Beauty. Thus, to use a Similitude, there

[1] Previously translated by Meric Casaubon, 1634. I have altered Collier's translation where I thought it necessary. It is very free, almost a paraphrase.

are Cracks, and little Breaks on the Surface of a Loaf, which tho' never intended by the Baker, have a sort of Agreeableness in them; which invite the Appetite. Thus Figs when they are most ripe, open and gape: And Olives when they fall of themselves and are near decaying, are particularly pretty to look at: To go on; The bending of an Ear of Corn, the Brow of a Lion, the Foam of a Boar, and many other Things, if you take them singly, are far enough from being handsome, but when they are look'd on with Reference, and Connexion to somewhat natural; are both Ornamental and Affecting. Thus, if a Man has but Feeling and Thought enough to examine the *Products* of the Universe; he'll find, even among those Things which are but mere Accessories and Appendages, nothing unaccountable nor without Matter of Delight. One thus prepared will perceive the Beauty of Life, as well as that of Imitation; and be no less pleased to see a Tyger grin in the *Tower*, than in a *Painter's* Shop. Such a one will be able to see the proper Ripeness and Maturity of old Age, whether in Man, or Woman, as well as the Allurement of Youth, with chaste and continent Eyes.

[Beauty is an absolute quality in things.]

iv. 20. Whatever is Beautiful, has that Quality from it self; 'tis finished by its own Nature, and Commendation is no part of it. Why then a thing is neither better, nor worse, for being prais'd. This holds concerning Things which are called *Beautiful* in the common way of speaking, as the products of Nature and Art; what do you think then of that which deserves this Character in the strictest Propriety? Do you imagine it wants any Thing Foreign to compleat the Idea? What is your Opinion of Truth, good Nature and Sobriety? Do any of these Beauties stand in need of a good Word; or are they the worse for a bad one? I hope a diamond will shine ne'er the less for a Mans being silent about the worth on't; Neither is there any Necessity of Flourishing upon a piece of Gold to preserve the Intrinsick of the Mettal.

PHILOSTRATUS

About A.D. 170–245

Life of Apollonius of Tyana [1]

[So-called imitation implies imagination, which is necessary in appreciating both art and nature.]

II. xxii. 'Well, then, Damis, is painting imitation?' 'What else could it be?' said he, 'for if it were not that it would be an absurd and childish daub.' 'But what about the shapes we see in the sky,' said Apollonius, 'when the clouds are dishevelled;—centaurs and unicorns, not to speak of wolves and horses? Will you not have to call them imitations?' 'I suppose so,' said he. 'Then, Damis, is God an animal-painter, that he should leave the chariot on whose wings he is borne through heaven and earth, ordering all that therein is, and should sit down to amuse himself by scribbling these things, like a child on the sands?' Damis blushed when he saw to what absurdity the argument was leading. But Apollonius, who was never overbearing in argument, went on in a friendly tone, 'Surely what you mean, Damis, is rather that all these cloud-pictures are without purpose or significance, so far as God is concerned, but that it is we who, from our instinct for imitation, endow them with regular form?' 'Let us choose that view, Apollonius; it is more probable and more attractive.' 'Then there are two kinds of imitation, Damis, and we may conclude that the one called painting can render things with the mind and the hand, but the other creates images with the mind only.' 'Not really two,' said Damis,' for we must consider the one which deserves the name of painting to be the more complete imitation, since it can render images with the mind and the hand; and the other to be only a part of it, since, even if a man be no draughtsman, he can appre-

---

[1] There is a translation by Conybeare (Loeb Classics).

hend and image with the mind, but cannot employ the hand for delineating.' 'Do you mean, Damis,' he said, 'that the man's hand is crippled by accident or disease?' 'Of course not;' he answered, 'what cripples it is never having handled colours or pencil or any other instrument and never having learned to draw.' 'Then we are both agreed, Damis, that "imitation" comes naturally to men, but draughtsmanship is an art. And the same would be true about sculpture. But I suppose you would not confine portraiture to coloured representation, for mono-chrome was enough for the older painters, and only as the art developed were four colours used, and later even more. We must call outlines portraiture, and also works composed of light and shade; for here too we find both likeness and essential character[1] as well as mind and honour and courage. Yet this is entirely divorced from colour and does not suggest the colour of blood or the tint of a man's hair or beard. But, however abstract, such compositions are real likenesses, whether of coloured men or white, so that if we were to draw one of these Indians in white chalk, he will look black enough, since his flat nose and stiff curls and heavy jaw and the nervous look of his eyes indicate an Indian and make you see black, if you know how to use your eyes. From which I argue that even for looking at pictures you need the "imitative" faculty.'

[Art is the work of imagination, not imitation.]

VI. xix. 'Are you going to tell me, then,' said Thespesion, 'that your Pheidias and Praxiteles went up into heaven and took casts of the gods' features[2] and then fashioned them artistically, or had they any other guidance in their modelling?' 'Yes,' said Apollonius, 'a guidance pregnant with wisdom.' 'What was it?' said he; 'surely you cannot mean anything but imitation?' 'Imagination,' replied the other, 'fashioned these works, a more cunning craftsman than imitation. For imitation will fashion what it has

---

[1] εἶδος, or perhaps here 'form'.   [2] εἶδος

seen, but imagination goes on to what it has not seen, which it will assume as the standard of the reality. And imitation is often baffled by awe, but imagination by nothing, for it rises unawed to the height of its own ideal.[1] If you have envisaged the character[2] of Zeus, you must see him with the firmament and the seasons and the stars, as Pheidias strove to do in this statue; and if you are to fashion Athene, you must have in your mind strategy and counsel and the arts and how she sprang from Zeus himself.

PLOTINUS

About A.D. 205–270

Plotinus has been considered both as carrying the Platonic philosophy to its logical conclusion and as degrading it by the introduction of an irrational mysticism. He accepted the distinction between the real unchanging essences (εἴδη), which are the objects of pure intelligence, and the particular things which are always changing and are the objects of sense. Intelligence, which is the same whether human or divine, must be akin to that which it apprehends; but, since they are not identical, both must have as the ground or source of their union the absolute One which transcends all existence both in reality and in goodness, and which may be called God. But of this we can know nothing except negatively that it is not any determinate thing. From the perfection of this One there emanates, as the expression of its perfection, the divine intelligence, in which we also participate, together with the essences which it knows. And from this again there issues a third divinity—the world-soul, which manifests itself also in our souls, and which creates the sensible world. Matter is the antithesis of the One; it is the extreme of plurality and division and of evil. All these successive emanations have the tendency to return in some way to that from which they come, except matter only.

Physical beauty, then, will be the unification of the formless multiplicity of matter by the unity of some essential character. In nature this will be produced by the world-soul; in art by the world-soul as manifested in a human soul. But more beautiful

---

[1] Cf. Longinus vii, p. 37, Kant on Sublimity, p. 118.   [2] εἶδος.

than any physical beauty is the essential character as apprehended or possessed by intelligence. For the ground of the
possibility of all unity, and therefore of all beauty, is the One.

Enneads [1]

[Beauty is not merely formal symmetry.]

 I. vi. I. Since the same bodies sometimes appear beautiful
and sometimes not, that which makes a thing a body is
not what makes it beautiful. Our first question then must
be what this is which enters into bodies. What is it which
opens the eyes of those who behold it, and attracts them,
nay, compels them towards itself, and makes them
rejoice in the vision of it? If we could discover that, we
could take our stand upon it to survey the wider field.
The almost universal reply is that a certain symmetry of
the parts, mutually, and with the whole, with the addition of appropriate colour, is what produces visible
beauty. Accordingly, for visible things and all others in
general, to be beautiful is to be symmetrical and proportioned. And on this theory no simple element could be
beautiful, but of necessity only the compound, and it
would be the whole which is beautiful.[2] Each individual
part would not by itself have beauty, but only so far as it
contributed to the beauty of the whole. Yet, if a whole
be beautiful, so must the parts be; beauty cannot be made
out of ugly things, it must have possessed them all. And
on this theory beautiful colours like sunlight, since they
are simple and could not get beauty by being symmetrical,
would be denied beauty. How could gold be beautiful?
Or in what way could midnight lightning be beautiful?
Likewise of sounds, the simple must be excluded, though
often each single note, of those which go to make up a
beautiful whole, is beautiful. And since the same face,
without change of symmetry, sometimes appears beautiful and sometimes not, how can we avoid saying that the

---

[1] There is a translation by McKenna and also of most of these passages by
Dodds.
[2] Cf. Coleridge, p. 133, Herbart, p. 153.

beauty is something supervening on the symmetry and that the symmetrical is beautiful for some other reason?

[Beauty is the expression, in matter, of reason, which is divine.]

2. What, then, is the primary beauty of bodies? There is such a beauty and it is perceived at first sight, and the soul, as being ware of it, calls it by name and, recognizing it, welcomes it and is wedded to it. But if the soul meet with the ugly, it shrinks from it and refuses and rejects it, not consenting with it, but alien. Our belief is that the soul, being what it is, and belonging to the world of true reality, when it sees what is akin to it or a trace of kinship, acknowledges it with transport and is reminded of itself and of its own things. But what likeness can there be between the beauties of this world and divine beauties? For if there is likeness we should have to say they were alike. Yet how can they be alike beautiful? Our belief is that the things of this world are beautiful by partaking in an essential character.[1] For everything that is formless, though its nature admits of form and essential character, so long as it is devoid of rationality and essential character is ugly and excluded from the divine and rational. That is the absolutely ugly. But a thing can also be ugly if it be not completely mastered by form and rationality, because its matter does not admit of being completely formed in accordance with an essential character. But when essential character has been added to a thing, so as to make it one by organizing its parts, it confers system and unity of plan and makes the thing coherent. For since the essential character was one, that which was formed by it had to become one, so far as the multiplicity of its parts allowed. Beauty is then enthroned upon the unity thus created, conferring itself both upon the parts and upon the whole. But when beauty takes possession of something simple and homogeneous, it confers itself upon the whole. For instance, sometimes a whole house receives beauty together with all its parts; sometimes a

[1] εἶδος

single stone receives it from the power of nature as the
house does from art. It is in this way that bodies become
beautiful by sharing in the rationality that comes from
the divine.

[Beauty can be contemplated without the aid of the senses.]

3. Beauty is recognized by a faculty designed for it,
a faculty which is more acute in judging its appropriate
objects than is any other even when the rest of the soul
concurs. Perhaps the soul pronounces by setting the
essential character which it comprehends beside the
objects and using that as a criterion of rightness. But
how can what is material be matched with what is prior
to matter? How can the architect compare the house
before him with the essential character of a house comprehended by his soul, and pronounce it beautiful? Is it
because the spatial house, if you could take away the
stones, would be the essence already comprehended by
his soul, but now extended as matter is in space?[1] The
essence is not spatial but it appears in what is extended.

[Physical beauty is expressive of spiritual dispositions.]

5. What is it which arouses this passionate emotion in
lovers? Not shape, nor colour, nor stature, but soul,
which itself has no colour, but which has discretion and
the splendour, itself colourless, of other excellencies. It is
when you see this in yourself, or behold in others 'greatness' of soul, and 'fairness' of mind, and 'transparent' discretion, and courage showing a stout 'face', and reserve
and modesty 'blooming' in a heart that is frank and free
and tranquil, with the divine gift of reason 'shining'
over all. These are what you love and delight in. . . .

6. The soul is beautiful in virtue of intelligence, and
other things are beautiful so far as the soul gives them
form—all things that are beautiful in actions and ways
of life. And it is soul which gives even bodies the right to
be called beautiful.[1] . . .

[1] Cf. Hegel, p. 162.

[But physical beauty really does express the spiritual.]

II. ix. 16. What man with music in his soul, beholding the harmony in the intelligible world, but must be moved by the harmony in sounds that are heard with the ear? Or who that is conversant with geometry and numbers but will take pleasure in the symmetry, the proportion, and the order which he can see with his eyes? Since even those who look with their eyes at pictures drawn by artists do not all see alike the same things, but if they recognize in what is given to their senses a representation of something in the world of thought, they are stirred to the recollection of the original. And when this happens love is born. But if one who sees beauty well presented in a face is emparadised, can any one be so dull and sluggish as to behold all the beauties of the visible world, all its symmetry and ordered vastness, and the distant stars revealing their essential nature,[1]—could any man behold all this and not be overcome by awe as he bethinks him whence such things must come? He could neither have had understanding of earthly things nor any vision of the heavenly.

[The nature and origin of artistic beauty.]

IV. iii. 18. Deliberate reasoning occurs in our mortal life when the soul is uncertain and troubled and not at its best. For the need of reasoning is a defect or inadequacy of apprehension. So in the arts; when artists falter, reasoning takes the reins; but when there is no hitch their imagination[2] governs them and achieves the work.

V. viii. 1. Suppose two things, two stones for instance, lying side by side in space, one shapeless and untouched by art, the other subdued already by art into the image of god or man, some Grace or Muse, perhaps, if it be divine, or, if human, not any individual, but composed of all beauties. That stone which the art has formed to the beauty of an essential character[3] is not beautiful in

[1] εἶδος

[2] In this and the next passage τέχνη seems to be almost exactly Coleridge's 'shaping spirit of imagination.' Cf. Bergson, p. 206.   [3] εἶδος

virtue of being a stone, for then the other would have been so equally, but in virtue of the character[1] which the art has given it. Now this essence or character was not in the material, but was in the conceiving mind, even before it entered into the stone. But it was in the artist not by virtue of his having eyes and hands, but by virtue of his imagination.[2] And this beauty, already comprehended in his imagination, was far greater. For this went not out of him into the stone, but abode with him and gave birth to a lesser beauty. And even so, this lesser beauty could not there preserve the purity of the design, but only so far as the stone was subdued to the art.[2] But if the external product of the art is after art's own nature and image, and if what art produces is beautiful so far as the nature of the product allows, then the shaping spirit[2] must be more highly and truly beautiful, since it has the truly artistic beauty, which is greater and more beautiful than exists in anything external. . . .

But if any one censure the arts on the ground that their products only copy the originals of nature,[3] we may reply that natural objects, too, are copies of an Original. And further we must recognize that the arts do not merely copy the visible world but ascend to the principles on which nature is built up; and further, that many of their creations are original. For they certainly make good the defects of things, as having the source of beauty in themselves. Thus Pheidias did not use any visible model for his Zeus, but apprehended him as he would appear if he deigned to show himself to our eyes.

[Physical beauties are produced by the art of the Creator.]

2. But let us leave the arts and consider what they are said to imitate, the acknowledged beauties of nature: rational animals and unreasoning things and especially such as achieve their end because the creative, shaping power[4] has subdued the material and attained the

---

[1] εἶδος   [2] See footnote 2, p. 47. Cf. Croce, p. 243.
[3] Cf. Plato, *Republic*, p. 21, Schopenhauer, p. 138.   [4] Cf. Schelling, p. 136.

essence[1] of its design. Wherein lies the beauty of such things? Certainly not in the blood and menses, whose colour is different from ours, and their shape either none or ugly, since they are a sort of crude material. What kindled Helen's beauty, for which nations fought, or all the beauties of women like the Queen of Love? What the beauty of that Queen herself or of any being that might be perfect in beauty, man or god, incarnate or unrevealed, yet possessed of beauty were it but visible?

Is it not the essential character[1] conferred on all these creatures by the creator which makes them beautiful, just as we said that it was conferred by the arts upon their products? What is the conclusion? Can products and the design carried out in matter be beautiful, and can that which is not materialized but is only in the creator not be beauty, though it is prior and immaterial and unextended? If mere extended material had been beautiful, the creative design, not being extended, could not have been beautiful. But if the same essence,[1] whether it be manifested on a large or a small scale, similarly affects and moves the beholder's soul by its native power, we cannot ascribe the beauty to the extended bulk. . . .

But Nature, which has created such beautiful things, is beautiful in a prior sense; yet we, who are wont to have no sense or knowledge of spiritual things, follow after material things, not recognizing that it is the spiritual which moves us. As if one seeing his own reflection, and knowing not whence it came, should pursue that.[2] . . .

VI. vii. 22. Even love of mortal bodies is not for their material substance but for the beauty embodied in them. . . . We meet, as it were, a beautiful face which yet cannot ravish our eyes, because there is no bloom of charm upon its beauty.

So we must admit that even here beauty is rather something which shines through symmetry than symmetry itself, and it is this beauty which is lovely. Else why is there a greater light of beauty in a living face, and only

[1] εἶδος [2] Cf. Croce, p. 244, Gentile, p. 327.

a vestige of it after death, even before the fleshly linea-
ments be wasted? And of portraits the more lively are
more beautiful, even though they be less regular. And
why does a living man, though less comely, surpass the
portrait of a beauty? Surely because his beauty is more
desirable, and that is because it has the soul of life.

ST. THOMAS AQUINAS
About 1225-74

Ultimate reality cannot be completely known by man, and such
knowledge as he can attain of it is not intuitive, but the result of
a laborious process of discursive thought. Yet nothing else than
a perfect knowledge of it would satisfy him, since what is ultimately real is ultimately good.

But in the immediate perception of *some* individual sensible
objects man attains, without discursive thought, a satisfaction
which is analogous, on a small scale, to the complete satisfaction.
This is so because the ultimate reality appears through or in the
individual sensible object.

The reason why it thus appears in or through *some* individual
sensible objects, is that there is a real difference in these objects,
not a difference in man's attitude to them. They are objects
where the matter and form or essential character are mutually
adequate, so that there is completeness and due proportion of
parts, and distinctness like the clarity of colour. Objects which
the form thus shines through or illuminates are peculiarly suited
to our faculties of perception and are beautiful. So beauty
appeals primarily to our intelligence and only incidentally to
our practical nature or desires.

This is a rather bold interpretation of the cursory and eclectic
but very suggestive remarks of St. Thomas about beauty. It
may read into him a closer resemblance to neo-Platonic tradition and more anticipation of post-Kantian idealism than he
would have liked. But the Christianity which influenced his
formulation of that tradition also influenced Schelling's.

Summa Theologica[1] (1267-73)

1. xxxix. 8. For beauty there are three requirements.
First, a certain wholeness or perfection, for whatever is

---

[1] There is a translation by the English Dominican Fathers.

incomplete is, so far, ugly; second, a due proportion or harmony; and third, clarity, so that brightly coloured things are called beautiful.

II. (2). cxlv. 2. The beauty of the body consists in a man having his bodily members well proportioned, together with a certain appropriate clarity of colour.

I. v. 4. Beauty and goodness are inseparable,[1] for they are based on the same thing, namely the form; and hence what is good is praised as being beautiful. But they are distinguishable;[2] since the good concerns desire and is what all desire, and is therefore conceived as the end, for desire is a kind of impulse towards something. But beauty concerns our cognitive faculty, for those things are called beautiful whose sight pleases. So beauty consists in due proportion, since sense delights in things duly proportioned as in things like to itself.[3] For sense is a kind of correspondence,[4] and so is every power of cognition. And since cognition is by assimilation [of the knower and the known] and assimilation is of the form, beauty belongs strictly to the category of the formal cause.

II. (1). xxvii. 1. The beautiful coincides with the good but is distinguishable. For since the good is 'that which all things desire,' it follows from our definition of the good that in it desire should be satisfied. But it is implied in the definition of beauty that by its very sight or recognition desire should be satisfied. Wherefore those senses are most concerned with beauty which are most concerned in apprehension, namely the sight and hearing, which minister to reason.[5] For we speak of beautiful sights and sounds, but do not give the name of beauty to the objects of the other senses, such as tastes or smells. Thus it is clear that beauty affords to our faculty of knowledge something ordered, over and above the good; so that what simply satisfies desire is called good, but that whose very apprehension pleases is called beautiful.

---

[1] *in subiecto idem.*   [2] *ratione differunt.*   [3] *in sibi similibus.*
[4] *ratio.* Cf. Aristotle, *De Anima*, 424ᵃ27, 426ᵇ3, Kant, p. 114.
[5] Cf. Plato, p. 15.

3778   H

Commentary on the Sentences (1254–6)

I. xxxi. 2. Beauty is not essentially[1] desirable, except so far as it partakes of the essence of the good. And to that extent truth also is desirable. But according to its own essence it has clarity.

SIR PHILIP SIDNEY
1554–86
An Apologie for Poetrie

Written about 1581;[2] first edition, 1595

The Metaphisick, though it be in the seconde and abstract notions, and therefore be counted supernaturall: yet doth hee indeede builde upon the depth of Nature: onely the Poet, disdayning to be tied to any such subjection, lifted up with the vigor of his owne invention, dooth growe in effect, another nature, in making things either better then Nature bringeth forth, or quite a newe formes such as never were in Nature, as the *Heroes*, *Demigods*, *Cyclops*, *Chimeras*, *Furies*, and such like: so as hee goeth hand in hand with Nature, not inclosed within the narrow warrant of her guifts, but freely ranging onely within the Zodiack of his owne wit.

Nature never set forth the earth in so rich tapistry, as divers Poets have done, neither with plesant rivers, fruitful trees, sweet smelling flowers: nor whatsoever els may make the too much loved earth more lovely. Her world is brasen, the Poets only deliver a golden: but let those things alone and goe to man, for whom as the other things are, so it seemeth in him her uttermost cunning is imployed, and knowe whether shee have brought

---

[1] *Non habet rationem appetibilis.*

[2] Sidney was probably answering the puritanical censures of poetry in Gosson's *School of Abuse* (1579, reprinted by Arber). The apologetic is traditional, being on the same lines as Boccaccio, *De Genealogia Deorum* (1472), and Daniello, *Poetica* (1536). See Saintsbury, *History of Criticism*. The alternative title—*The Defence of Poesie*—has equal authority. For similar English works of the time see Gregory Smith, *Elizabethan Critical Essays*.

foorth so true a lover as *Theagines*, so constant a friende as *Pilades*, so valiant a man as *Orlando*, so right a Prince as *Xenophons Cyrus*: so excellent a man every way, as *Virgils Aeneas*: neither let this be jestingly conceived, because the works of the one be essentiall: the other, in imitation or fiction, for any understanding knoweth the skil of the Artificer: standeth in that *Idea* or fore-conceite of the work, and not in the work it selfe. And that the Poet hath that *Idea*, is manifest, by delivering them forth in such excellencie as hee hath imagined them. Which delivering forth also, is not wholie imaginative, as we are wont to say by them that build Castles in the ayre: but so farre substantially it worketh, not onely to make a *Cyrus*, which had been but a particuler excellencie, as Nature might have done, but to bestow a *Cyrus* upon the worlde, to make many *Cyrus's*, if they wil learne aright why, and how that Maker made him.

Neyther let it be deemed too sawcie a comparison to ballance the highest poynt of mans wit with the efficacie of Nature: but rather give right honor to the heavenly Maker of that maker: who having made man to his owne likenes, set him beyond and over all the workes of that second nature, which in nothing hee sheweth so much as in Poetrie: when with the force of a divine breath, he bringeth things forth far surpassing her dooings. . . .

Poesie therefore is an arte of imitation, for so *Aristotle* termeth it in his word *Mimesis*, that is to say, a representing, counterfetting, or figuring foorth: to speake metaphorically, a speaking picture: with this end, to teach and delight. . . .

Nowe therein of all Sciences, (I speak still of humane, and according to the humaine conceits) is our Poet the Monarch. For he dooth not only show the way, but giveth so sweete a prospect into the way, as will intice any man to enter into it. Nay, he dooth as if your journey should lye through a fayre Vineyard, at the first give you a cluster of Grapes: that full of that taste, you may long to passe further. He beginneth not with obscure

definitions, which must blur the margent with interpretations, and load the memory with doubtfulnesse: but
hee commeth to you with words sent in delightfull proportion, either accompanied with, or prepared for the
well inchaunting skill of Musicke; and with a tale for-
sooth he commeth unto you: with a tale which holdeth
children from play, and old men from the chimney
corner. And pretending no more, doth intende the win-
ning of the mind from wickednesse to vertue: even as the
childe is often brought to take most wholsom things, by
hiding them in such other as have a pleasant tast: which
if one should beginne to tell them, the nature of *Aloes*, or
Rubarb they shoulde receive, woulde sooner take their
Phisicke at their eares, then at their mouth.[1] . . .

For even those harde harted evill men, who thinke vertue a schoole name, and knowe no other good, but *indul-
gere genio*, and therefore despise the austere admonitions
of the Philosopher, and feele not the inward reason they
stand upon; yet will be content to be delighted: which is
al, the good felow Poet seemeth to promise: and so steale
to see the forme of goodnes (which seene they cannot
but love) ere themselves be aware, as if they tooke a
medicine of Cherries. . . .

Certainly I must confesse my own barbarousnes, I
never heard the olde song of *Percy* and *Duglas*, that I
found not my heart mooved more then with a Trumpet.

FRANCIS BACON, LORD VERULAM

1561–1626

The Proficience and Advancement of Learning (1605)

II. xiii. The vse of this FAINED HISTORIE hath beene to
giue some shadowe of satisfaction to the minde of Man
in those points wherein the Nature of things doth denie
it, the world being in proportion inferiour to the soule;
by reason whereof there is agreeable to the spirit of Man

[1] Cf. Croce, p. 237.

a more ample Greatnesse, a more exact Goodnesse, and a more absolute varietie then can bee found in the Nature of things. Therefore, because the Acts or Euents of *true Historie* haue not that Magnitude which satisfieth the minde of Man, *Poesie* faineth Acts and Euents Greater and more Heroicall; because *true Historie* propoundeth the successes and issues of actions not so agreable to the merits of Vertue and Vice, therefore *Poesie* faines them more iust in Retribution and more according to Reuealed Prouidence; because *true Historie* representeth Actions and Euents more ordinarie and lesse interchanged, therefore *Poesie* endueth them with more Rarenesse and more vnexpected and alternatiue Variations: So as it appeareth that *Poesie* serueth and conferreth to Magnani-mitie, Moralitie, and to delectation. And therefore it was euer thought to haue some participation of diuineness, because it doth raise and erect the Minde, by submitting the shewes of things to the desires of the Mind, whereas reason doth buckle and bowe the Mind vnto the Nature of things. And we see that by these insinuations and con-gruities with mans Nature and pleasure, ioyned also with the agreement and consort it hath with Musicke,[1] it hath had accesse and estimation in rude times and barbarous Regions, where other learning stoode excluded. . . .

And the cause was for that it was then of necessitie to expresse any point of reason which was more sharpe or subtile then the vulgar in that maner, because men in those times wanted both varietie of examples and sub-tiltie of conceit: And as *Hierogliphikes* were before Letters, so parables were before arguments. . . . Neuerthelesse in many the like incounters, I doe rather think that the fable was first and the exposition deuised then that the Morale was first & thereupon the fable framed. . . .

But to ascribe vnto it that which is due for the expressing of affections, passions, corruptions and customes, we are beholding to Poets more then to the Philosophers workes, and for wit and eloquence not much lesse then to

[1] Cf. Dante, *De Vulgari Eloquio*, 'Fictio rhetorica in musica posita.'

Orators harangues. But it is not good to stay too long in the Theater: let vs now passe on to the iudicial Place or Pallace of the Mind, which we are to approach and view with more reuerence and attention.[1]

Essayes or Counsels, XLIII. Of Beauty (1607–1625)[2]

That is the best part of beauty, which a picture cannot express; no nor the first sight of the life. There is no excellent beauty that hath not some strangeness in the proportion. A man cannot tell whether Apelles or Albert Durer were the more trifler; whereof the one would make a personage by geometrical proportions; the other, by taking the best parts out of divers faces, to make one excellent. Such personages, I think, would please nobody but the painter that made them. Not but I think a painter may make a better face than ever was; but he must do it by a kind of felicity, (as a musician that maketh an excellent air in music,) and not by rule. A man shall see faces, that if you examine them part by part, you shall find never a good; and yet altogether do well.

THOMAS HOBBES
1588–1679[3]
Leviathan (1651)

vi. Whatsoever is the object of any mans Appetite or Desire; that is it, which he for his part calleth *Good*: And the object of his Hate, and Aversion, *Evill*; And of his Contempt, *Vile*, and *Inconsiderable*. For these words of Good, Evill, and Contemptible, are ever used with relation to the person that useth them: There being nothing simply and absolutely so; nor any common Rule of Good and Evill, to be taken from the nature of the objects themselves. . . . Of Good there be three kinds; Good in the Promise, that is *Pulchrum*; Good in Effect, as the end

---

[1] Cf. Hegel, p. 175.   [2] Three versions, with much variety of spelling.
[3] For the critical works of Hobbes and other writers of the period see Spingarn, *Critical Essays of the XVIIth Century.*

desired, which is called *Jucundum, Delightfull*; and Good
as the Means, which is called *Vtile, Profitable*.

.   .   .   .   .   .

Sudden Glory, is the passion which maketh those *grimaces*
called LAUGHTER; and is caused either by some sudden
act of their own, that pleaseth them; or by the apprehension of some deformed thing in another, by comparison
whereof they suddenly applaud themselves.

GOTTFRIED WILHELM LEIBNIZ
1646–1716
Meditations on Knowledge, Truth, and Ideas (1684)

An *obscure* or vague idea is one that does not suffice for
the recognition of its object. . . . If I can recognize the
thing I have *clear* or vivid knowledge of it, but this again
may be either confused [sensuous] or distinct [intellectual].
It is confused [1] if I cannot enumerate one by one the
marks which suffice for distinguishing the thing from
others. . . . Thus we see painters and other artists well
enough aware what is right and what is faulty, but
often unable to give any reason for their taste: if asked,
they reply that the work they dislike lacks a *je ne sais quoi*.[2]

Theodicy (1710)

ii. 148. The chief end . . . of poetry should be to teach
prudence and virtue by examples.
[i.e. in vivid, 'confused' ideas].

GIAN VINCENZO GRAVINA
1664–1718
A Discourse on the Ancient Fictions (1696)[3]

I. i. All the passions beget in us a kind of delirium in
greater or less degree according to the greater or less

---

[1] Cf. Baumgarten, *Philosophical Thoughts*, p. 82.   [2] Bouhours, *Entretiens*.
[3] Practically reproduced in his *Della Ragion Poetica*, 1708.

violence of the spirits which assail the fancy. This is so above all with ambition and love, for these impress their objects—the desired honour or face—with greater strength, and occupy almost the whole sphere of our imagination. The reason for this is that the idea of distance in space or time is excluded from our imagination, and so in fact are all ideas which suggest the absence of the honour or the face to which these passions refer. Consequently the mind embraces the imagined rank or beauty as if it were truly present. And so it comes about that for the most part men dream with open eyes.

ii. Now poetry besieges our imagination on all sides with lively pictures and appearances which have an effective likeness to the truth, and it keeps far from us the images of contrary things, which disprove the reality of what the poet expresses. . . . Hence the poet, by images referring to nature and by lively pictures resembling the true existence and nature of the imagined things, moves and excites the imagination, exactly as the realities do.

vii. Poetry is a kindly magician, it is a delirium which purges us of madness. . . . Vulgar minds, which are almost entirely wrapped in the mists of imagination, are closed to the stimulus of truth and of knowledge through universals. If these are to find entrance there, they must be embodied in figures apt to the fancy.

xi. By means of sensible images, the laws of nature and of God are introduced into the popular mind, and the seeds of religion and morality are sown.

JOHN DENNIS

1657–1734

The Advancement and Reformation of Modern Poetry
(1701)

Epistle Dedicatory. The end of Poetry is to Instruct and Reform. . . . Passion is the principle thing in Poetry. . . . I am no further pleas'd nor instructed by any Tragedy, than as it excites Passion in me. . . . A Poet is capacitated by that which is commonly call'd Regularity, to excite the ordinary Passions more powerfully by the constitution of the Fable.

Pt. I, ch. v. Poetry then is an imitation of Nature by a pathetick and numerous Speech. . . . Passion is still more necessary to it than Harmony. For Harmony only distinguishes its instrument from that of Prose, but Passion distinguishes its very nature and character. For therefore Poetry is Poetry, because it is more passionate and sensual[1] than Prose. . . . For Passion can please without Harmony, but Harmony tires without Passion. And in Tragedy and in Epick Poetry a man may instruct without Harmony but never without Passion. . . . There must be Passion every where in Poetry and Painting.

vi. Most of our thoughts are naturally attended with some sort and some degree of Passion. And 'tis the expression of this Passion which gives us so much pleasure, both in Conversation and in Human Authors. . . . . But these passions that attend upon our thoughts are seldom so strong, as they are in those kind of thoughts which we call Images.

xv. Nature is the same thing with Genius, and Genius and Passion are all one.

II. i. As the misery of man proceeds from the discord and those civil jars that are maintained within him, it follows that nothing can make him happy, but what can remove that discord, and restore the Harmony of the Human Faculties.[2] So that must be the best and the nobler Art, which makes the best Provision at the same time for the satisfaction of all the Faculties, the Reason, the Passions, the Sences. . . . In a sublime and accom-

---

[1] Cf. Milton, *Treatise of Education* (1650), 'Poetry . . . simple, sensuous and passionate'.

[2] Cf. Richards, p. 282. Dennis is surely influenced by Dryden, *Defence of an Essay of Dramatic Poesy* (1668): 'Delight is the chief, if not the only end of poetry; instruction can be admitted but in the second place, for poesy only instructs as it delights.' And in general see Ker, *Essays of John Dryden*. Cf. Castelvetro, *Aristotle's Poetics* (1570) 'Poetry was invented merely to delight and entertain . . . the minds of the vulgar.'

plish'd Poem, the Reason and Passions and Sences are pleas'd at the same time superlatively . . . The Reason further finds its account, in the exact perpetual Observance of Decorums, and in beholding itself exalted by the exaltation of the Passions. . . . Those very Passions which plague and torment us in life, please us, nay, transport us in Poetry. . . . He who is entertain'd with an accomplish'd Poem, is for a time at least restor'd to Paradise. . . . But nothing that is meerly Human can be on all sides perfect. The Delight which Poetry gives is neither perpetual, nor are all men capable of it. Religion alone can provide man a pleasure that is lasting, as it may be universal.[1]

LUDOVICO ANTONIO MURATORI
1672–1750
The Perfection of Italian Poetry (1706)

I. iv. Moral philosophy has found another daughter or minister, even more delightful and useful than history: poetry, an art that partakes both of history and of rhetoric. . . .Poetry, as an imitative art and composer of poems, has for its end delight; as an art subordinate to moral philosophy or politics its end is to be of service to others. . . . By *beautiful* we generally understand whatever, when seen, heard, or understood, delights, pleases, and ravishes us by causing within us agreable sensations and love. God is the most beautiful of all things. . . .

vi. Truth and goodness are the two ultimate ends to which the desires of our intellect and our will always and naturally tend. The former faculty longs to know all that is within or without us; the latter to obtain that which by its goodness may make us happy. And these two mighty appetites never rest until they come to enjoy the beatific vision, which is the vision of God, in whom are conjoined the supreme truth and supreme goodness.[2] But since in our fallen and banished state many obstacles, by occasion

[1] Cf. Schopenhauer, p. 148; Hegel, p. 165.   [2] Cf. St. Thomas, p. 51.

of the body and of evil passions, every day can hinder the soul in these two flights, natural though they be, God has willed, by stamping beauty upon truth and goodness, greatly to strengthen the natural inclination of our souls. . . .

In poetry, which delights our understanding, is found an element of beauty which belongs to the sense of hearing, namely the harmony and music of the verse. But such beauty is a superficial ornament, necessary indeed to beautiful poetry, but not able to make it truly and intrinsically beautiful. . . . The beauty which by its sweetness delights and moves the human understanding is nothing else than an illumination or resplendent aspect of the truth. This light, this aspect, whenever it succeeds in illuminating our soul, and by its sweetness driving out ignorance (one of the most grievous penalties bequeathed us by our first father) causes in us a delicious pleasure, a most grateful emotion. This illumination consists in brevity or clarity[1] or evidence or force or novelty, nobility, usefulness, magnificence, proportion, arrangement, probability, and other virtues which can accompany truth. . . . Poetry on the one hand depicts and represents the truth as it is, or rather as it should and could be, and on the other depicts it simply for the sake of depicting or imitating, and by this imitation furnishing delight. . . .

vii. Now poetry may delight in two ways; either by the things and truths which it imitates, or by its manner of imitating them. The truths and things represented by the poet may delight us either because they are new and marvellous in themselves or because they become so in the poet's hands. . . . This office [of finding or making what is wonderful and new] belongs to the intellect and to the imagination. . . .

xiv. The power or faculty of the mind which apprehends and recognizes sensible objects or, to speak more accurately, their images, is the imagination or fancy; which, being placed, as we hold, in the inferior part of the soul,

[1] Cf. St. Thomas, p. 51.

we may conveniently call *Inferior Apprehension.*[1] Our soul has another apprehension of things, which we call *Superior,*[1] because it is placed in the superior, reasonable, and divine part, and which is commonly named *Understanding.* The office of the imagination is not to inquire or know if things are true or false but merely to apprehend them; it is the office of the understanding to know and to inquire whether these are true or false. When we reflect or think, these two powers co-operate, the inferior supplying the superior with images or shadows of objects out of its store-house without fresh recourse to the senses. Or the inferior by itself may make use of these shadows to imagine things already apprehended, or to fashion from them new shadows, since it has the power of conceiving new images. So the imagination governs this private arsenal or secret treasury of our soul, where are assembled, as it were in miniature, so many and so various sensible objects, destined to give, so to speak, material body to the thoughts and internal operations of man. As these images, which are also called *idols,* are apprehended by the inferior faculty and arranged like so much merchandise in a great market-place or fair, with more or less order, either the imagination itself or the understanding itself proceeds instantaneously to select those from which our thoughts are formed, joining some hitherto separate, rejecting others, and not deigning even a glance at some. If in time we wish to bring forth what we have conceived and impart it to others, with marvellous swiftness this same imagination furnishes us with images of words apt to clothe our thought and communicate it to the ears or eyes of men. . . . Now images are formed in three ways. Either the understanding forms them itself with its divine and penetrating power, the imagination supplying nothing but the seed. Or the understanding and imagination unite to form them together. Or else the imagination conceives them alone, taking no counsel with the understanding. . . .

[1] Cf. Baumgarten, p. 84.

For example [of the first activity], our understanding sees many images of men apprehended by the imagination and impressed on it. It unites them, and, from so many particular images which the inferior apprehension had collected, it extracts and forms an image, which was not yet present, conceiving e.g. that 'Every man has the power of laughter.' . . .

The third activity occurs when imagination holds absolute sway in the soul and gives little or no heed to the counsels of the understanding. This is experienced by us in dreams, in violent excitements of passion, in delirium. . . . Our concern is confined to the consideration of those images which are conceived in the second way, that is, when the understanding and the imagination unite harmoniously[1] to conceive things and to set them forth. Now imagination allied with understanding (and therefore pledged to seek some kind of truth) can and does produce images which are either (1) *directly true* to the imagination and *directly* also appear so to the understanding, as when we vividly and appropriately describe a rainbow, a single combat, a spirited horse. . . . Such images represent a truth furnished by sense to the imagination and also recognized as such by the understanding. Or (2) the images are *directly* only *probable* to both imagination and intellect, as, for instance, the imagination of the tragic scene from the fall of Troy . . . the madness of Orlando, and such-like imaginary things, which both to the imagination and the understanding appear perfectly possible and probable. Or (3) the images are *directly true* or *probable to the imagination* but only *indirectly* appear so *to the understanding*, as when, for example, the imagination, seeing the infinite meanders of a stream through a lovely landscape, imagines, what seems to it true or probable, that the stream is enamoured of the flowery lawn and cannot or will not leave it. This image makes the understanding conceive the truth, namely the loveliness of the spot and the

[1] Cf. Kant, p. 113.

voluptuous windings of the stream, not directly (for the literal sense is false) but indirectly.[1] . . .

xv. There are some images which are directly true or probable to the imagination by reason of passion. And truly of these the poet's treasury must be full. . . . These are formed by the imagination when, excited by some passion, it unites two simple and natural images and gives them a shape and nature different from the representation of the senses. In doing this, the imagination pictures for the most part lifeless things as alive. . . . In a lover the imagination is compact of these images, inspired in him by the beloved object. His violent passion makes him, for example, conceive the company and the caresses of his beloved to be bliss so rare and enviable that he truly and naturally imagines all other beings, even grass and flowers, to burn and sigh for that felicity. . . . This is the delusion of a love-sick imagination; but the poet represents this delusion to others, as it was born in his imagination, to make them apprehend vividly the violence of his own passion.

II. x. Having spoken of the intellect and the imagination, it remains that I should say something about the judgement, which among other names is also called *discretion, immediate reason,* and sometimes *good taste,* and is a part, virtue, or faculty of the understanding itself. . . . Judgement is a virtue founded on the consideration of individuals and particular things; and as these may be called innumerable, so are also the laws and rules of judgement. . . . It is that *Virtue of the understanding which teaches us to avoid and pass over all that is inept or prejudicial to the theme we have undertaken and to select all that becomes it.* It is the *Light that discovers to us, according to the circumstances, those extremes between which beauty lies.*

[1] Cf. Ruskin, p. 179.

ANTHONY ASHLEY COOPER, LORD SHAFTESBURY

1671–1713

Characteristicks

ii. *Of Wit and Humour* (1709). We may imagine what we please of a substantial solid Part of Beauty: but were the Subject to be well criticiz'd, we shou'd find, perhaps, that what we most admir'd, even in the Turn of *outward* Features, was but a mysterious Expression, and a kind of shadow of something *inward* in the Temper.

v. *The Moralists* (1709). *The Beautiful, the Fair, the Comely*, were never in the *Matter*, but in the *Art* and *Design*; never in *Body* it-self, but in the *Form* or *Forming Power*. . . .

Never can the *Form* be of real force where it is uncontemplated, unjudg'd of, unexamin'd, and stands only as the accidental Note or Token of what appeases provok'd Sense, and satisfies the brutish Part. . . . *Beauty* and *Good* are still the same.

JOSEPH ADDISON

1672–1719

The Spectator [1] (1712)

411. By the Pleasures of the Imagination or Fancy (which I shall use promiscuously) I here mean such as arise from visible Objects, either when we have them actually in our View, or when we call up their Ideas in our Minds by Paintings, Statues, Descriptions, or any the like Occasion. We cannot indeed have a single Image in the Fancy that did not make its first Entrance through the Sight; but we have the Power of retaining, altering and compounding those Images, which we have once received, with all the varieties of Picture and Vision that are most agreeable . . .The Pleasures of the Imagination,

---

[1] Translated into German, 1745.

taken in the full Extent, are not so gross as those of Sense, nor so refined as those of the Understanding.[1] . . . We immediately assent to the Beauty of an Object, without enquiring into the particular Causes and Occasions of it.

412. I shall first consider those Pleasures of the Imagination, which arise from the actual View and Survey of outward Objects: And these, I think, all proceed from the Sight of what is *Great*, *Uncommon*, or *Beautiful*. . . .

By *Greatness*, I do not mean the Bulk of any single Object, but the Largeness of a whole View, considered as one entire Piece. Such are the Prospects of an open Champian Country, a vast uncultivated Desart, of huge Heaps of Mountains, high Rocks and Precipices, or a wide Expanse of Waters, where we are not struck with the Novelty or Beauty of the Sight, but with that rude kind of Magnificence which appears in many of these stupendous Works of Nature. Our Imagination loves to be filled with an Object, or to grasp at anything that is too big for its Capacity. We are flung into a pleasing Astonishment at such unbounded Views, and feel a delightful Stillness and Amazement in the Soul at the Apprehensions of them. The Mind of Man naturally hates everything that looks like a Restraint upon it.[2] . . . But if there be a Beauty or Uncommonness joined with this Grandeur, as in a troubled Ocean, a Heaven adorned with Stars and Meteors, or a spacious Landskip cut out with Rivers, Woods, Rocks, and Meadows, the Pleasure still grows upon us, as it rises from more than a single Principle.

Every Thing that is *new* or *uncommon* raises a Pleasure in the Imagination, because it fills the Soul with an agreeable Surprize, gratifies its Curiosity, and gives it an Idea of which it was not before possest. . . . It is this that bestowes Charms on a Monster, and makes even the Imperfections of Nature please us. It is this that recommends Variety. . . . But there is nothing that makes its Way more directly to the soul than *Beauty*, which im-

[1] Cf. Kant, pp. 113, 117.   [2] Cf. Longinus, xxxv, p. 38; Kant, § 25, p. 119.

mediately diffuses a secret Satisfaction and Complacency through the Imagination. . . . There is not perhaps any real Beauty or Deformity more in one Piece of Matter than another, because we might have been so made, that whatsoever now appears loathsome to us, might have shewn itself agreeable; but we find by Experience, that there are several Modifications of Matter which the Mind, without any previous Consideration, pronounces at first Sight Beautiful or Deformed. Thus we see that every different Species of sensible Creatures has its different Notions of Beauty, and that each of them is most affected with the Beauties of its own kind. . . .

There is a second Kind of *Beauty* that we find in the several Products of Art and Nature, which does not work in the Imagination with that Warmth and Violence as the Beauty that appears in our proper Species, but is apt, however, to raise in us a secret Delight, and a kind of Fondness for the Places or Objects in which we discover it. This consists either in the Gaiety or Variety of Colours, in the Symmetry and Proportion of Parts, in the Arrangement and Disposition of Bodies, or in a just Mixture and Concurrence of all together. . . .

413. One of the Final Causes of our Delight, in anything that is *great*, may be this. The Supreme Author of our Being has so formed the Soul of Man, that nothing but himself can be its last, adequate, and proper Happiness.[1] . . .

414. If we consider the Works of *Nature* and *Art*, as they are qualified to entertain the Imagination, we shall find the last very defective, in Comparison of the former; for though they may sometimes appear as Beautiful or Strange, they can have nothing in them of that Vastness and Immensity, which afford so great an Entertainment to the Mind of the Beholder.[2] The one may be as Polite and Delicate as the other, but can never shew herself so August and Magnificent in the Design. There is

[1] Cf. St. Thomas, p. 51, Muratori, p. 60.
[2] Cf. Kant's restriction of sublimity to nature, p. 118.

something more bold and masterly in the rough careless
Strokes of Nature, than in the nice Touches and Em-
bellishments of Art. . . . Yet we find the Works of Nature
still more pleasant, the more they resemble those of Art:
For in this case our Pleasure arises from a double Principle; from the Agreeableness of the Objects to the Eye,
and from their Similitude to other Objects. . . . Hence it
is that we take Delight . . . in anything that hath such a
Variety or Regularity as may seem the Effect of Design,
in what we call the Works of Chance.[1] . . .

418. Anything that is disagreeable when looked upon,
pleases us in an apt Description. . . . There is yet another
Circumstance which recommends a Description more
than all the rest, and that is if it represents to us such
Objects as are apt to raise a secret Ferment in the Mind
of the Reader, and to work, with Violence, upon his
Passions. For, in this Case, we are at once warmed and
enlightened, so that the Pleasure becomes more Universal, and is several ways qualified to entertain us. Thus in
Painting, it is pleasant to look on the Picture of any Face,
where the Resemblance is hit, but the Pleasure increases,
if it be the Picture of a Face that is Beautiful, and is still
greater, if the Beauty be softened with an Air of Melancholy or Sorrow. The two leading Passions which the
more serious Parts of Poetry endeavour to stir up in us,
are Terror and Pity. . . . But how comes it to pass, that we
should take delight in being terrified or dejected by a
Description, when we find so much Uneasiness in the
Fear or Grief which we receive from any other Occasion?
If we consider, therefore, the Nature of this Pleasure, we
shall find that it does not arise so properly from the Description of what is terrible, as from the Reflection we
make on ourselves at the time of reading it. When we
look on such hideous Objects, we are not a little pleased
to think we are in no danger of them. . . .

420. Nothing is more pleasant to the Fancy, than to
enlarge itself by Degrees, in its Contemplation of the

[1] Cf. Kant's Adaptation without design, p. 114.

various Proportions which its several Objects bear to
each other, when it compares the Body of Man to the
Bulk of the whole Earth, the Earth to the Circle it describes round the Sun, that circle to the Sphere of the
fixt Stars, the Sphere of the fixt Stars to the Circuit of the
whole Creation, the whole Creation itself to the infinite
Space[1] that is everywhere diffused about it. . . . The
Understanding, indeed, opens an infinite Space on every
side of us, but the Imagination, after a few faint Efforts,
is immediately at a stand.[1] . . .

421. The Pleasures of the Imagination are not wholly
confined to such particular Authors as are conversant in
material Objects, but are often to be met with among the
Polite Masters of Morality, Criticism, and other Speculations abstracted from Matter, who, tho' they do not
directly treat of the visible Parts of Nature, often draw
from them their Similitudes, Metaphors and Allegories.
By these Allusions a Truth in the Understanding is as it
were reflected by the Imagination; we are able to see
something like Colour and Shape in a Notion, and to discover a Scheme of Thoughts traced out upon Matter.
And here the Mind receives a great deal of Satisfaction,
and has two of its Faculties gratified at the same time,
while the Fancy is busie in copying after the Understanding, and transcribing Ideas out of the Intellectual
World into the Material.[2] . . . The most entertaining
(Allusions) lie in the Works of Nature, which are obvious
to all Capacities, and more delightful than what is to be
found in Arts and Sciences. It is this Talent of affecting
the Imagination . . . that has something in it like Creation.

[1] Cf. Longinus ix, p. 37, Kant, § 25, p. 120.
[2] Cf. Kant, pp. 113, 123–4.

FRANCIS HUTCHESON

1694–1740

An Enquiry into the Original of our Ideas of Beauty and Virtue

1725, third edition 1729[1]

I

viii. The only Pleasure of Sense, which many Philosophers seem to consider, is that which accompanys the simple ideas of Sensation: But there are far greater Pleasures in those complex Ideas of Objects, which obtain the Names of *Beautiful, Regular, Harmonious*. . . . So in Musick, the Pleasure of *fine Composition* is incomparably greater than that of any one Note, how sweet, full, or swelling soever. . . .

x. I should rather choose to call our Power of perceiving these Ideas, an internal Sense. . . . Many Men have in the common Meaning, the Senses of Seeing and Hearing perfect enough; they perceive all the *simple Ideas* separately, and have their Pleasures; . . . And yet perhaps they shall find no Pleasure in Musical Compositions, in Painting, Architecture, natural Landskip; or but a very weak one in comparison of what others enjoy. . . .

xiii. This superior Power of Perception is justly called *a Sense*, because of its Affinity to the other Senses in this, that the Pleasure does not arise from any *Knowledge* of Principles, Proportions, Causes, or of the Usefulness of the Object; but strikes us at first with the Idea of Beauty. . . .

xvii. Beauty is either *Original* or *Comparative*; or if any like the Terms better, *Absolute*, or *Relative*:[2] Only let it be observ'd, that by *Absolute* or *Original* Beauty, is not understood any Quality suppos'd to be in the Object, which should of itself be beautiful, without any Relation to any Mind which perceives it: For Beauty, like other Names of sensible Ideas, properly denotes the *Perception* of some

[1] Translated into German, 1762.　　[2] Cf. Home, iii, p. 94, Kant, § 16, p. 116.

Mind. . . . We therefore by *Absolute* Beauty understand only that Beauty, which we perceive in Objects without *comparison* to any thing external, of which the Object is suppos'd an imitation, or Picture; such as that Beauty perceiv'd from the *Works of Nature, artificial Forms, Figures, Theorems. Comparative* or *Relative* Beauty is that which we perceive in Objects, commonly considered as *Imitations* or *Resemblances* of something else. . . .

II. *Of* Original *or* Absolute Beauty

iii. What we call Beautiful in Objects, to speak in the Mathematical Style, seems to be in a compound *Ratio* of *Uniformity* and *Variety*: so that where the *Uniformity* of Bodys is equal, the Beauty is as the *Variety*; and where the *Variety* is equal, the Beauty is as the *Uniformity*. . . .

ix. As to that most powerful Beauty in *Countenances, Airs, Gestures, Motion,* we shall shew in the second Treatise,[1] that it arises from some imagin'd *Indication* of morally good Dispositions of Mind. In motion there is also a natural Beauty, when at fixed periods like Gestures and Steps are regularly repeated. . . .

x. The *Beauty* arising from Mechanism, apparently adapted to the Necessitys and Advantages of any Animal; which pleases us, even tho there be no Advantage to our selves ensuing from it; will be consider'd under the Head of *Relative Beauty*, or *Design*. . . .

xiii. Under *Original Beauty* we may include *Harmony,* or *Beauty of Sound*, if that Expression can be allow'd, because *Harmony* is not usually conceiv'd as an Imitation of anything else. *Harmony* often raises Pleasure in those who know not what is the Occasion of it: and yet the Foundation of this Pleasure is known to be a sort of *Uniformity* . . .

IV. *Of* Relative *or* Comparative Beauty

i. This *Beauty* is founded on a *Conformity* or a kind of *Unity* between the Original and the Copy. . . . To obtain

[1] *An Enquiry Concerning Moral Good and Evil*, VI. iii.

comparative Beauty alone, it is not necessary that there be any Beauty in the Original.

iv. Everything in *Nature*, by our strange inclination to *Resemblance*, shall be brought to represent other things, even the most remote, especially the Passions and Circumstances of human Nature in which we are more nearly concern'd.

V. *Concerning our Reasoning about* Design *and* Wisdom *in the* Cause, *from the* Beauty *or* Regularity *of* Effects

i. As there are an Infinity of *Forms* possible into which any System may be reduc'd, an Infinity of *Places* in which Animals may be situated, and an Infinity of *Relishes* or *Senses* in these Animals is suppos'd possible; that in the immense Spaces any one Animal should by chance be plac'd in a System agreeable to its Taste, must be improbable as *infinite* to one at least.[1] . . . There is another kind of *Beauty* from which we conclude Wisdom in the Cause, as well as Design, *when we see many useful or beautiful Effects flowing from one general Cause.* . . . How incomparably more *beautiful* is this Structure, than if we suppos'd so many *distinct Volitions* in the DEITY, producing every particular Effect, and preventing some of the incidental Evils which casually flow from the *General Law.*[2]

VI. *Of the* Universality *of the* Sense of Beauty *among* Men

i. Since we know not how great a *Variety* of Senses there may be among Animals, there is no Form in *Nature* concerning which we can pronounce, 'That it has no *Beauty*;' for it may still please some *perceiving Power*.[3] But our *Inquiry* is confin'd to Men. . . . There is no Form which seems necessarily disagreeable of itself, when we dread no other Evil from it, and compare it with nothing better of the Kind. . . . No Composition of Objects which give not unpleasant simple Ideas seems positively unpleasant.

[1] Cf. Kant, § 14, p. 114.

[2] Cf. Kant, *Critique of Judgement*, Introduction v and Part II (neither is included in this book).

[3] Cf. ROSS, p. 319.

. . . Our *Sense of Beauty* seems design'd to give us positive Pleasure, but not positive Pain or Disgust, any further than what arises from disappointment. . . .

VII. *Of the Power of* Custom, Education *and* Example, *as to our* Internal Senses

i. There is a *natural* Power of *Perception*, or *Sense of Beauty* in Objects, antecedent to all *Custom*, *Education*, or *Example*. . . .

iii. *Education* and *Custom* may influence our *internal Senses*, where they are antecedently, by enlarging the Capacity of our Minds to retain and compare the Parts of complex Compositions: And then if the finest Objects are presented to us, we grow conscious of a Pleasure far superior to what common Performances excite. But all this presupposes our *Sense* of *Beauty* to be *natural*.

VIII. *Of the* Importance *of the* Internal Senses *in Life, and the* final Causes *of them*

ii. Those Objects of Contemplation in which there is *Uniformity amidst Variety*, are more distinctly and easily comprehended and retain'd than *irregular Objects*. . . . Hence we see how suitable it is to the *sagacious Bounty* which we suppose in the DEITY, to constitute our *internal Senses* in the manner in which they are; by which Pleasure is join'd to the Contemplation of *those Objects* which a finite *Mind* can best imprint and retain the Ideas of with the least Distraction.[1]

GIAMBATTISTA VICO
1668–1744
The New Science
First edition 1725, second 1730, third 1744

The Elements, 36. Strength of imagination is in proportion to weakness of reasoning.

The Elements, 53. Men at first feel without perception,

---

[1] Cf. Kant, § 14, p. 115.

then they perceive with a confused and disturbed mind, finally they reflect with the pure intellect.

This axiom is the principle of poetical statements, which are formed with feelings of passion and emotion, whereas philosophical statements are formed by reflection with reasoning. Hence the latter approach truth as they rise to the universals, the former are more certain the nearer they approach the particulars.

ii. *Introduction*. As much as had been first felt by poets in the way of crude[1] knowledge was later understood in the way of abstract[2] knowledge by the philosophers, so that we might call the former the senses and the latter the mind of the human race. Of which in general might be said what Aristotle said of each man in particular: 'There is nothing in the intellect unless it has first been in the senses.'

Heroic Statements. Abstract statements belong to philosophers since they are about universals, and reflections thereon are the feelings of false and frigid poets.

Poetical figures of speech. In all languages most of the names for lifeless things are transferred from the human body and its parts or from human feelings and passions.

GEORGE BERKELEY, BISHOP OF CLOYNE
1685–1753
The New Alciphron (1732)

iii. 8. *Euphranor*. Pray tell me, Alciphron, are all mankind agreed in the notion of a beauteous face?

Alciphron. Beauty in human-kind seems to be of a mixed and various nature; forasmuch as the passions, sentiments, and qualities of the soul, being seen through and blending with the features, work differently on different minds, as the sympathy is more or less. But with regard to other things is there no steady principle of beauty? Is there upon earth a human mind without the idea of order, harmony, and proportion?

---

[1] *volgare*   [2] *riposta*

Euph. O Alciphron, it is my weakness that I am apt to be lost and bewildered in abstractions and generalities, but a particular thing is better suited to my faculties. I find it easy to consider and keep in view the objects of sense: let us therefore try to discover what their beauty is, or wherein it consists; and so, by the help of these sensible things, as a scale or ladder, ascend to moral and intelligible beauty. Be pleased then to inform me, what is it we call beauty in the objects of sense?

Alc. Every one knows beauty is that which pleases.

Euph. There is then beauty in the smell of a rose, or the taste of an apple?

Alc. By no means. Beauty is, to speak properly, perceived only by the eye.

Euph. It cannot therefore be defined in general—that which pleaseth?[1]

Alc. I grant it cannot.

Euph. How then shall we limit or define it?

Alciphron, after a short pause, said that beauty consisted in a certain symmetry or proportion pleasing to the eye.

Euph. Is this proportion one and the same in all things, or is it different in different kinds of things?

Alc. Different, doubtless. The proportions of an ox would not be beautiful in a horse. And we may observe also in things inanimate, that the beauty of a table, a chair, a door, consists in different proportions.

Euph. Doth not this proportion imply the relation of one thing to another?

Alc. It doth.

Euph. And are not these relations founded in size and shape?

Alc. They are.

Euph. And, to make the proportions just, must not those mutual relations of size and shape in the parts be such as shall make the whole complete and perfect in its kind?

Alc. I grant they must.

---

[1] Cf. Plato, p. 13.

Euph. Is not a thing said to be perfect in its kind when it answers the end for which it was made?[1]

Alc. It is.

Euph. The parts, therefore, in true proportions must be so related, and adjusted to one another, as that they may best conspire to the use and operation of the whole?

Alc. It seems so.

Euph. But the comparing parts one with another, the considering them as belonging to one whole, and referring this whole to its use or end, should seem the work of *reason*: should it not?

Alc. It should.

Euph. Proportions, therefore, are not, strictly speaking, perceived by the sense of sight, but only by reason through the means of sight.

Alc. This I grant.

Euph. Consequently beauty, in your sense of it, is an object, not of the eye, but of the mind.

Alc. It is.

Euph. The eye, therefore, alone cannot see that a chair is handsome, or a door well proportioned.

Alc. It seems to follow; but I am not clear as to this point.

Euph. Let us see if there be any difficulty in it. Could the chair you sit on, think you, be reckoned well proportioned or handsome, if it had not such a height, breadth, wideness, and was not so far reclined as to afford a convenient seat?

Alc. It could not.

Euph. The beauty, therefore, or symmetry of a chair cannot be apprehended but by knowing its use, and comparing its figure with that use; which cannot be done by the eye alone, but is the effect of judgment. It is, therefore, one thing to *see* an object, and another to *discern its beauty.*[2]

Alc. I admit this to be true.

9. *Euph.* The architects judge a door to be of a beautiful

[1] Cf. Xenophon, p. 1. [2] Cf. Moore, p. 246.

proportion, when its height is double of the breadth. But if you should invert a well-proportioned door, making its breadth become the height, and its height the breadth, the figure would still be the same, but without that beauty in one situation which it had in another. What can be the cause of this, but that, in the fore-mentioned supposition, the door would not yield convenient entrances to creatures of a human figure? But, if in any other part of the universe there should be supposed rational animals of an inverted stature, they must be supposed to invert the rule for proportion of doors; and to them that would appear beautiful which to us was disagreeable.

Alc. Against this I have no objection.

Euph. Tell me, Alciphron, is there not something truly decent and beautiful in dress?

Alc. Doubtless, there is.

Euph. Are any likelier to give us an idea of this beauty in dress than painters and sculptors, whose proper business and study it is to aim at graceful representations?

Alc. I believe not.

Euph. Let us then examine the draperies of the great masters in these arts: how, for instance, they use to clothe a matron, or a man of rank. Cast an eye on those figures (said he, pointing to some prints after Raphael and Guido, that hung upon the wall)—what appearance do you think an English courtier or magistrate, with his Gothic, succinct, plaited garment, and his full-bottomed wig; or one of our ladies in her unnatural dress, pinched and stiffened and enlarged, with hoops and whale-bone and buckram, must make, among those figures so decently clad in draperies that fall into such a variety of natural, easy, and ample folds, that appear with so much dignity and simplicity, that cover the body without encumbering it, and adorn without altering the shape?

Alc. Truly I think they must make a very ridiculous appearance.

Euph. And what do you think this proceeds from? Whence is it that the Eastern nations, the Greeks, and

the Romans, naturally ran into the most becoming
dresses; while our Gothic gentry, after so many centuries
racking their inventions, mending, and altering, and
improving, and whirling about in a perpetual rotation
of fashions, have never yet had the luck to stumble on any
that was not absurd and ridiculous? Is it not from hence
—that, instead of consulting use, reason, and convenience,
they abandon themselves to irregular fancy, the unnatural parent of monsters? Whereas the ancients, considering the use and end of dress, made it subservient to
the freedom, ease, and convenience of the body; and,
having no notion of mending or changing the natural
shape, they aimed only at shewing it with decency and
advantage. And, if this be so, are we not to conclude that
the beauty of dress depends on its subserviency to certain
ends and uses?

Alc. This appears to be true.

Euph. This subordinate relative nature of beauty, perhaps, will be yet plainer, if we examine the respective
beauties of a horse and a pillar. Virgil's description of
the former is—

> Illi ardua cervix,
> Argutumque caput, brevis alvus, obesaque terga,
> Luxuriatque toris animosum pectus.[1]

Now, I would fain know whether the perfections and uses
of a horse may not be reduced to these three points,
courage, strength, and speed; and whether each of the
beauties enumerated doth not occasion or betoken one of
these perfections? After the same manner, if we inquire
into the parts and proportions of a beautiful pillar, we
shall perhaps find them answer to the same idea. Those
who have considered the theory of architecture tell us
the proportions of the three Grecian orders were taken
from the human body, as the most beautiful and perfect
production of nature. Hence were derived those graceful
ideas of columns, which had a character of strength
without clumsiness, or of delicacy without weakness.

[1] *Georgics*, iii. 79.

Those beautiful proportions were, I say, taken originally from nature, which, in her creatures, as hath been already observed, referreth them to some end, use, or design. The *gonfiezza* also, or swelling, and the diminution of a pillar, is it not in such proportion as to make it appear strong and light at the same time? In the same manner, must not the whole entablature, with its projections, be so proportioned, as to seem great but not heavy, light but not little; inasmuch as a deviation into either extreme would thwart that reason and use of things wherein their beauty is founded, and to which it is subordinate? The entablature, and all its parts and ornaments, architrave, frieze, cornice, triglyphs, metopes, modiglions, and the rest, have each a use or appearance of use, in giving firmness and union to the building, in protecting it from the weather and casting off the rain, in representing the ends of beams with their intervals, the production of rafters, and so forth. And if we consider the graceful angles in frontispieces, the spaces between the columns, or the ornaments of their capitals—shall we not find, that their beauty riseth from the appearance of use, or the imitation of natural things, whose beauty is originally founded on the same principle? which is, indeed, the grand distinction between Grecian and Gothic architecture; the latter being fantastical, and for the most part founded neither in nature nor in reason, in necessity nor use, the appearance of which accounts for all the beauty, grace, and ornament of the other.

Crito. What Euphranor has said confirms the opinion I always entertained—that the rules of architecture were founded, as all other arts which flourished among the Greeks, in truth, and nature, and good sense. But the ancients, who, from a thorough consideration of the grounds and principles of art, formed their idea of beauty, did not always confine themselves strictly to the same rules and proportions; but, whenever the particular distance, position, elevation, or dimension of the fabric or its parts seemed to require it, made no scruple to depart from them, without deserting the original principles of beauty, which governed whatever deviations they made. This latitude or licence might not, perhaps, be safely trusted with most modern architects, who in their bold sallies seem to act without aim or design; and to be governed by no idea, no reason, or principle of art, but pure caprice, joined with a thorough contempt of that noble simplicity of the ancients, without which there can be no unity, gracefulness, or grandeur in their works; which of consequence must serve only to disfigure and dishonour the nation, being so many monuments to future ages of the opulence and ill taste of the present; which, it is to be feared, would succeed as wretchedly, and make as mad work in other affairs, were men to follow, instead of rules, precepts, and morals, their own taste and first thoughts of beauty.

Alc. I should now, methinks, be glad to see a little more distinctly the use and tendency of this digression upon architecture.

Euph. Was not beauty the very thing we inquired after?

Alc. It was.

Euph. What think you, Alciphron, can the appearance of a thing please at this time, and in this place, which pleased two thousand years ago, and two thousand miles off, without some real principle of beauty?

Alc. It cannot.

Euph. And is not this the case with respect to a just piece of architecture?

Alc. Nobody denies it.

Euph. Architecture, the noble offspring of judgment and fancy, was gradually formed in the most polite and knowing countries of Asia, Egypt, Greece, and Italy. It was cherished and esteemed by the most flourishing states and most renowned princes, who with vast expense improved and brought it to perfection. It seems, above all other arts, peculiarly conversant about order, proportion, and symmetry. May it not therefore be supposed, on all accounts, most likely to help us to some rational notion of the *je ne sais quoi* in beauty? And, in effect, have we not learned from this digression that, as there is no beauty without proportion, so proportions are to be esteemed just and true, only as they are relative to some certain use or end, their aptitude and subordination to which end is, at bottom, that which makes them please and charm?

Alc. I admit all this to be true.

BARON CHRISTIAN VON WOLFF[1]
1679–1764
Empirical Psychology (1732)

543. What pleases is called beautiful, what displeases ugly.

544. Beauty consists in the perfection of a thing so far as the thing is apt thereby to produce pleasure in us. . . . [e.g. We call a picture beautiful because of its resemblance to its subject.]

545. Beauty may be defined as a fitness for pleasing us or as obvious perfection.

546. True beauty arises from perfection. Apparent beauty from apparent perfection.
[Our pleasure in the apparently beautiful thing is not caused by it but by our false opinion of its perfection.]

ALEXANDER GOTTLIEB BAUMGARTEN
1714–62

Baumgarten's positive contribution to *aesthetics* was slight. It consisted chiefly in having, so far as is known, first used that word to designate the philosophy of beauty. Besides this he has some historical importance as having applied the Leibnizian tradition, handed down through Wolff, to aesthetics in detail, and as having provided Kant with a text-book.

Philosophical thoughts on matters connected with Poetry
(1735)

3. Ideas received through our inferior faculty of knowledge are called sensuous (*Repraesentationes sensitivae*).

[1] Wolff has some historical importance as influencing Baumgarten and Kant.

8. A sensuous discourse is perfect in proportion as its component parts arouse many sensuous ideas.

9. A perfect sensuous discourse is a poem.

12. Sensuous ideas are either obscure or clear.

13. Clear or vivid ideas are more poetical than obscure or faint ones.

14. Ideas which can be distinctly conceived, and which are adequate and perfect, are not sensuous and, consequently, not poetical.

15. Since clear or vivid ideas are poetical, but distinct ideas are not, it is only confused [i.e. sensuous] but vivid[1] ideas which are poetical.

16. If one idea comprehends more than others, though all obscurely, it has a greater amount of clearness or vividness (*extensive clarior*) than they.

18. The more definitely things are thought of, the more is comprehended in the idea of them. The more elements are combined in a sensuous idea, so much the greater is its amount of clearness or vividness and so much the more poetical is it.

19. Individuals are perfectly definite; so ideas of individuals are eminently poetical.

20. The idea of a species is more poetical than that of the genus.

24. Our ideas of some present change in ourselves are feelings (*repraesentationes sensuales*); consequently they are sensuous and poetical.

25. Passions are notable degrees of pleasure or pain; consequently such feelings are presented, to the man who is apprehending something, as confused or sensuous ideas of good and evil. Consequently they afford poetical ideas —and it is poetical to arouse passions.

26. When we have an idea of anything as good or bad the idea is, thereby, more comprehensive. So ideas which present themselves in a confused or sensuous way as good or evil have a greater amount of clearness, and are more

[1] Cf. Leibniz, p. 57.

poetical for that reason. But such ideas arouse passions. So to arouse passions is poetical.

27. Stronger feelings are the more clear or vivid.

28. Mental images are sensuous ideas.

29. Images are less clear or vivid than feelings and, therefore, less poetical. Since feelings are occasioned by the excitement of passions, a poem which arouses passion is more perfect than one full of cold imagery. It is more poetical to rouse the passions than to create mere imagery.

65. The connexion of poetical ideas should be apt to arouse sensuous knowledge, that is to say it should be poetical.[1]

77. Since words are among the elements of a poem they should be poetical.

78. In words we distinguish the articulate sounds from the meaning. The more poetical both are, the more perfect the poem.

79. Since metaphorical expressions are mostly the appropriate indications of sensuous ideas, picturesque phrases (*tropi*) are poetical; for the ideas introduced by such figures are sensuous and therefore poetical, because poetical figures furnish composite confused ideas.

109. If we are to call a poem an imitation of nature or of actions, what is thereby required is that its effect should resemble that of nature.

110. Ideas produced by nature, i.e. by the inner principle of change in the universe, and by actions arising out of nature, are never immediately distinct and intellectual, but sensuous; on the other hand they have a very great amount of clearness or vividness. So they are poetical. Consequently the products of nature . . . and of the poet resemble one another.[2] A poem, therefore, is an imitation of nature and of natural actions.

111. When a poem is defined as a metrical discourse in which actions or nature are imitated, we have two essen-

[1] Cf. Alison, p. 105, Croce, p. 241, Richards, p. 278.
[2] Cf. Schelling, p. 135.

tial characteristics not mutually connected.[1] Our theory provides the connexion.

[Because metre pleases [2] the ear and thereby produces attention for many ideas ; this produces a clear or vivid and sensuous or confused idea; and nature also produces such an idea; so metre *is* an imitation of nature[2]—or nature of metre.]

116. The Greek philosophers and the Fathers of the Church already sufficiently distinguished *aistheta* from *noeta* (objects of thought). But obviously for them *aistheta* were not to be identified with things perceptible by the senses, for objects not actually present, namely imaginations, were so called. *Noeta*, as what can be known by the higher faculty of knowledge, are the object of logic; *aistheta* belong to the aesthetical science or to Aesthetic.

Metaphysics (1739)

521. An indistinct idea is called a sensuous idea. My vital powers, then, give me sensuous perceptions by means of an inferior faculty.[3]

662. The appearance of perfection, or perfection obvious to taste in the wide sense, is *beauty*; the corresponding imperfection is ugliness. Hence beauty, as such, delights the observer; ugliness, as such, is disgusting.

Aesthetics (1750)

1. Aesthetics (the theory of the fine arts, the theory of the lower kind of knowledge, the art of thinking beautifully, the art of analogical reasoning) is the science of sensuous knowledge.

14. The end of aesthetics is perfection of sensuous knowledge as such. This is beauty (*Metaphysics*, §§ 511, 662). The defect of sensuous knowledge, to be avoided, is ugliness.

18. Ugly things, as such, may be thought of in a beautiful way, and more beautiful things in an ugly way.

---

[1] Cf. Aristotle, p. 31.

[2] Cf. Reynolds, vii, p. 97. 'Whatever pleases has in it what is analogous to the mind and is, therefore, in the highest sense, natural.' Cf. Dryden, *Essay of Dramatic Poetry*.   [3] Cf. Muratori, p. 62.

91. [Among predisposing causes of beautiful thinking are] all passions of the mind which are not so violent that their appearance suppresses all symbolical knowledge.

483. That of which we have not complete certainty, though we do not apprehend any falsehood in it, is probable. So aesthetic truth, which should rather be called probability, is that grade of truth, which, though not carried to complete certainty, yet contains no obvious falsehood.

484. What the spectators or audience secretly anticipate as they watch or listen, what generally happens or what is the custom, what is popularly believed to happen, or what is at all like these things—whether it be false (in the widest logical sense) or true (in the strictest logical sense), —all that is not easily rejected by our senses, all this is the εἰκός or probable which, on the authority of Aristotle and Cicero, the artistic mind should pursue.

DAVID HUME
1711–76

A Treatise of Human Nature (1738)

II. i. 8. Beauty is such an order and construction of parts, as, either by the *primary constitution* of our nature, by *custom*, or by *caprice*, is fitted to give a pleasure and satisfaction to the soul. This is the distinguishing character of beauty, and forms all the difference betwixt it and deformity, whose natural tendency is to produce uneasiness. Pleasure and pain, therefore, are not only necessary attendants of beauty and deformity, but constitute their very essence. And, indeed, if we consider that a great part of the beauty which we admire either in animals or in other objects is derived from the idea of convenience and utility, we shall make no scruple to assent to this opinion. That shape which produces strength is beautiful in one animal; and that which is a sign of agility, in another. The order and convenience of a palace are no less essential to its beauty than its mere figure and appearance. In like manner the rules of architecture require, that the top of a pillar should be more slender than its base, and that because such a figure conveys to us the idea of security, which is pleasant; whereas the contrary form gives us the apprehension of danger, which is uneasy.

II. ii. 5. It is evident that nothing renders a field more agreeable than its fertility, and that scarce any advantages of ornament or situation will be able to equal this beauty. . . . I know not but a plain overgrown with furze and broom, may be, in itself, as beautiful as a hill covered with vines or olive-trees, though it will never appear so to one who is acquainted with the value of each. But this is a beauty merely of imagination, and has no foundation in what appears to the senses.[1] Fertility and value have a plain reference to use; and that to riches, joy, and plenty, in which, though we have no hope of partaking, yet we enter into them by the vivacity of the fancy, and share them in some measure with the proprietor.

Essay XXIII.   Of the Standard of Taste (1757)

The great variety of Taste, as well as of opinion, which prevails in the world, is too obvious not to have fallen under every one's observation. . . . As this variety of taste is obvious to the most careless enquirer; so will it be found, on examination, to be still greater in reality than in appearance. . . . Every voice is united in applauding elegance, propriety, simplicity, spirit in writing; and in blaming fustian, affectation, coldness and a false brilliancy: But when critics come to particulars, this seeming unanimity vanishes; and it is found, that they had affixed a very different meaning to their expressions. In all matters of opinion and science, the case is opposite: The difference between men is there oftener found to lie in generals than in particulars; and to be less in reality than in appearance. An explanation of the terms commonly ends the controversy, and the disputants are surprized

[1] Cf. Ruskin, p. 178.

to find, that they had been quarrelling, while at bottom they agreed in their judgment. . . .

But though all the general rules of art are founded only on experience and on the observation of the common sentiments of human nature, we must not imagine, that, on every occasion, the feelings of men will be conformable to these rules. . . . A perfect serenity of mind, a recollection of thought, a due attention to the object; if any of these circumstances be wanting, our experiment will be fallacious, and we shall be unable to judge of the catholic and universal beauty. . . . It appears then, that, amidst all the variety and caprice of taste, there are certain general principles of approbation or blame, whose influence a careful eye may trace in all operations of the mind. Some particular forms or qualities, from the original structure of the internal fabric, are calculated to please, and others to displease, and if they fail of their effect in any particular instance, it is from some apparent defect or imperfection in the organ. . . . If, in the sound state of the organ, there be an entire or a considerable uniformity of sentiment among men, we may thence derive an idea of the perfect beauty. . . . But notwithstanding all our endeavours to fix a standard of taste, and reconcile the discordant apprehensions of men, there still remain two sources of variation, which are not sufficient indeed to confuse all the boundaries of beauty and deformity, but will often serve to produce a difference in the degree of our approbation or blame. The one is the different humours of particular men; the other, the particular manners and opinions of our age and country. . . . Where there is such a diversity in the internal frame or external situation as is entirely blameless on both sides, and leaves no room to give one the preference above the other; in that case a certain degree of diversity in judgment is unavoidable, and we seek in vain for a standard, by which we can reconcile the contrary sentiments.

WILLIAM HOGARTH
1697–1764
The Analysis of Beauty (1753)

[The first element in beauty is Fitness, the second Variety, and the third Regularity, but of Regularity only so much as Fitness requires.]

Though all sorts of waving lines are ornamental when properly applied; yet, strictly speaking, there is but one precise line, properly to be called the line of *beauty*. . . . So there is only one precise serpentine line that I call the *line of grace*.

EDMUND BURKE
1729–97

A Philosophical Enquiry into the Origin of our Ideas on the Sublime and Beautiful (1756)[1]

Fifth edition, with an Introductory Discourse concerning Taste, 1767

1. vii. Whatever is fitted in any sort to excite the ideas of pain, and danger, that is to say, whatever is in any sort terrible, or is conversant about terrible objects, or operates in a manner analogous to terror, is a source of the *sublime*; that is it is productive of the strongest emotion which the mind is capable of feeling. I say the strongest emotion, because I am satisfied the ideas of pain are much more powerful than those which enter on the part of pleasure. . . .

When danger or pain press too nearly, they are incapable of giving any delight, and are simply terrible; but at certain distances and with certain modifications, they may be, and they are delightful, as we every day experience.

xiii. Sympathy must be considered as a sort of substitution, by which we are put into the place of another man,

---

[1] Translated into German, 1773.

and affected in many respects as he is affected; so that
this passion may either partake of those which regard
self-preservation, and turning upon pain, may be a source
of the sublime; or it may turn upon ideas of pleasure;
and then whatever has been said of the social affections,
whether they regard society in general, or only some
particular modes of it, may be applicable here. . . .

xiv. I am convinced we have a degree of delight, and
that no small one, in the real misfortunes and pains of
others . . . for terror is a passion which always produces
delight when it does not press too close, and pity is a
passion accompanied with pleasure, because it arises
from love and social affection. . . .

xv. It is thus in real calamities. In imitated distresses the
only difference is the pleasure resulting from the effects
of imitation. . . . When you have collected your audience,
just at the moment when their minds are erect with
expectation, let it be reported that a state criminal of
high rank is on the point of being executed in the
adjacent square; in a moment the emptiness of the
theatre would demonstrate the comparative weakness of
the imitative arts. . . . We delight in seeing things, which
so far from doing, our heartiest desires would be to see
redressed. . . .

ii. i. The passion caused by the great and sublime in
nature, when those causes operate most powerfully, is
astonishment or that state of the soul, in which all its
motions are suspended with some degree of horror. In
this case the mind is so entirely filled with its object, that
it cannot entertain any other. . . .

ii. Whatever therefore is terrible, with regard to sight, is
sublime too, whether this cause of terror, be endued with
greatness of dimension or not.[1] . . .

iii. To make anything very terrible, obscurity seems in
general to be necessary.

iv. The ideas of eternity, and infinity, are among the
most affecting we have; and perhaps there is nothing

---

[1] Cf. Kant, §§ 23–8, pp. 117–20.

of which we really understand so little, as of infinity, and eternity. . . . Hardly anything can strike the mind with its greatness, which does not make some sort of approach towards infinity;[1] which nothing can do whilst we are able to perceive its bounds; but to see an object distinctly, and to perceive its bounds, is one and the same thing. A clear idea is therefore another name for a little idea.[2] There is a passage in the book of Job amazingly sublime, and this sublimity is principally due to the terrible uncertainty of the thing described. *In thoughts from the visions of the night, when deep sleep falleth upon men, fear came upon me and trembling, which made all my bones to shake. Then a spirit passed before my face. The hair of my flesh stood up. It stood still,* but I could not discern the form thereof; *an image was before mine eyes; there was silence; and I heard a voice,—Shall mortal man be more just than God?* . . .

v. Besides these things which *directly* suggest the idea of danger, and those which produce a similar effect from a mechanical cause, I know of nothing sublime which is not some modification of power.

vi. All *general* privations are great, because they are all terrible; *Vacuity, Darkness, Solitude,* and *Silence.*

vii. Greatness of dimension is a powerful cause of the sublime. . . . Extension is either in length, height, or depth. Of these the length strikes least; an hundred yards of even ground will never work such an effect as a tower an hundred yards high, or a rock or mountain of that altitude. I am apt to imagine likewise, that height is less grand than depths; . . . as the great extreme of dimension is sublime, so the last extreme of littleness is in some measure sublime likewise. . . . For division must be infinite as well as addition. . . .

viii. Infinity has a tendency to fill the mind with that sort of delightful horror, which is the most genuine effect, and truest test of the sublime. There are scarce any things which can become the objects of our senses, that are really and in their own nature infinite. But the eye not

---

[1] Cf. Kant, § 25, p. 119.   [2] Cf. Reynolds, vii, p. 97.

being able to perceive the bounds of many things, they seem to be infinite, and they produce the same effects as if they were really so. We are deceived in the like manner, if the parts of some large object are so continued to any indefinite number, that the imagination meets no check which may hinder its extending them at pleasure. . . .

xiii. *Magnificence* is likewise a source of the sublime. A great profusion of things which are splendid or valuable in themselves, is magnificent. The starry heaven, though it occurs so very frequently to our view, never fails to excite an idea of grandeur. . . .

xxii. My first observation will be found very nearly true; that the sublime is an idea belonging to self-preservation; that it is therefore one of the most affecting we have; that its strongest emotion is an emotion of distress; and that no pleasure from a positive cause belongs to it.

III. i. By beauty I mean, that quality or those qualities in bodies, by which they cause love, or some passion similar to it. . . . The passion caused by beauty, which I call love, is different from desire, though desire may sometimes operate along with it. . . .

ii. Beauty hath usually been said to consist in certain proportions of parts. On considering the matter I have great reason to doubt, whether beauty be at all an idea belonging to proportion. Proportion relates almost wholly to convenience, as every idea of order seems to do; and it must therefore be considered as a creature of the understanding, rather than a primary cause acting on the senses and imagination. . . . Proportion is the measure of relative quantity. Since all quantity is divisible, it is evident that every distinct part into which any quantity is divided, must bear some relation to the other parts or to the whole. . . .

iv. You may assign any proportions you please to every part of the human body; and I undertake that a painter shall religiously observe them all, and notwithstanding produce, if he pleases, a very ugly figure. The same painter shall considerably deviate from these proportions, and produce a very beautiful one. . . . Are these proportions exactly the same in all handsome men? or are they at all the proportions found in beautiful women? nobody will say they are; yet both sexes are undoubtedly capable of beauty, and the female of the greatest. . . .

v. The general idea of beauty can be no more owing to customary than to natural proportion. Deformity arises from the want of the common proportions; but the necessary result of their existence in any object is not beauty. . .

vi. It is said that the idea of utility, or of a part's being well adapted to answer its end, is the cause of beauty, or indeed beauty itself. . . . The stomach, the lungs, the liver, as well as other parts, are incomparably well adapted to their purposes; yet they are far from having any beauty. Again, many things are very beautiful, in which it is impossible to discern any idea of use. . . . What idea of use is it that flowers excite?. . . .

ix. So far is perfection, considered as such, from being the cause of beauty; that this quality, where it is highest in the female sex, almost always carries with it an idea of weakness and imperfection. Women are very sensible of this. . . . I know it is in everybody's mouth that we ought to love perfection. This is to me a sufficient proof, that it is not the proper object of love. Who ever said, we *ought* to love a fine woman? . . .

xviii. On the whole, the qualities of beauty, as they are merely sensible qualities, are the following. First, to be comparatively small. Secondly, to be smooth. Thirdly, to have a variety in the direction of the parts; but, fourthly, to have those parts not angular, but melted as it were into each other. Fifthly, to be of a delicate frame, without any remarkable appearance of strength. Sixthly, to have its colours clear and bright, but not very strong and glaring. Seventhly, or if it should have any glaring colour, to have it diversified with others. . . .

xxv. . . . that sinking, that melting, that languor, which is the characteristical effect of the beautiful, as it regards every sense. The passion excited by beauty is in fact nearer to a species of melancholy, than to jollity and mirth. . . .

iv. iii. The only difference between pain and terror is, that things which cause pain operate on the mind, by the intervention of the body; whereas things that cause terror, generally affect the bodily organs by the operation of the mind suggesting the danger; but both agreeing, either primarily, or secondarily, in producing a tension, contraction, or violent emotion of the nerves, they agree likewise in everything else. For it appears very clearly to me, from this, as well as from many other examples, that when the body is disposed, by any means whatsoever, to such emotions as it would acquire by the means of a certain passion; it will of itself excite something very like that passion in the mind. . . .

vii. As common labour, which is a mode of pain, is the exercise of the grosser, a mode of terror is the exercise of the finer parts of the system; and if a certain mode of pain be of such a nature as to act upon the eye or the ear, as they are the most delicate organs, the affection approaches more nearly to that which has a mental cause. In all these cases, if the pain and terror are so modified as not to be actually noxious; if the pain is not carried to violence, and the terror is not conversant about the present destruction of the person, as these emotions clear the parts, whether fine or gross, of a dangerous and troublesome incumbrance, they are capable of producing delight;[1] not pleasure, but a sort of delightful horror, a sort of tranquillity tinged with terror; which, as it belongs to self-preservation, is one of the strongest of all the passions. Its object is the sublime. . . .

xix. When we have before us such objects as excite love and complacency, the body is affected, so far as I could observe, much in the following manner. The head reclines something on one side; the eye-lids are more closed than usual, and the eyes roll gently with an inclination to the object; the mouth is a little opened, and the breath

[1] Cf. Spencer, p. 182.

drawn slowly, with now and then a low sigh: the whole body is composed, and the hands fall idly to the sides. All this is accompanied with an inward sense of melting and languor. . . . From this description it is almost impossible not to conclude, that beauty acts by relaxing the solids of the whole system. There are all the appearances of such a relaxation; and a relaxation somewhat below the natural tone seems to me to be the cause of all positive pleasure.

HENRY HOME, LORD KAMES
1696–1782
Elements of Criticism (1762) [1]

II. vi. Many emotions have some resemblance to their causes. . . . When force is exerted with any effort, the spectator feels a similar effort, as of force exerted within his mind. A large object swells the heart. An elevated object makes the spectator stand erect.[2] Sounds also produce emotions or feelings that resemble them. A sound in a low key brings down the mind.

III. Considering attentively the beauty of visible objects, we discover two kinds. The first may be termed *intrinsic*[3] beauty, because it is discovered in a single object viewed apart without relation to any other. . . . The other may be termed *relative*[3] beauty, being founded on the relation of objects. . . . Intrinsic beauty is a perception of sense merely; for to perceive the beauty of a spreading oak or of a flowing river, no more is required but singly an act of vision. Relative beauty is accompanied with an act of understanding and reflection; for of a fine instrument or engine, we perceive not the relative beauty, until we be made acquainted with its use and destination. . . . Both are equally perceived as belonging to the object . . . an old Gothick tower, that has no beauty in itself, appears

---

[1] Translated into German, 1763, and reviewed, perhaps by Kant himself, in the *Königsbergsche gelehrte und politische Zeitungen* of 5 March 1764. See Schlapp, *Anfänge von Kant's Kritik des Geschmacks.*

[2] Cf. Lipps, p. 257. [3] Cf. Hutcheson, I. xvii, p. 70, and Kant, § 16, p. 116.

beautiful, considered as proper to defend against an enemy. Regularity, uniformity, order and simplicity contribute each of them to readiness of apprehension; and enable us to form more distinct images of objects. . . .

Beauty in its very nature refers to a percipient.

iv. St. Peter's Church at Rome, the great pyramid of Egypt, the Alps towering above the clouds, a great arm of the sea, and above all a clear and serene sky are grand, because besides their size, they are beautiful in an eminent degree.[1]

v. No quality nor circumstance contributes more to grandeur than force.

ix. Nothing can be more happily accommodated to the inward constitution of man, than that mixture of uniformity with variety, which the eye discovers in natural objects.[2]

xxv. Doth it not seem whimsical, and perhaps absurd, to assert, that a man *ought not* to be pleased when he is, or that he *ought* to be pleased when he is not? . . . Do we not talk of a good and a bad taste? . . . The conviction of a common nature or standard and of its perfection, accounts clearly for that remarkable conception we have of a right and a wrong sense or taste.[3]

SIR JOSHUA REYNOLDS

1723-92

Discourses delivered at the Royal Academy

ii. (1769). Style in painting is the same as in writing, a power over materials, whether words or colours, by which conceptions or sentiments are conveyed.

iii (1770). The power of discovering what is deformed in Nature, or, in other words, what is particular and uncommon, can be acquired only by experience; and the whole beauty and grandeur of the Art consists, in my opinion, in being able to get above all singular forms,

[1] Cf. Kant, § 26, p. 119.   [2] Cf. Kant, § 11, p. 114.
[3] Cf. Kant, §§ 8, 17, 20, pp. 112, 117.

local customs, particularities, and details of every kind. All the objects which are exhibited to our view by Nature, upon close examination will be found to have their blemishes and defects. The most beautiful forms have something about them like weakness, minuteness, or imperfection. But it is not every eye that perceives these blemishes. It must be an eye long used to the contemplation and comparison of the forms; and which, by a long habit of observing what any set of objects of the same kind have in common, has acquired the power of discerning what each wants in particular. This long laborious comparison should be the first study of the Painter who aims at the greatest style. By this means, he acquires a just idea of beautiful forms; he corrects Nature by herself, her imperfect state by her more perfect. . . .

Though the most perfect of each of the general divisions of the human figure are ideal, and superior to any individual form of that class; yet the highest perfection of the human figure is not to be found in any one of them. . . . For perfect beauty in any species must combine all the characters that are beautiful in that species. . . . There is, likewise, a kind of symmetry, or proportion, which may properly be said to belong to deformity. A figure lean or corpulent, tall or short, though deviating from beauty, may still have a certain union of the various parts, which may contribute to make them on the whole not unpleasing. . . . As the idea of beauty is of necessity but one, so there can be but one great mode of painting.

IV. (1771). The great end of the Art is to strike the imagination.

V. (1772). If you mean to preserve the most perfect beauty *in its most perfect state*, you cannot express the passions, all of which produce distortion and deformity, more or less, in the most beautiful faces.[1]

VI (1774). What we now call Genius, begins, not where rules, abstractly taken, end; but where known vulgar and trite rules have no longer any place. It must of necessity

[1] Cf. Schelling, p. 135.

be, that even works of Genius, like every other effect, as they must have their cause, must likewise have their rules.

VII (1776). Obscurity . . . is one sort of the sublime.[1] . . .

The natural appetite or taste of the human mind is for Truth; whether that truth results from the real agreement or equality of original ideas among themselves; from the agreement of the representation of any object with the thing represented; or from the correspondence of the several parts of any arrangement with each other. It is the very same taste which relishes a demonstration in geometry, that is pleased with the resemblance of a picture to an original, and touched with the harmony of music. All these have unalterable and fixed foundations in nature. . . . Colouring is true, when it is naturally adapted to the eye, from brightness, from softness, from harmony, from resemblance; because these agree with their object, Nature, and therefore are true; as true as a mathematical demonstration; but known to be true only to those who study these things.

But besides real, there is also apparent truth, or opinion, or prejudice. With regard to real truth, when it is known, the taste which conforms to it is, and must be, uniform. With regard to the second sort of truth, which may be called truth upon sufferance, or truth by courtesy, it is not fixed but variable. However, whilst these opinions and prejudices, on which it is founded, continue, they operate as truth; and the art whose office is to please the mind, as well as instruct it, must direct itself according to opinion, or it will not attain its end. . . . Whatever pleases has in it what is analogous to the mind, and is, therefore, in the highest and best sense of the word, natural. . . . Well-turned periods in eloquence, or harmony of numbers in poetry, which are in those arts what colouring is in painting, however highly we may esteem these, can never be considered as of equal importance with the art of unfolding truths that are useful to mankind, and which make us better or wiser. Nor can

---

[1] Blake thought that all sublimity is founded on minute discrimination.

those works which remind us of the poverty and meanness of our nature, be considered as of equal rank with
what excites ideas of grandeur, or raises and dignifies
humanity.

IX (1780). The Art which we profess has beauty for its
object; this it is our business to discover and to express;
the beauty of which we are in quest is general and intellectual; it is an idea that subsists only in the mind;
the sight has never beheld it, nor has the hand expressed
it: it is an idea residing in the breast of the artist, which
he is always labouring to impart, and which he dies at
last without imparting.

X (1780). Imitation is the means, and not the end of
Art; it is employed by the sculptor as the language by
which his ideas are presented to the mind of the spectator.
Poetry and elocution of every sort make use of signs, but
those signs are arbitrary and conventional. The sculptor
employs the representation of the thing itself; but still as
a means to a higher end—as a gradual ascent always
advancing towards faultless form and perfect beauty. It
may be thought at the first view, that even this form,
however perfectly represented, is to be valued and take
its rank only for the sake of a still higher object, that of
conveying sentiment and character, as they are exhibited
by attitude, and expression of the passions. But we are
sure from experience, that the beauty of form alone,
without the assistance of any other quality, makes of
itself a great work.

XI (1782). There is nothing, however unpromising in
appearance, but may be raised into dignity, convey
sentiment and produce emotion, in the hands of a painter
of genius.

XIII (1786). I observe, as a fundamental ground, common to all the arts with which we have any concern in this
discourse, that they address themselves only to two faculties of the mind, its imagination and its sensibility.

All theories which attempt to direct or to control the
art, upon any principles falsely called rational, which

we form to ourselves upon a supposition of what ought in reason to be the end or means of art, independent of the known first effect produced by objects on the imagination, must be false and delusive. For though it may appear bold to say it, the imagination is here the residence of truth. . . .

The great end of all those arts is, to make an impression on the imagination and the feeling. The imitation of nature frequently does this. Sometimes it fails, and something else succeeds. I think, therefore, the true test of all the arts is not solely whether the production is a true copy of nature, but whether it answers the end of art, which is to produce a pleasing effect upon the mind. . . .

To pass over the effect produced by that general symmetry and proportion by which the eye is delighted, as the ear is with music, architecture certainly possesses many principles in common with poetry and painting. Among those which may be reckoned as the first is, that of affecting the imagination by means of association of ideas. Thus, for instance, as we have naturally a veneration for antiquity, whatever building brings to our remembrance ancient customs and manners, such as the castles of the Barons of ancient chivalry, is sure to give this delight. . . . For this purpose, Vanbrugh appears to have had recourse to some of the principles of the Gothic architecture; which, though not so ancient as the Grecian, is more so to our imagination, with which the artist is more concerned than with absolute truth. . . . It often happens that additions have been made to houses at various times, for use or pleasure. As such buildings depart from regularity, they now and then acquire something of scenery by this accident, which I should think might not unsuccessfully be adopted by an architect in an original plan, if it does not too much interfere with convenience. Variety and intricacy are beauties and excellencies in every other of the arts which address the imagination.

THOMAS REID
1710–96
Essays on the Intellectual Powers (1785)
Essay VIII: on Taste

I. Of Taste

When a beautiful object is before us, we may distinguish the agreeable emotion it produces in us, from the quality of the object which causes that emotion. When I hear an air in music that pleases me, I say, it is fine, it is excellent. This excellence is not in me; it is in the music. ... Though some of the qualities that please a good taste resemble the secondary qualities of body, and therefore may be called occult qualities, as we only feel their effect, and have no more knowledge of the cause, but that it is something which is adapted by nature to produce that effect—this is not always the case. Our judgment of beauty is in many cases more enlightened. A work of art may appear beautiful to the most ignorant, even to a child. It pleases, but he knows not why. To one who understands it perfectly, and perceives how every part is fitted with exact judgment to its end, the beauty is not mysterious; it is perfectly comprehended; and he knows wherein it consists, as well as how it affects him. .... Internal taste ought to be accounted most just and perfect, when we are pleased with things that are most excellent in their kind. ... In some cases, that superior excellence is distinctly perceived, and can be pointed out; in other cases, we have only a general notion of some excellence which we cannot describe.

II. Of Novelty

Novelty is not properly a quality of the thing to which we attribute it, far less is it a sensation in the mind to which it is new; it is a relation which the thing has to the knowledge of the person.

III. *Of Grandeur*

Grandeur . . . seems to be nothing else but such a degree of excellence, in one kind or another, as merits admiration. . . . At first men are prone by nature and by habit to give all their attention to things external. . . . An external existence is ascribed to things which are only conceptions or feelings of the mind. . . . From the time of Des Cartes philosophy took a contrary turn. . . . It was then a very natural progress to conceive, that beauty, harmony, and grandeur, the objects of taste, as well as right and wrong, the objects of the moral faculty, are nothing but feelings of the mind. . . . If we hearken to the dictates of common sense, we must be convinced that there is real excellence in some things, whatever our feelings or constitution be. . . . There is therefore a real intrinsic excellence in some qualities of mind. . . . But it may be asked, Is there no real grandeur in material objects? It will, perhaps, appear extravagant to deny that there is; yet it deserves to be considered, whether all the grandeur we ascribe to objects of sense be not derived from something intellectual, of which they are the effects or signs, or to which they bear some relation or analogy. Besides the relations of effect and cause, of sign and thing signified, there are innumerable similitudes and analogies between things of very different nature, which lead us to connect them in our imagination, and to ascribe to the one what properly belongs to the other. Every metaphor in language is an instance of this; and it must be remembered that a very great part of language, which we now account proper, was originally metaphorical; for the metaphorical meaning becomes the proper, as soon as it becomes the most usual. . . . Grandeur is found, originally and properly, in qualities of mind; it is discerned, in objects of sense, only by reflection, as the light we perceive in the moon and planets is truly the light of the sun; and those who look for grandeur in mere matter, seek the living among the dead. . . .

IV. *Of Beauty*

All the objects we call beautiful agree in two things, which seem to concur in our sense of beauty. *First*, when they are perceived, or even imagined, they produce a certain agreeable emotion or feeling in the mind; and, *secondly*, This agreeable emotion is accompanied with an opinion or belief of their having some perfection or excellence belonging to them. . . . Our determinations with regard to the beauty of objects, may, I think, be distinguished into two kinds; the first we may call instinctive, the other rational. Some objects strike us at once, and appear beautiful at first sight, without any reflection, without our being able to say why we call them beautiful, or being able to specify any perfection which justifies our judgment. . . . The beauty of the object may in such cases be called an occult quality. We know well how it affects our senses; but what it is in itself we know not. But this, as well as other occult qualities, is a proper subject of philosophical disquisition; and by a careful examination of the objects to which Nature hath given this amiable quality, we may perhaps discover some real excellence in the object, or, at least, some valuable purpose that is served by the effect which it produces upon us. This instinctive sense of beauty, in different species of animals, may differ as much as the external sense of taste, and in each species be adapted to its manner of life. . . . As far as our determinations of the comparative beauty of objects are instinctive, they are no subject of reasoning or of criticism; they are purely the gift of nature, and we have no standard by which they may be measured. But there are judgments of beauty that may be called rational, being founded on some agreeable quality of the object which is distinctly conceived, and may be specified. . . . An expert mechanic views a well constructed machine. . . . He pronounces it to be a beautiful machine. He views it with the same agreeable emotion as the child viewed the pebble; but he can

give a reason for his judgment, and point out the particular perfections of the object on which it is grounded. . . .

There is nothing more common in the sentiments of all
mankind, and in the language of all nations, than what
may be called a communication of attributes; that is,
transferring an attribute, from the subject to which it
properly belongs, to some related or resembling subject.
. . . It is therefore natural, and agreeable to the strain of
human sentiments and of human language, that in many
cases the beauty which originally and properly is in
the thing signified, should be transferred to the sign;
that which is in the cause to the effect; that which is in
the end to the means; and that which is in the agent to the
instrument. . . . I apprehend, therefore, that it is in the
moral and intellectual perfections of mind, and in its
active powers, that beauty originally dwells; and that
from this as the fountain, all the beauty which we perceive in the visible world is derived. . . .

Even in the inanimate world, there are many things
analogous to the qualities of mind; so that there is hardly
anything belonging to mind which may not be represented by images taken from the objects of sense; and,
on the other hand, every object of sense is beautified, by
borrowing attire from the attributes of mind. Thus, the
beauties of mind, though invisible in themselves, are
perceived in the objects of sense, on which their image is
impressed. If we consider, on the other hand, the qualities
in sensible objects to which we ascribe beauty, I apprehend we shall find in all of them some relation to mind,
and the greatest in those that are most beautiful. . . .

In a composition of sounds, or a piece of music, the
beauty is either in the harmony, the melody, or the
expression. The beauty of expression must be derived,
either from the beauty of the thing expressed, or from the
art and skill employed in expressing it properly. In
harmony the very names of concord and discord are
metaphorical, and suppose some analogy between the
relations of sound, to which they are figuratively applied,

and the relations of minds and affections, which they originally and properly signify. . . . With regard to melody, I leave it to the adepts in the the science of music, to determine whether music, composed according to the established rules of harmony and melody, can be altogether void of expression; and whether music that has no expression can have any beauty.

In every species, the more perfectly any individual is fitted for its end and manner of life, the greater is its beauty. . . . As, amongst us, one man prefers a fair beauty, another a brunette, without being able to give any reason for this preference; this diversity of taste has no standard in the common principles of human nature, but must arise from something that is different in different nations, and in different individuals of the same nation. . . . Thus, I think, all the ingredients of human beauty . . . terminate in expression; they either express some perfection of the body, as a part of the man, and an instrument of the mind, or some amiable quality or attribute of the mind itself. It cannot, indeed, be denied that the expression of a fine countenance may be unnaturally disjoined from the amiable qualities which it naturally expresses; but we presume the contrary till we have clear evidence; and even then we pay homage to the expression, as we do to the throne when it happens to be unworthily filled.

ARCHIBALD ALISON
1757–1839
Essays on the Nature and Principles of Taste (1790)
Sixth edition 1825

Introduction. The Effect which is produced upon the Mind, when the Emotions of Beauty or Sublimity are felt . . . is not in fact a Single, but a Complex Emotion; it involves, in all cases, *1st*, the production of some Simple Emotion, or the exercise of some moral affection, and, *2dly*, the consequent Excitement of a

peculiar [1] Exercise of the Imagination. . . . The Qualities
of Matter are not beautiful or sublime in themselves, but
as they are, by various means, the Signs or Expressions
of Qualities capable of producing Emotion.

I

ii, 1. Whenever the emotions of Sublimity or Beauty
are felt, that exercise of Imagination is produced, which
consists in the indulgence of a train of Thought; . . . it is
obvious that this is not every train of thought of which
we are capable. . . . This difference consists in two things.
1st, In the Nature of the ideas or conceptions which compose such trains: and 2dly, in the Nature or Law of their
succession.[2] . . . (1) Every individual idea of such a succession is in itself productive of some simple Emotion
or other. . . . (2) There is always some general principle
of connexion which pervades the whole, and gives them
some certain and definite character. They are either gay,
or pathetic. . . .

2. It is not only impossible for us to imagine an
Object of Taste, that is not an Object of Emotion;
but it is impossible to describe any such object, without
resting the description upon that quality, or those
qualities in it, that are productive of Simple Emotion. . . .
The productions that all men peculiarly admire, are
those which suit that peculiar strain of Emotion, to
which, from their original constitution, they are most
strongly disposed. . . . To a man under some present
impression of joy, we should not venture to appeal with
regard to the Beauty of any melancholy or pathetic
composition. To a man under the dominion of sorrow,
we should much less presume to present even the most
beautiful composition, which contained only images of joy.
In both cases, we should feel, that the compositions in
question demanded different emotions from those that the
persons in question had in their power to bestow.[3] . . .

[1] Cf. Richards, p. 278.
[2] Cf. Baumgarten, p. 83, Croce, p. 241, Richards, p. 279.
[3] Cf. Croce, p. 244.

3. Those trains of thought which attend the Emotions of Taste, are uniformly distinguished by some general principle of connexion; . . . no Composition of Objects or qualities in fact produces such emotions, in which this Unity of character or of emotion is not preserved. . . . Every object that is not suited to the character of the scenes, or that has not an effect in strengthening the expression by which it is distinguished, we condemn as an intrusion.

II

i. Although the qualities of matter are in themselves incapable of producing emotion, or the exercise of any affection, yet it is obvious that they may produce this effect, from their association with other qualities, and as being either the signs or expressions of such qualities as are fitted by the constitution of our nature to produce Emotion. Thus, in the human body, particular forms or colours are the signs of particular passions or affections. . . . In such cases, the constant connexion between the sign and the thing signified, between the material quality and the quality productive of Emotion, renders at last the one expressive to us of the other. . . . There are analogies between Silence and Tranquillity,—between the bustle of Morning, and the gaiety of Hope. . . .

ii. 1. The tones of the Human Voice . . . are beautiful or sublime only as they express Passions or Affections which excite our sympathy. . . . To a man in Grief, the tone of Cheerfulness is simply painful.

2. The Key or fundamental Tone of every composition, from its relation to the Tones of the human Voice, is naturally expressive to us of those qualities or affections of mind which are signified by such Sounds. . . . The Time of musical Composition is also expressive to us of various affecting or interesting qualities. . . .

iii. 1. Wherever Colours are felt as producing the Emotion of Beauty,—it is by means of their Expression, and not from any original fitness in the Colours themselves to produce this effect. . . .[1]

[1] Cf. Kant, p. 121.

iv. With regard to inanimate Forms, the principal expressions which they have to us, seem to me to be, 1*st*, The expressions of such qualities as arise from the nature of the bodies distinguished by such Forms; and 2*dly*, The expression of such qualities as arise from their being the subject or production of Art. The first of these constitutes what may be called their *Natural* Beauty; the second, what may be called their *Relative* Beauty.[1] There is also another source of expression in such qualities from accidental Association, and which perhaps may be termed their *Accidental* Beauty. . . .

1. If the Composition of Uniformity and Variety in Forms, were in itself beautiful, it would necessarily follow, that in every case where this Composition was found, the Form would be beautiful. The greater part of Forms, both in Art and Nature, are possessed of this union. The greater part of these Forms, however, are not beautiful. . . .

2. The considerations of Design, of Fitness, and of Utility may be considered as the three great sources of the Relative Beauty of Forms. In many cases this Beauty arises from all these Expressions together. . . . It is obvious, however, that we often perceive the Expression of Design in Forms, both in Art and Nature, in which we discover neither Fitness nor Utility.[2] By what means then, do we infer the existence of Design in such cases; and are there any qualities of Form, which are in themselves expressive to us of Design and Intention? . . . The material quality which is most naturally and most powerfully expressive to us of Design, is *Uniformity* or *Regularity*. . . .

In the view which I have now presented to the Reader, the qualities of Uniformity and Variety are considered as beautiful from their Expression of Design. In the preceding section, on the other hand, these qualities are considered as beautiful from the effect of their Composition, in maintaining and promoting the Emotion which

[1] Cf. Hutcheson, p. 71, Kant, § 16, p. 116.
[2] Cf. Kant's *Adaptation without design*, § 10, p. 114.

the subject itself is capable of exciting. . . . The confounding of these distinct Expressions, has also, I believe, been the cause of the greater part of mistakes which have been made in the investigation of the Beauty of these qualities. . . . The superiority[1] of the Beauty of Expression or Character, seems to consist in three things: 1*st*, in the greater and more affecting Emotion, which is produced by it, than what is produced by the mere Expression of Design; 2*dly*, In this Beauty being more universally felt, as being dependent only upon Sensibility, while the Beauty of Design is felt only fully by those who are proficients in the Art, and who are able accordingly to judge of the Skill or Taste which is displayed: and 3*dly*, In the permanence of this Beauty, as arising from certain invariable principles of our Nature, while the Beauty of Design is dependent upon the period of the Art in which it is displayed, and ceases to be beautiful, when the Art has made a further progress either in improvement or decline. . . . In the Arts of Taste, whose object is Beauty, and in which the Taste or Genius of the Artist is in like manner most surely displayed by the production of beautiful Form, it is . . . absurd to sacrifice the superior Beauty of Character or Expression, to that meaner and less permanent Beauty, which may arise from the display of his own ability or art. However obvious or important the principle which I have now stated may be, the fine Arts have been unfortunately governed by a very different principle: and the undue preference which Artists are naturally disposed to give to the Display of Design, has been one of the most powerful causes of that decline and degeneracy which has uniformly marked the history of the fine Arts, after they have arrived at a certain period of perfection. . . . It is by the Expression of Character therefore, that the Generality of Men determine the Beauty of Forms. It is by the Expression of Design that the Artist determines it. . . . There is no quality, however, which has a more powerful effect upon our imagination

[1] Cf. Herbart, p. 156, Bell, p. 264.

than Novelty. The Taste of the generality of mankind, therefore, very naturally falls in with the invention of the Artist. . . . They willingly therefore submit their opinions to the guidance of those who, by their practice in these arts, appear the most competent to judge. . . . Certain Proportions affect us with the Emotion of Beauty, not from any original capacity in such qualities to excite this Emotion, but from their being expressive to us of the Fitness of the parts to the End designed.

IMMANUEL KANT

1724–1804

Kant held that we can have no theoretic certainty about the ultimate nature of reality. The only objects of such knowledge are things as they must appear to beings with faculties like our own. These are the *phenomena* of science. All that comes to the mind is a chaos of sensations; all form or order is entirely due to the mind's nature. The chaotic sensations are unified into *phenomena* by the imagination guided by the conceptions of the understanding. In every perception these two faculties must act together. In such judgements as Fire melts wax, the imagination unites the sensations both under the forms of time and space and also under a conception (causality) of the understanding and so gives us knowledge of the phenomenon. But in such a judgement as That is beautiful, we use no conception of the thing's nature. We are aware, by the very fact that we perceive anything, of a harmonious action of our faculties of perception; but here the harmony is one of free play, not of subordination to a conception or law presupposed as necessary. Things must be apprehended as causal, substantial, quantitative, qualified, and so on, if they are to be apprehended at all. They need not be beautiful. So the judgement that a thing is beautiful is 'reflective', not 'determinant'; it is not one that seems forced upon us if we are to apprehend the thing at all, but rather one about the thing's relation to our powers of apprehension. To call a thing beautiful is really to assert that what is 'given' seems designed, but designed for no other purpose than to facilitate our unification of it by imagination and understanding. Our faculties of apprehension are stimulated to harmonious interaction without being necessitated. And our pleasure arises from our conviction that all men's faculties, when applied to the same sensuous matter, can harmonize in the same way, as surely as they do in apprehension of scientific fact, but freely. We are thus confirmed by beauty in our assurance of the possibility both of knowledge and of communication. For we have found an instance when what is given to us seems gratuitously to facilitate its apprehension, since we could have apprehended it without that particular kind of facility; and yet this depends on the fitness of what is given, not to anything personal, but to those very faculties which make possible our common experience of a world. Such at least is my understanding of Kant.

The Critique of Judgement [1] (1790)

1. *The judgement of taste is aesthetic.* The judgement of taste is not a judgement of knowledge, and is consequently not scientific but aesthetic; by which I mean that it is a judgement for which the ground can only be subjective. All our ideas,[2] even those of sensation, can, however, refer to objects (and then they signify a reality corresponding to an empirical idea), except only those which refer to the feelings of pleasure and pain. Here nothing is indicated in the object, but we have a feeling of ourselves as we are affected by the idea. . . .

2. *The satisfaction which occasions the judgement of taste is disinterested.* The satisfaction connected with our idea of the existence of an object is called interest. This satisfaction is therefore always also related to the faculty of desire, either as affecting it or as necessarily connected with what affects it. But when the question is whether a thing be beautiful, we do not want to know whether anything depends or can depend, for us or for anybody else, on the existence of the object, but only how we estimate it in mere contemplation. . . .

3. *The satisfaction in the pleasant is interested.* . . . It involves desire. . . .

[1] There are translations by Bernard and Meredith. Cf. my ' Sources and Effects in England of Kant's Philosophy of Beauty ' in *Bicentenary Papers read at North Western University* (Chicago, 1925). [2] *Vorstellungen.*

4. *The satisfaction in the good is interested.* Everything which pleases us through our reason when we simply conceive of it is *good.* What thus pleases us only as a means to something else we call useful or *good for something*; other things which please us for their own sake we call *good in themselves.* Both always imply the conception of a purpose, and consequently the relation of our reason to an act, or possible act, of will, and therefore a satisfaction in the existence of an object or an act, that is to say, some sort of interest.

To deem anything good I must always know what sort of thing it ought to be; I must have a conception of it. To find beauty in a thing, this is not necessary. Flowers, arabesques, decorative intertwining of lines in what is called foliation, mean nothing and depend on no definite conception, and yet please us. . . .

5. Of all these three kinds of satisfaction, we may say that the satisfaction of taste in the beautiful is the only one that is disinterested and free. . . .

Taste is the faculty of estimating an object or a type of idea in respect of satisfaction or dissatisfaction without any interest. The object of such satisfaction is called *beautiful.*

6. *The beautiful is that which is thought of as the object of a universal satisfaction apart from any conception.* . . . A thing of which every one recognises that his own satisfaction in its beauty is without any interest, must be estimated by him to afford a ground of satisfaction for all men. For since his satisfaction does not depend upon any inclination of his own (nor upon any other conscious interest), and since he feels himself absolutely free in the satisfaction which he accords to the object, he can find no private peculiarity, affecting him alone, as the cause of his satisfaction; and consequently he must regard the satisfaction as caused by something which he can presuppose in every other man. So he must think he has reason for attributing a like satisfaction to every man. Hence he will speak of beauty as if it were a quality of the object, and

as if his judgement were scientific—that is, constituted
a knowledge of the object by conceptions of it,—though
it is only aesthetical. . . . So a claim to subjective universality must be implied in the judgement of taste.[1] . . .

7. A man says The *thing* is beautiful; he does not merely
expect the assent of others to his judgement of satisfaction
because they have agreed with him before; he *demands*
it of them. He blames them when they judge differently,
and denies their taste . . .

8. *The universality of our satisfaction is represented in the
judgement of taste as only subjective.* If we estimate objects
merely by conceptions, all idea of beauty is lost. So
there can be no rule by which anybody can be compelled
to recognize anything as beautiful. No one allows his
judgement on the beauty of a coat, a house, a flower, to
be coerced by reasons or principles. He wants to have the
thing before him, just as if his satisfaction were sensuous;
yet, if he then calls it beautiful, he claims to have the universal
voice on his side, whereas sensation is private and decides
nothing beyond the satisfaction of the man who has it. . .

9. If the pleasure in a given object came first and only
the universal communicability of the pleasure were to be
attributed to the idea of the object by the judgement of
taste, we should have a contradiction. For such a pleasure
would be nothing but mere pleasantness of sensation, and
so could naturally only have private validity, as depending immediately on our perception of the object.

Consequently it is the universal communicability of our
state of mind, in having the idea, which must occasion in
our minds the judgement of taste and be a condition of it;
and the pleasure in the thing must be the result of this.
But nothing can be universally communicated except
knowledge, and ideas so far as they belong to knowledge.
For only so far are ideas objective, and only so have they
a common point of reference in which the ideas of all
men are bound to agree. Now when we have to think
that what makes us judge our idea to be universally

[1] Cf. Stace, ii, p. 302.

communicable is merely subjective,—is in fact no conception of the object,—it can be nothing but the state of
mind consisting in the mutual relation of our faculties for
forming ideas, so far as these faculties employ a perception
for purposes of knowledge in general.

The faculties of knowledge brought into play by the
idea are in such a case in free play,[1] because no definite
conception of the object's nature confines them to any
particular principle of knowledge. So the state of mind
in having such an idea must be a feeling of the free play
of our faculties for ideas in using a perception for purposes of knowledge in general. Now for any idea of an
object, and so for knowledge in general, there are required
Imagination[2] to combine the manifold apprehended[3] and
Understanding[2] to afford a conception which can unify
the ideas.[4] This state of the free play of our faculties of
knowledge in the idea of an object must be one that
can be shared universally; for knowledge (being the
distinction of an object, with which all perceptions, to
whomever they belong, must agree) is the only kind of
idea that is valid for every man. . . .

This merely subjective (aesthetic) estimation of the
object, or of our idea of it, precedes our pleasure in it,
and occasions this pleasure in the harmony of our
faculties of knowledge. And the universal, though subjective, validity of that satisfaction which we connect with
the idea of the object which we call beautiful, is effected
solely by the universality in men of these subjective conditions for estimating objects. . . .In a judgement of taste
we impute, as necessary, to everybody the pleasure we
feel ourselves; as if the beauty we ascribe to a thing were
to be considered a property following from the conception of it; though beauty, apart from relation to our
feeling, is itself nothing.[5] . . .

---

[1] Cf. Schiller, xv, p. 126.   [2] Cf. Muratori, p. 63, and Addison, p. 66.
[3] *die Zusammensetzung des Mannigfaltigen der Anschauung.*
[4] *die Einheit des Begriffs der die Vorstellungen vereinigt.*
[5] Cf. Hutcheson, I. xvii, p. 70.

10. So far as the faculty of desire can be stimulated to activity by conceptions, that is by a purpose, it is called the will. But a thing or a state of mind or an action is said to be adapted to purpose,[1] though its possibility does not necessarily presuppose a purpose.[2] This is so whenever we can only explain or understand the thing's possibility by supposing it to be brought about by a final cause, or in other words to have been devised by a will according to the idea of some principle. The adaptation,[3] then, can be without a purpose,[4] so far as we do not attribute the thing's arrangement to a will, though we could only give any intelligible account of its possibility by so attributing it. . . .

11. Any purpose, regarded as the cause of our pleasure, implies an interest to occasion our judgement about the pleasing object. So it can be no purpose of ours which occasions the judgement of taste [which is without interest]. Nor can the judgement of taste be occasioned by any idea of an objective purpose (that is, of the object's possibility depending on design) or by any conception of the good. For it is an aesthetic, not a scientific judgement, and so involves no conception of the thing's character nor of its possibility through causes within or without itself, but only the relation set up between our faculties for forming ideas. . . . So the occasion for a judgement of taste can be nothing but a seeming[5] adaptation in our idea of an object, without any purpose either objective or belonging to ourselves. And a seeming adaptation is the merely general form of adaptation in our perception of objects, so far as we are aware of it. This effects the satisfaction, which we estimate as universally communicable though we are using no conception; and that is the occasion of a judgement of taste.[6] . . .

---

[1] *zweckmässig.*   [2] *die Vorstellung eines Zwecks.*
[3] *Zweckmässigkeit.*   [4] *ohne Zweck.* Cf. Alison, p. 107.   [5] *subjective.*
[6] This perhaps means that though the thing we have an idea of does not seem to be designed for any good purpose nor to give us any pleasure, yet the play of our faculties in apprehending it does seem designed and

14. A mere colour, for instance the green of a lawn, and a mere tone (as distinguished from sound and noise), for instance that of a violin, are by most people called beautiful in themselves, though both seem to depend upon the mere matter [as opposed to form] of our ideas, namely simple sensations, and so only to deserve the name of pleasant or charming. We may, however, note here that the sensations of colour and tone have the claim to be counted beautiful, so far, but so far only, as they are *pure*. For purity is a character of their form and also the only character of these ideas which can certainly be universally appreciated. . . .

In painting, sculpture, and indeed all the arts of form such as architecture and gardening, so far as these are fine arts, the essential thing is the design. And herein it is not what pleases the senses, but what satisfies us by its form, that fundamentally concerns taste. . . .

The form of all sensible objects, both of those that are external, and also indirectly of those that are internal, is either shape or play. The latter is either play of shapes in space (pantomine and dance) or mere play of sensations in time. The charm of colour or the pleasant tone of the instrument may be added, but in shape the design, and in play the composition, are the proper objects of pure judgements of taste. . . .

Emotion, a feeling in which pleasure is aroused only through a momentary check and ensuing stronger outflow of our vital force, has nothing to do with beauty. But sublimity, which involves the feeling of emotion, demands a criterion other than that on which taste relies. The pure judgement of taste is occasioned neither by charm nor emotion.

15. *The judgement of taste is quite independent of the conception of perfection.* . . . The formal element in the idea of a thing, that is the harmonizing of its multifarious constituents into a unity, without any thought what this

pleases us. He here contradicts the view that the communicability precedes the pleasure. Cf. my *Theory of Beauty*, v, § 5. Cf. Hutcheson, pp. 72–3.

unity ought to be, indicates by itself absolutely no objective adaptation; for, since we do not consider this unity as the end which the thing ought to fulfil, there remains nothing but the adaptation of ideas in our mind. This announces indeed a certain adaptation of our mental condition and a fitness therein to picture a presented shape, but not the perfection of any object. For the object is not thought of as serving any purpose.

16. *The judgement of Taste which declares an object beautiful with reference to a definite conception is not pure.* There are two different kinds of beauty: free beauty (*pulchritudo vaga*), and merely dependent beauty[1] (*pulchritudo adhaerens*). The former does not presuppose any conception of what the thing ought to be; the latter does, and presupposes also the thing's conformity to it. . . . Greek decorative designs, foliation for margins or on wallpapers, and so on, mean nothing in themselves; they represent nothing of which we have any definite conception and are free beauties. We can also count as belonging to the same class what in music are called Fantasies, or compositions without theme, and in fact all music without words. . . . But the beauty of mankind, whether man, woman, or child, of a horse and of a building, whether church, palace, arsenal, or summer-house, presupposes a purpose which settles what the thing ought to be (that is, a conception of its ideal) and is consequently only dependent beauty. Just as we saw that to combine what is sensuously pleasant with beauty, which should properly consist in form only, prevents a pure judgement of taste, so also, we now see, does the combination of the good with beauty. . . . Properly, perfection gains nothing through beauty, nor beauty through perfection; but when we compare our perception of an object with our conception of what it ought to be, since we cannot help combining the idea at the same time with our own feeling about it, the whole faculty of forming ideas of things profits by the harmony of the two mental states.

[1] Cf. Hutcheson, p. 71, Alison, p. 107.

. . . By this distinction we can adjust many differences between critics of beauty, by pointing out that one is emphasizing free and the other dependent beauty.

17. There can be no objective rule of taste to determine by conceptions what is to be beautiful.[1] . . .

23. The beautiful agrees with the sublime in this, that both please us in themselves, and that neither presupposes a judgement of sense nor yet a scientific judgement (about the nature of an object)[2] but a reflective judgement. Consequently the satisfaction in neither depends on a sensation, as that in the pleasant does, nor yet on a definite conception, as does that in the good. . . . But there are important and obvious differences between them. The beautiful in nature belongs to the form of a thing, which consists in having boundaries; the sublime, on the other hand, can be found even in a formless thing, so far as in it or by occasion of it we find an idea of boundlessness[3] and yet attach to it the thought of a whole. So the beautiful seems to be taken as representing some quite indefinite conception of the understanding, the sublime as representing a similar conception of the reason.[4] So our satisfaction in beauty is connected with the idea of quality, that of sublimity with one of quantity. And they are clearly different in kind. Beauty brings with it directly a feeling of vital stimulus, and so can be united with charm and play of imagination. But our feeling for the sublime is only an indirect pleasure, since it is produced by the experience of a momentary check to our vital powers,[5] which are thereby stimulated immediately to a correspondingly stronger outflow. Consequently, as an emotion, it seems to be no play of our imagination but its serious employment. So it cannot be united with charm.[6] And as the mind is not merely attracted by the object,

---

[1] Cf. Home, xxv, p. 95.   [2] Cf. Addison, p. 66.

[3] Cf. Longinus, xxxv, p. 38, and Addison, pp. 66, 69.

[4] Cf. Kant, *Prolegomena*, § 59. Reason forbids understanding to dogmatize beyond possible experience but also reveals the ideal which alone would satisfy the understanding, namely the absolute, unconditioned whole.

[5] Cf. Burke, pp. 89, 93.   [6] Cf. Santayana, § 57, p. 202.

but also, alternately, repelled, our satisfaction in sublimity implies less a positive pleasure than admiration or respect, and might well be called a negative pleasure.[1]

The fundamental and most important difference between the sublime and the beautiful is, however, as follows. (In the first instance we naturally consider only the sublimity of natural things, for in art sublimity is conditioned by agreement with nature[2]). The independent beauty of nature has a fitness of form, whereby the thing seems, as it were, intended for our judgement, and so becomes in itself an object of satisfaction. On the contrary, whatever arouses in us, by its mere perception and without reasoning, the feeling of sublimity, may have a form that seems very ill-fitted to our judgement, unsuited to our powers of perception, and, as it were, doing violence to our imagination; and yet it will be judged all the more sublime.

We at once see from this that we generally express ourselves incorrectly when we call any natural thing sublime, though we can quite properly call many such things beautiful. For how can we designate with a term of approval that which we apprehend as in its nature chaotic?[3] We can only say that the thing serves to present to us a sublimity which is to be found in the mind. For the sublime proper can be embodied in no sensible form.[4] . . .

24. The analysis of sublimity involves a division, which was not needed by that of beauty, into the Mathematical and the Dynamic sublime. The feeling of sublimity is characterized by an emotion connected with our estimation of the object; whereas taste for beauty must find and maintain the mind in calm contemplation.[5] But since the sublime pleases us, this emotion must be estimated as if it were adapted.[6] Consequently the emotion is related, through the imagination, either to the faculty of knowledge or to that of desire. In either relation we

---

[1] Cf. Burke, p. 93. [2] Cf. Addison, p. 67. [3] *zweckwidrig*.
[4] Cf. Longinus, ix, xxxv, pp. 37–8. [5] Cf. Addison, p. 67.
[6] i.e. as if our faculties were adapted to the object or vice versa.

only estimate the perception as adapted to the faculty, not to any end or interest. So what is really the suitability of an emotion to our faculty of knowledge is ascribed to the object as something mathematically affecting our imagination, but its suitability to our faculty of desire as doing so dynamically. So the object can be found sublime in either of these two ways. . . .

[The Mathematical Sublime]

25. The [mathematical] sublime is that in comparison with which everything else is small. . . . Thus considered, nothing which can be an object of the senses is to be called sublime.[1] Our imagination strives for a progress to infinity, but our reason demands a complete totality as an idea to be realized. So the very fact that our power of measuring sensible objects is inadequate to this idea, awakes the feeling of a power in us superior to sense. It is the use which we naturally make of certain objects to arouse this feeling, when we judge about them, that is absolutely great, though the object of sense is not; and any other use is comparatively trivial. So not the object should be called sublime, but rather the state of mind caused by an idea which excites our reflective faculty of judgement. So we can add to our previous formulas for explaining sublimity this: a thing is sublime, if the mere power of thinking it is evidence of a mental power surpassing all standards of sense. . . .

26. Examples of mathematical sublimity in nature[2] for mere intuition are afforded by all instances where we are given not so much a larger numerical conception as a large unit to be a standard of measurement for the imagination. A tree, which is itself measured by the height of a man, gives us a standard for measuring a mountain; and if this were a mile high it could serve as the unit for the number expressing the earth's diameter,

[1] Cf. Longinus, xxxv, p. 38, Addison, *Spectator*, 420, p. 69, and Burke II, iv, p. 89.

[2] Kant denies that art can be properly sublime, yet instances the pyramids and St. Peter's, both instanced by Home (Lord Kames), *Elements of Criticism*, iv, p. 95.

so as to make the latter intuitable. The earth's diameter
serves as a standard for the known planetary system, that
again for the milky way; and the immeasurable host of
milky way systems, which are called nebulae, and which
presumably in their turn compose a system of the same
kind, forbids us to expect any limit here.[1] . . .

[The Dynamic Sublime]

28. When we estimate nature as being dynamically
sublime, our idea of it must be fearful. . . . We can, however, consider an object as fearful without fearing it, if we
so estimate it that we imagine circumstances in which we
might choose to resist it, and that then all resistance would
be perfectly vain. . . . A man in a state of fear is as incapable of judging nature to be sublime as one possessed
by longing or appetite is of judging about beauty. . . .
Bold, overhanging rocks which seem to threaten us,
storm-clouds piled up in heaven and moving on their
way with lightnings and thunders, volcanoes with all
their destructive might, hurricanes leaving a wake of
devastation, the boundless ocean in its anger, a high
waterfall in a mighty river:—such things reduce our
power of resistance to impotence as compared with their
might. But the sight of them is attractive in proportion to
their fearfulness so long as we find ourselves in security,
and we readily call such things sublime because they
elevate the powers of our souls above their wonted level
and discover in us a faculty for resistance of quite a different kind, which encourages us to measure ourselves
against the apparent omnipotence of nature. . . . Nature is
not aesthetically estimated to be sublime so far as it
excites fear, but because it calls up in us the power,
which is beyond nature, to regard all that we care for—
wealth, health, life itself—as small. Thus we come to
regard the might of nature, on which for all these things
we are utterly dependent, as nevertheless, in relation to us
and our personality, a power beneath which we need not

[1] Cf. Longinus, ix, p. 37, and Addison, *Spectator*, 420, p. 69; also Wordsworth, p. 130.

bend if the maintenance of our highest principles were at stake. So nature is here called elevated or sublime[1] just because she elevates[2] the imagination to picture situations in which the mind can realize the proper sublimity of its own destiny as surpassing nature itself. . . .

42. The charms of beautiful nature which are to be met with in such plenty, fused in her beautiful forms, belong either to the modifications of light (in colouring) or of sound (in tones). For these are the only sensations which afford not only mere sense-feeling but reflection upon the form of these affections of our senses; and consequently contain, as it were, a language which nature speaks to us and which seems to have an inward meaning. So the whiteness of lilies seems to affect the mind with ideas of innocence; and, following the order of the seven colours from red to violet, we get the ideas of (1) Sublimity, (2) Courage, (3) Candour, (4) Friendliness, (5) Modesty, (6) Constancy, (7) Tenderness.[3] . . .

56. The following contradiction arises about the principle of taste:

(1) *Thesis.* The judgements of taste cannot depend on conceptions, for otherwise we could argue about them, that is to say, give conclusive proofs.

(2) *Antithesis.* The judgements of taste must depend on conceptions, for otherwise, however much they differed, we could not even quarrel about them, that is to say, demand that other people should necessarily agree with us. [We do not make this demand about mere sensations.] . . .

57. All contradiction disappears if we say that the judgement of taste does depend on a conception, but only on a general conception of some reason for the seeming adaptation of nature to our powers of judgement. From such a conception nothing could be learned or proved about the nature of an object, since no particular object can be *known* to exemplify such a conception.[4]

---

[1] *erhaben.*   [2] *erhebt.*   [3] Cf. Alison, p. 106.

[4] *weil er an sich unbestimmbar und zur Erkenntniss untauglich ist.* Cf. Stace, iii, p. 303.

[As a billiard-cannon exemplifies Causality or Caesar exemplifies Man.] Yet by this very conception the judgement acquires validity for every man (though a singular judgement, which immediately accompanies his perception),[1] because what occasions the judgement is perhaps a conception of the supersensible reality which underlies human nature [and the world of sense]. . . .

58. [On an empirical or sensationalist theory of taste] the object of aesthetic satisfaction would be merely pleasant, but on a rationalist theory (if the judgement depended on definite conceptions) it would be merely good. So beauty would be shuffled out of the world, and all that would be left would be a particular name given perhaps to a certain mixture of these two kinds of satisfaction.[2] But we have shown that there are grounds of satisfaction other than empirical, and therefore consistent with the rationalist principle, although they cannot be grasped as definite conceptions.

Such rationalist principles of taste must further be distinguished according as they take the apparent adaptation [of art and nature to our faculties] to be really designed or only accidental.[3] . . .

One fact positively proves that, as the ground of our aesthetic judgements, we assume only an apparent adaptation[4] of beautiful nature, to the exclusion of any explanation which asserts its real adaptation[5] to our perceptive faculties. I mean the fact that, whenever we estimate beauty, we do not seek any criterion from experience, but judge for ourselves aesthetically whether the thing is beautiful.[6] This could not be if we assumed a designed adaptation of nature, for then we should have to learn from nature what we had to find beautiful, and the judgement of taste would have to bow to experience. But such an estimation does not depend on what nature is

---

[1] *bei jedem zwar als einzelnes, die Anschauung unmittelbar begleitendes Urtheil.*

[2] Cf. Sidney, p. 54, Muratori, p. 60.

[3] This is a free paraphrase. I believe it gives the meaning. Cf. Santayana, p. 200.   [4] *Idealität der Zweckmässigkeit.*

[5] *Realismus eines Zwecks.*   [6] *die ästhetische Urtheilskraft selbst gesetzgebend ist.*

or even on how it is in fact adapted to us, but on how we look at it. If nature had produced its forms for our satisfaction, that would in the end be an objective design in nature, not a merely apparent suitability to us [1] resting on the free play of our imagination; it would be a grace done to us by nature, whereas in fact we confer one upon her. [2] In beautiful art it is even easier to recognize that the adaptation can only be known as apparently designed. . . . The fact that the beauties of art by their nature must be considered as products not of scientific understanding, but of genius, plainly shows that, even on a rationalistic theory, it is only apparent and not necessarily real design which accounts for our satisfaction. . . .

59. Now I say that the beautiful is the symbol [3] of the morally good; and only from this point of view (which every man naturally takes and thinks it the duty of others to take) do we claim that all men should agree about the pleasure it gives. . . . In the faculty of taste the judgement does not find itself, as in judging by experience, constrained by empirical laws; it legislates for itself on the objects of so pure a satisfaction, just as reason legislates autonomously on the faculty of desire in morality. And owing to this capacity in ourselves and to the capacity in external nature to harmonize therewith, the judgement finds in itself a reference to something in us and also outside us, which is neither physical necessity nor moral freedom but is allied to the supersensible [though intelligible] conditions of freedom. In this supersensuous reality, the theoretical faculty [of judgement] and the practical faculty [of moral reason] are mutually and mysteriously interwoven. [4] . . .

Even common understanding pays respect to this analogy, and we often call beautiful objects of nature or

[1] *subjective Zweckmässigkeit.*   [2] Cf. Herbart, *Practical Philosophy,* i. § 15, p. 152.

[3] Kant has just given as an instance of what he means by symbolism that a hand-mill is a symbol of despotism, because, though they are not alike, the ways in which we have to think about their internal relations are alike. Similarly a living organism is a symbol of constitutional monarchy.

[4] Cf. Hegel, pp. 161–4.

R

art by names which imply a moral estimate. We call trees and buildings majestic or dignified and meadows smiling or gay; even colours are called pure, chaste, tender, because they arouse feelings analogous to those aroused by moral judgements. Taste facilitates a gradual transition from sensuous charm to an habitual interest in morality,[1] since it exhibits the imagination as at once free and adapted to conform to the understanding, and so accustoms us to find a satisfaction that is free from sensuous allurement even in the objects of sense.

SIR UVEDALE PRICE

1747–1829

Essays on the Picturesque (1794)

iii. The qualities which make objects picturesque, are not only as distinct as those which make them beautiful or sublime, but are equally extended to all our sensations by whatever organs they are received; and music (though it appears like a solecism) may be as truly picturesque, according to the general principles of picturesqueness, as it may be beautiful or sublime. . . . The two opposite qualities[2] of roughness, and of sudden variation, joined to that of irregularity, are the most efficient causes of the picturesque. . . . iv. I do not mean to infer from the instances I have given, that an object to be picturesque must be old and decayed; but that the most beautiful objects will become so from the effects of age and decay. . . .

[1] Cf. Schiller, *Letters*, xiv, p. 125.
[2] Opposite to the smoothness and gradual variation attributed by Burke to beauty. Price is answering Payne Knight, who denied the distinction (cf. his *Principles of Taste*, 1805, I. v, § 19 and II. ii, §§ 15–27 and 79), but who suggests, as equally plausible, one between the beautiful and the *grottesque*. A good idea of the fondness for such discussions in England and Scotland at this time is given by Hussey, *The Picturesque*. Cf. also Peacock, *Headlong Hall* (1816), iv: 'Allow me,' said Mr. Gall, 'I distinguish the picturesque and the beautiful, and I add to them, in the laying out of grounds, a third and distinct character, which I call *unexpectedness*.' 'Pray, sir,' said Mr. Milestone, 'by what name do you distinguish this character, when a person walks round the grounds for the second time?' Cf. Ruskin, p. 176.

v. It seldom happens that these two qualities [beauty and picturesqueness] are perfectly unmixed; and I believe it is for want of observing how nature has blended them, and from attempting to make objects beautiful by dint of smoothness and flowing lines, that so much insipidity has arisen. . . . We must acknowledge ['irritation'] to be the source of our most active and lively pleasures.

JOHANN CHRISTOPH FRIEDRICH VON SCHILLER
1759–1805

Letters on the Aesthetic Education of Mankind (1795)

xiv. When we passionately embrace a person who is worthy of our contempt, we feel bitterly the compulsion of nature. When we are hostile to one who extorts our respect, we feel bitterly the compulsion of reason. But so soon as one both attracts our inclinations and earns our respect, the coercions of sense and of reason alike vanish and we begin to love; that is we begin to play both with our inclination and our respect.[1]

xv. The object of the sensuous impulse may be defined, according to its universal conception, as life in the widest sense. This conception covers all physical existence and all that is immediately present in sense. The object of the rational impulse[2] may be defined according to its universal conception as form both in the wider and the narrower sense. This conception covers all the formal characters of things and their relations to our rational faculties. The object of the play-impulse may consequently be defined, if we picture it under a general figure, as living form.[3] This conception seems to describe all the aesthetic qualities of phenomena and in fact all that we call beautiful in the widest sense. This explanation, if I may so call it, neither extends beauty to the

[1] Cf. Kant, § 59, p. 123.
[2] *Formtrieb,* i.e. impulse towards form or order. Cf. Aristotle, *Poetics,* p. 31.
[3] Cf. Bell, p. 264.

whole realm of life nor yet confines it to that realm. A block of marble, though it must ever be lifeless, can none the less become living form in the hands of the architect or sculptor; a man, though he lives and has form, may be far from being a living form. For that, it is requisite that his form should be life and his life form. So long as we merely *think* about his form it is a lifeless abstraction; so long as we merely *feel* his life, it is a formless sense-impression. Only so far as his form lives in our feeling and his life has form for our understanding is he living form, and this will always be so when we call him beautiful. . . . Man, we know, is neither exclusively matter nor exclusively spirit. Consequently beauty, which is the consummation of his nature, cannot on the one hand be purely physical,[1] as the degrading taste of our day would have it, and as has been held by shrewd observers (like Burke) who relied too much on empirical evidence; nor, on the other hand, can it be pure form, as has been thought by speculative philosophers, who left experience too far behind, and by philosophizing artists who in their definition let themselves be too much influenced by the requirements of art. Beauty is the common object of both impulses, that is to say it is the object of the play impulse.[2] Ordinary language fully justifies this name, for it commonly gives the name of play to whatever is not forced upon us whether by nature or our own mind and yet is not accidental with respect to either. . . . Man only plays when he is man in the full meaning of the term, and he is only fully man when he plays.

xvi. We have seen that beauty results from the interplay of two opposed impulses and the union of two opposed principles.[3] Its highest ideal, therefore, must be looked for in the completest possible unity and balance of reality or life and form. But this balance remains a mere idea never actually attained. Actually one element will always outweigh the other; and the best we can exper-

---

[1] *blosses Leben.*   [2] Cf. Kant, § 9, p. 113, and Spencer, p. 182.
[3] Cf. Aristotle, *Poetics*, iv, p. 31, Nietzsche, p. 185, Stevenson, p. 198.

ience will be a fluctuation between the two, in which now reality or life, now form preponderates.

xxii. The unique secret of art which all great masters know is to sublimate the matter by the form. The more impressive, importunate, or seductive the subject-matter is of itself, and the more violently it imposes its effects upon us, or the more we are tempted to yield to its influence, just so much the greater is the triumph of the art which masters it and sways us. . . . Art, and beautiful art, dealing with passion there is, but a beautiful passionate art is a contradiction in terms, for the inevitable effect of beauty is freedom from the passions. No less contradictory is the idea of beautiful art which is didactic or edifying, for nothing is so inconsistent with the idea of beauty as to give the mind a definite direction.

xxiii. The transition from the passive state of feeling to the active state of thought and will can only come about through a middle state of aesthetic freedom.[1]

xxiv. In his physical stage man merely suffers the forces of nature, in his aesthetic stage he frees himself from these forces, in his moral stage he overcomes them.

xxvii. In the hearts of the terrifying realm of natural forces and of the awe-inspiring realm of moral law, the impulse for form secretly consolidates its third and joyous realm of play and of appearance, which when a man enters, the fetters that link him to things are struck off and he is freed from his slavery both to natural and to moral law.[2] . . .

Material goods can only make one man happy, for they depend on appropriation which is always exclusive; and even of that one they can only make one part happy, for his whole personality is not involved. Absolute goods can only make us happy under conditions that cannot be universally presupposed; for truth is only the reward of self-denial and only a pure heart believes in the pure will. Beauty alone makes all the world happy, and under its charm every creature forgets his bonds.

[1] Cf. Croce.   [2] Cf. Schopenhauer, p. 142.

WILLIAM WORDSWORTH
1770–1850
Preface to Lyrical Ballads (1800)

All good poetry is the spontaneous overflow of powerful feelings. . . . What is a Poet? To whom does he address himself? And what language is to be expected from him? He is a man speaking to men: a man, it is true, endowed with more lively sensibility, more enthusiasm and tenderness, who has a greater knowledge of human nature, and a more comprehensive soul, than are supposed to be common among mankind; a man pleased with his own passions and volitions, and who rejoices more than other men in the spirit of life that is in him; delighting to contemplate similar volitions and passions as manifested in the goings-on of the Universe,[1] and habitually impelled to create them where he does not find them. To these qualities he has added a disposition to be affected more than other men by absent things as if they were present; an ability of conjuring up in himself passions, which are indeed far from being the same as those produced by real events, yet (especially in those parts of the general sympathy which are pleasing and delightful) do more nearly resemble the passions produced by real events, than anything which, from the motions of their own minds merely, other men are accustomed to feel in themselves:—whence, and from practice, he has acquired a greater readiness and power in expressing what he thinks and feels, and especially those thoughts and feelings which, by his own choice, or from the structure of his own mind, arise in him without immediate external excitement. . . . The Poet writes under one restriction only, namely the necessity of giving immediate pleasure to a human Being possessed of that information which may be expected of him, not as a lawyer, a physician, a mariner, an astronomer, or a natural philosopher, but as a Man. . . . He considers man and nature as essentially adapted

[1] Cf. Schopenhauer, p. 146.

to each other, and the mind of man as naturally the mirror of the fairest and most interesting properties of nature.[1] . . . Poetry is the breath and finer spirit of all knowledge; it is the impassioned expression which is in the countenance of all Science . . . carrying sensation into the midst of the objects of the science itself. . . . The Poet is chiefly distinguished from other men by a greater promptness to think and feel without immediate external excitement, and a greater power of expressing such thoughts and feelings as are produced in him in that manner. But these passions and thoughts and feelings are the general passions and thoughts and feelings of men.[2]

The end of Poetry is to produce excitement in coexistence with an overbalance of pleasure. . . . . The copresence of something regular [e.g. metre], something to which the mind has been accustomed in various moods, and in a less excited state, cannot but have a great efficacy in tempering and restraining the passion by an intermixture of ordinary feeling and of feeling not strictly and necessarily connected with the passion. . . . [Metre] will be found greatly to contribute to impart passion to the words.[3] I have said that poetry is the spontaneous overflow of powerful feelings: it takes its origin from emotion recollected in tranquillity:[4] the emotion is contemplated till, by a species of reaction, the tranquillity gradually disappears, and an emotion, kindled to that which was before the subject of contemplation, is gradually produced, and does itself actually exist before the mind.

Essay Supplementary to the Preface (1815)

The appropriate business of poetry (which nevertheless, if genuine, is as permanent as pure science), her appropriate employment, her privilege and her *duty*, is to treat of things not as they *are*, but as they *appear*; not as they exist in themselves, but as they seem to exist to the *senses*, and to the *passions*. . . .

[1] Cf. Wordsworth, *The Recluse*.
[2] Cf. Richards, pp. 277–8, and Gentile, p. 326.
[3] Cf. Santayana, § 57, p. 200.   [4] Cf. Schopenhauer, p. 141.

Men who read from religious or moral inclinations, even when the subject is of that kind which they approve, are beset with misconceptions and mistakes peculiar to themselves. Attaching so much importance to the truths which interest them, they are prone to over-rate the Authors by whom those truths are expressed and enforced. They come prepared to impart so much passion to the Poet's language, that they remain unconscious how little, in fact, they receive from it.[1] . . .

Preface to Poems (1815)

(Imagination) recoils from everything but the plastic, the pliant, and the indefinite. She leaves it to Fancy to describe Queen Mab as coming,

> In shape no bigger than an agate-stone
> On the fore-finger of an alderman.[2]

Having to speak of stature, she does not tell you that her gigantic Angel was as tall as Pompey's Pillar; much less that he was twelve cubits, or twelve hundred cubits high; or that his dimensions equalled those of Teneriffe or Atlas; because these, and, if they were a million times as high, it would be the same, are bounded: The expression is, 'His stature reached the sky!' the illimitable firmament![3]

Letter to a Friend of Burns

(To James Gray, 1816)

Who, but some impenetrable dunce or narrow-minded puritan in works of art, ever read without delight the picture which he has drawn of the convivial exaltation of the rustic adventurer, Tam o' Shanter? The poet fears not to tell the reader in the outset that his hero was a desperate and sottish drunkard, whose excesses were frequent as his opportunities. This reprobate sits down to his cups, while the storm is roaring, and heaven and earth are in confusion;—the night is driven on by song

[1] Cf. Richards, p. 283. [2] Shakespeare, *Romeo and Juliet*, I. iv. 55.
[3] Milton, *Paradise Lost*, iv. 988. Cf. Kant, p. 120.

and tumultuous noise—laughter and jest thicken as the
beverage improves upon the palate—conjugal fidelity
archly bends to the service of universal benevolence—
selfishness is not absent, but wearing the mask of social
cordiality—and, while these various elements of humanity
are blended into one proud and happy composition of
elated spirits, the anger of the tempest without doors
only heightens and sets off the enjoyment within.—I
pity him who cannot perceive that, in all this, though
there was no moral purpose, there is a moral effect.

> Kings may be blest, but Tam was glorious,
> O'er a' the *ills* of life victorious.

SAMUEL TAYLOR COLERIDGE

1772–1834

Dejection, an Ode [1] (1802)

III

My genial spirits fail;
    And what can these avail
To lift the smothering weight from off my breast?
    It were a vain endeavour,
    Though I should gaze for ever
On that green light that lingers in the west:
I may not hope from outward forms to win
The passion and the life, whose fountains are within.

IV

O William! we receive but what we give,
And in our life alone does Nature live:
Ours is her wedding garment, ours her shroud!
    And would we aught behold, of higher worth,
Than that inanimate cold world allowed
To the poor loveless ever-anxious crowd,
    Ah! from the soul itself must issue forth

[1] I have selected the various readings which seemed aptest to my purpose.
See the critical apparatus in the *Poetical Works*, ed. E. H. Coleridge, Clarendon Press, 1912.

A light, a glory, a fair luminous cloud
  Enveloping the Earth—
And from the soul itself must there be sent
  A sweet and potent voice, of its own birth,
Of all sweet sounds the life and element.[1]

V

O pure of heart! thou need'st not ask of me
What this strong music in the soul may be!
What, and wherein it doth subsist,
This light, this glory, this fair luminous mist,
This beautiful and beauty-making power.
  Joy, O beloved, joy that ne'er was given,
Save to the pure, and in their purest hour,
Life, and Life's effluence, cloud at once and shower,
Joy, William, is the spirit and the power,
Which wedding Nature to us gives in dower
  A new Earth and new Heaven,
Undreamt of by the sensual and the proud—
Joy is the sweet voice; Joy the luminous cloud—
  We in ourselves rejoice!
And thence flows all that charms or ear or sight,
  All melodies an echo of that voice,
All colours a suffusion from that light.
Calm steadfast Spirit, guided from above,
O Wordsworth! friend of my devoutest choice,
Great son of genius! full of light and love
  Thus, thus dost thou rejoice.
To thee do all things live from pole to pole,
Their life the eddying of thy living soul.
Brother and friend of my devoutest choice
Thus mayst thou ever, evermore rejoice!

VI

There was a time when, though my path was rough,
  This joy within me dallied with distress,
And all misfortunes were but as the stuff
  Whence Fancy made me dreams of happiness;

[1] Cf. Plotinus, p. 46.

For hope grew round me like the twining vine,
And fruits, and foliage, not my own, seemed mine,
But now afflictions bow me down to earth:
Nor care I that they rob me of my mirth;
    But oh! each visitation
Suspends what nature gave me at my birth,
    My shaping spirit of Imagination.

On the Principles of Sound Criticism (1814)

I. All the fine arts are different species of poetry. The same spirit speaks to the mind through different senses by manifestations of itself, appropriate to each. . . . The common essence of all consists in the excitement of emotion for the immediate purpose of pleasure through the medium of beauty; herein contra-distinguishing poetry from science, the immediate object and primary purpose of which is truth and possible utility. . . .

II. The venison is agreeable because it gives pleasure; while the Apollo Belvedere is not beautiful because it pleases, but it pleases us because it is beautiful. . . . There exists in the constitution of the human soul a sense, and a regulative principle, which may indeed be stifled and latent in some, and be prevented and denaturalized in others, yet is nevertheless universal in a given state of intellectual and moral culture; which is independent of local and temporary circumstances, and dependent only on the degree in which the faculties of the mind are developed. . . .

III. The BEAUTIFUL, contemplated in its essentials, that is, in kind and not in degree, is that in which the many, still seen as many, becomes one. . . . So far is the Beautiful from depending wholly on association, that it is frequently produced by the mere removal of associations. . . .

It seems evident then, first, that beauty is harmony, and subsists only in composition,[1] and secondly, that the first species of the Agreeable can alone be a component part of the beautiful, that namely which is naturally consonant with our senses by the pre-established harmony between

[1] Cf. Plotinus, p. 44.

nature and the human mind; and thirdly, that even of this species, those objects only can be admitted (according to rule the first) which belong to the eye and ear, because they alone are susceptible of distinction of parts. . . . The result, then, of the whole is that the shapely (i.e. *formosus*) joined with the naturally agreeable, constitutes what, speaking accurately, we mean by the word beautiful (i.e. *Pulcher*). . . . *The sense of beauty subsists in simultaneous intuitive[1] of the relation of parts, each to each, and of all to a whole: exciting an immediate and absolute complacency, without intervenence,[1] therefore, of any interest sensual or intellectual.* The Beautiful is thus at once distinguished both from the agreeable, which is beneath it, and from the GOOD which is above it: for both these have an interest necessarily attached to them: both act on the Will, and excite a desire for the actual existence of the image or idea contemplated: while the sense of beauty rests gratified in the mere contemplation. . . . But may not the sense of beauty originate in our perception of the fitness of the means to the end in and for the animal itself? Or may it not depend on a law of proportion? No!

On Poesy or Art (1818)

Art, used collectively for painting, sculpture, architecture and music, is the mediatress between, and reconciler of, nature and man. It is, therefore, the power of humanizing nature, of infusing the thoughts and passions of man into every thing which is the object of his contemplation; colour, form, motion, and sound, are the elements which it combines, and it stamps them into unity in the mould of a moral idea.[2] . . .

By excitement of the associative power passion itself imitates order, and the order resulting produces a pleasurable passion, and thus (poetry) elevates the mind by making its feelings the object of its reflexion. So likewise, whilst it recalls the sights and sounds that had accompanied the occasions of the original passions,

[1] So printed by Cottle, *Early Recollections* (1837), vol. ii, p. 230, from Felix Farley's *Bristol Journal*, 1814. [2] Cf. Croce, p. 241.

poetry impregnates them with an interest not their own by means of the passions, and yet tempers the passion by the calming power which all distinct images exert on the human soul. . . .

The Fine Arts . . . all, like poetry, are to express intellectual purposes, thoughts, conceptions, and sentiments which have their origin in the human mind, not, however, as poetry does, by means of articulate speech, but as nature or the divine art does, by form, colour, magnitude, proportion, or by sound, that is, silently or musically.[1]

FRIEDRICH WILHELM JOSEPH VON SCHELLING
1775–1854
The Relation of the arts of form to Nature[2] (1807)

If we look at the mere empty shape of things and not at their essential nature, they do not speak to our hearts. We must read in them our own soul and spirit if they are to answer us. What is the perfection of an individual thing? Nothing but the creative life within it, its power of self-maintenance. While our careless glance sees nature as a dead thing, we shall never experience the chemical change which precipitates the pure gold of beauty and truth. . . . By what power is the soul created in and with the body, as by a single breath? If art cannot do this, as nature does, it can create nothing. . . . Works which start from mere form, however far developed from that side, betray their origin by an incurable emptiness just where we look for the last and essential perfection. . . . How can we melt the apparently hard forms of nature so that the pure energy of things may fuse into one mould together with the energy of our own minds? We must go behind the form in order to come back to it as intelligible, alive and really felt. What remains in the

[1] For Coleridge's relation to Schelling see *Biographia Literaria*, edited by Shawcross.

[2] This lecture was provoked by Winckelmann's distinction between beauty, as mere form, and the character or meaning which might be added to it.

most beautiful form if you abstract from this active principle? Only superficial qualities of extension and spatial relation. . . .

The artist must strive to emulate that real Spirit of Nature which speaks from within things, and uses their shape and form as its mere sensuous symbols. . . . If the form could subsist in independence of an essential content, and in its own right, it could only be an alien limitation of that content. But how could the essential meaning feel itself limited by that which itself creates, which exists only with and through it?[1] . . . Definition of form in nature is never merely negative or formal, it always has positive character.[2]

ARTHUR SCHOPENHAUER
1788–1860

In Schopenhauer we may see the influence of the Kantian point of view upon a very different temperament. Kant had been by nature or training pious and rationalistically dogmatic. His philosophical study and acumen had forced him to take into account difficulties such as those raised by Hume. Schopenhauer was by temperament pessimistic and sceptical, with the imaginative impulse to personify abstractions. He readily accepted Kant's criticism of the intellect as unable to afford knowledge of ultimate reality, and also his doctrine that in practical activity we somehow experience this unknowable. But the irreconcilable conflict of desire and duty had seemed to Kant to imply God, 'freedom', and immortality as the realities which underlie the apparent contradictions of life. To Schopenhauer they suggested an ultimate reality not only careless of our happiness but condemned by our moral reason. Post-Kantian idealism seemed to him complacently to present 'the best of all possible worlds, in which everything is a necessary evil.' Our own and every other existence, according to Schopenhauer, is the outcome of a primordial 'Will', or tendency to live, which realizes itself in the various grades of phenomenal being, and

[1] Cf. Stevenson, p. 198.
[2] Cf. Blake: 'All sublimity is founded on minute discrimination'; and Reynolds, p. 97, and Bosanquet, p. 190.

finally becomes conscious and, in man, self-conscious. But the 'Will' is insatiable—'man never is but always to be blest'—and it is cruel. In our lust and fear we destroy one another. There is no abiding happiness and no peace but annihilation. Our duty is to conquer the Will by asceticism. Suicide or manslaughter, while destroying the phenomenal individual, merely realize the fundamental 'Will'; they are manifestations of passion and fear. Only if all men could, by attaining the ideal of Christian or eastern ascetics, wholly free themselves from the body and its self-seeking, would Nirvana be attained.

But in the meantime, we have, unexpectedly enough, our intervals of respite. In the self-consciousness of man the 'Will' has overreached itself. For even if the moral reason which self-consciousness brings with it be too weak to conquer the will, and can only add remorse to our ever-recurring lust and satiety, man also has knowledge. And so far as knowledge is not will, nor in the service of the will, it is peace. But, according to Schopenhauer, all that usually goes by the name of knowledge, all science, which deals with abstract Universals, is in the service of the will. We only understand in order to use for our purposes. The only disinterested knowledge is aesthetic contemplation. There, with no ulterior aim, we survey the spectacle of the Universe (that is, the 'Will') either in the detail of its phenomenal manifestations in space and time, or, through music, in its essential reality. Art is the only positively good thing in life. Asceticism is but a means to annihilation.

The World as Will and Idea (1818)

(Translated by R. B. Haldane and J. Kemp, 1883)

iii. 30. In the First Book the world was explained as mere *idea*,[1] object for a subject. In the Second Book we considered it from its other side, and found that in this aspect it is *will*, which proved to be simply that which this world is besides being idea. In accordance with this knowledge we called the world as idea, both as a whole and in its parts, the *objectification of will*, which therefore means the will become object, i.e. idea. . . .

33. Knowledge, now, as a rule, remains always subordi-

[1] *Vorstellung.*

nate to the service of the will, as indeed it originated for this service, and grew, so to speak, to the will, as the head to the body. In the case of brutes this subjection of knowledge to the will can never be abolished. . . . This human excellence is exhibited in the highest degree by the Apollo of the Belvedere; the head of the God of the Muses, with eyes fixed on the far distance, stands so freely on his shoulders that it seems wholly delivered from the body, and no more subject to its cares.

34. If, raised by the power of the mind, a man relinquishes the common way of looking at things, gives up tracing, under the guidance of the forms of the principle of sufficient reason, their relations to each other, the final goal of which is always a relation to his own will; if he thus ceases to consider the where, the when, the why, and the whither of things, and looks simply and solely at the *what*; if, further, he does not allow abstract thought, the concepts of the reason, to take possession of his consciousness, but, instead of all this, gives the whole power of his mind to perception, sinks himself entirely in this, and lets his whole consciousness be filled with the quiet contemplation of the natural object actually present, whether a landscape, a tree, a mountain, a building, or whatever it may be; inasmuch as he *loses* himself in this object (to use a pregnant German idiom), i.e. forgets even his individuality, his will, and only continues to exist as the pure subject, the clear mirror of the object, so that it is as if the object alone were there, without any one to perceive it, and he can no longer separate the perceiver from the perception, but both have become one, because the whole consciousness is filled and occupied with one single sensuous picture; if thus the object has to such an extent passed out of all relation to something outside it, and the subject out of all relation to the will, then that which is so known is no longer the particular thing as such; but it is the *Idea*,[1] the eternal form, the immediate

---

[1] *Idee* (ἰδέα, εἶδος), the essential character of some kind of thing, is translated by Idea, *Vorstellung* by idea. Cf. Plotinus, p. 48.

objectivity of the will at this grade; and, therefore, he who is sunk in this perception is no longer individual, for in such perception the individual has lost himself; but he is *pure*, will-less, painless, timeless *subject of knowledge*. . . .

Whoever now has, after the manner referred to, become so absorbed and lost in the perception of nature that he only continues to exist as the pure knowing subject, becomes in this way directly conscious that, as such, he is the condition, that is, the supporter, of the world and all objective existence; for this now shows itself as dependent upon his existence. Thus he draws nature into himself, so that he sees it to be merely an accident of his own being. In this sense Byron says—

> Are not the mountains, waves, and skies, a part
> Of me and of my soul, as I of them?[1]

36. The common mortal, that manufacture of Nature which she produces by the thousand every day, is, as we have said, not capable, at least not continuously so, of observation that in every sense is wholly disinterested, as sensuous contemplation,[2] strictly so called, is. He can turn his attention to things only so far as they have some relation to his will, however indirect it may be. Since for this purpose, which never demands anything but the knowledge of relations, the abstract conception of the thing is sufficient, and for the most part even better adapted for use, the ordinary man does not linger long over the mere perception, does not fix his attention long on one object, but in all that is presented to him hastily seeks merely the concept under which it is to be brought, as the lazy man seeks a chair; and then it interests him no further. This is why he is so soon done with everything, with works of art, objects of natural beauty, and indeed everywhere with the truly significant contemplation of all the scenes of life. He does not linger; only seeks to know his own way in life, together with all that

[1] *Childe Harold*, iii. lxxv.
[2] 'sensuous contemplation': *Beschaulichkeit*.

might at any time become his way. Thus he makes topographical notes in the widest sense; over the consideration of life itself as such he wastes no time. The man of genius, on the other hand, whose excessive power of knowledge frees it at times from the service of will, dwells on the consideration of life itself, strives to comprehend the Idea of each thing, not its relations to other things; and in doing this he often forgets to consider his own path in life, and therefore for the most part pursues it awkwardly enough. While to the ordinary man his faculty of knowledge is a lamp to lighten his path, to the man of genius it is the sun which reveals the world. . . .

37. Aesthetic pleasure is one and the same whether it is called forth by a work of art or directly by the contemplation of nature and life. The work of art is only a means of facilitating the knowledge in which this pleasure consists. That the Idea comes to us more easily from the work of art than directly from nature and the real world, arises from the fact that the artist, who knew only the Idea, no longer the actual, has reproduced in his work the pure Idea, has abstracted it from the actual, omitting all disturbing accidents. The artist lets us see the world through his eyes. That he has these eyes, that he knows the inner nature of things apart from all their relations, is the gift of genius, is inborn; but that he is able to lend us this gift, to let us see with his eyes, is acquired, and is the technical side of art. . . .

38. In the aesthetical mode of contemplation we have found *two inseparable constituent parts*—the knowledge of the object, not as individual thing but as Platonic Idea, that is, as the enduring form of this whole species of things; and the self-consciousness of the knowing person, not as individual, but as *pure will-less subject of knowledge*. The condition, under which both these constituent parts appear always united, was found to be the abandonment of the method of knowing which is bound to the principle of sufficient reason, and which, on the other hand, is the only kind of knowledge that is of value for the service of

the will and also for science. Moreover, we shall see that
the pleasure which is produced by the contemplation of
the beautiful arises from these two constituent parts,
sometimes more from the one, sometimes more from the
other, according to what the object of the aesthetical
contemplation may be.

All *willing* arises from want, therefore from deficiency,
and therefore from suffering. The satisfaction of a wish
ends it; yet for one wish that is satisfied there remain at
least ten which are denied. Further, the desire lasts long,
the demands are infinite; the satisfaction is short and
scantily measured out. But even the final satisfaction is
itself only apparent; every satisfied wish at once makes
room for a new one; both are illusions; the one is known
to be so, the other not yet. No attained object of desire
can give lasting satisfaction, but merely a fleeting grati-
fication; it is like the alms thrown to the beggar, that
keeps him alive to-day that his misery may be prolonged
till the morrow. Therefore, so long as our consciousness
is filled by our will, so long as we are given up to the
throng of desires with their constant hopes and fears, so
long as we are the subject of willing, we can never have
lasting happiness nor peace. It is essentially all the same
whether we pursue or flee, fear injury or seek enjoyment;
the care for the constant demands of the will, in whatever
form it may be, continually occupies and sways the consciousness; but without peace no true well-being is possible. The subject of willing is thus constantly stretched
on the revolving wheel of Ixion, pours water into the sieve
of the Danaids, is the ever-longing Tantalus.

But when some external cause or inward disposition
lifts us suddenly out of the endless stream of willing, and
delivers knowledge from the slavery of the will, the attention is no longer directed to the motives of willing, but
comprehends things free from their relation to the will,
and thus observes them without personal interest, without
subjectivity, purely objectively, and gives itself entirely up
to them so far as they are ideas, but not in so far as they are

motives.[1] Then all at once the peace which we were always seeking, but which always fled from us on the former path of the desires, comes to us of its own accord, and it is well with us. It is the painless state which Epicurus prized as the highest good and as the state of the gods; we are for the moment set free from the miserable striving of the will; we keep the Sabbath of the penal servitude of willing; the wheel of Ixion stands still.[2]

But this is just the state which I described above as necessary for the knowledge of the Idea, as pure contemplation, as sinking oneself in perception, losing oneself in the object, forgetting all individuality, surrendering that kind of knowledge which follows the principle of sufficient reason, and comprehends only relations; the state by means of which at once and inseparably both the perceived particular thing is raised to the Idea of its whole species, and the knowing individual to the pure subject of will-less knowledge, and as such they are both taken out of the stream of time and all other relations. It is then all one whether we see the sun set from the prison or from the palace.

Inward disposition, the predominance of knowing over willing, can produce this state under any circumstances. This is shown by those admirable Dutch artists who directed this purely objective perception to the most insignificant objects, and established a lasting monument of their objectivity and spiritual peace in their pictures of *still life*, which the aesthetic beholder does not look on without emotion; for they present to him the peaceful, still frame of mind of the artist, free from will, which was needed to contemplate such insignificant things so objectively, to observe them so attentively, and to repeat this perception so intelligently; and as the picture enables the onlooker to participate in this state, his emotion is often increased by the contrast between it and the unquiet frame of mind, disturbed by vehement willing, in which he finds himself. In the same spirit,

[1] Cf. Bergson, p. 206.   [2] Cf. Schiller, p. 127.

landscape-painters, and particularly Ruisdael, have often painted very insignificant country scenes, which produce the same effect even more agreeably.

38. Lastly, it is this blessedness of will-less perception which casts an enchanting glamour over the past and distant, and presents them to us in so fair a light by means of self-deception. For as we think of days long gone by, days in which we lived in a distant place, it is only the objects which our fancy recalls, not the subject of will, which bore about with it then its incurable sorrows just as it bears them now; but they are forgotten, because since then they have often given place to others. Now, objective perception acts with regard to what is remembered just as it would in what is present, if we let it have influence over us, if we surrendered ourselves to it free from will. Hence it arises that, especially when we are more than ordinarily disturbed by some want, the remembrance of past and distant scenes suddenly flits across our minds like a lost paradise. The fancy recalls only what was objective, not what was individually subjective, and we imagine that the objective stood before us then just as pure and undisturbed by any relation to the will as its image stands in our fancy now; while in reality the relation of the objects to our will gave us pain then just as it does now. We can deliver ourselves from all suffering just as well through present objects as through distant ones whenever we raise ourselves to a purely objective contemplation of them and so are able to bring about the illusion that only the objects are present and not we ourselves. Then, as the pure subject of knowledge, freed from the miserable self, we become entirely one with these objects, and, for the moment, our wants are as foreign to us as they are to them. The world as idea alone remains, and the world as will has disappeared. . . .

Sight, unlike the affections of the other senses, cannot, in itself, directly and through its sensuous effect, make the *sensation* of the special organ agreeable or disagreeable; that is, it has no immediate connexion with the will. . . .

In the case of hearing this is to some extent otherwise; sounds can give pain directly, and they may also be sensuously agreeable, directly and without regard to harmony or melody. Touch, as one with the feeling of the whole body, is still more subordinated to this direct influence upon the will; and yet there is such a thing as a sensation of touch which is neither painful nor pleasant. But smells are always either agreeable or disagreeable, and tastes still more so. Thus the last two senses are most closely related to the will, and therefore they are always the most ignoble, and have been called by Kant the subjective senses. The pleasure which we experience from light is in fact only the pleasure which arises from the objective possibility of the purest and fullest perceptive knowledge, and as such it may be traced to the fact that pure knowledge, freed and delivered from all will, is in the highest degree pleasant, and of itself constitutes a large part of aesthetic enjoyment.[1] . . .

39. All these reflections are intended to bring out the subjective part of aesthetic pleasure; that is to say, that pleasure so far as it consists simply of delight in perceptive knowledge as such, in opposition to will. And as directly connected with this, there naturally follows the explanation of that disposition or frame of mind which has been called the sense of the *sublime*.

We have already remarked above that the transition to the state of pure perception takes place most easily when the objects bend themselves to it, that is, when by their manifold and yet definite and distinct form[2] they easily become representatives of their Ideas, in which beauty, in the objective sense, consists. This quality belongs preeminently to natural beauty, which thus affords even to the most insensible at least a fleeting aesthetic satisfaction.

41. When we say that a thing is *beautiful*, we thereby assert that it is an object of our aesthetic contemplation,

---

[1] Cf. Plato, *Hippias*, p. 15.

[2] A few lines later Schopenhauer uses the phrase 'significant form' (*Bedeutsamkeit Formen*); cf. Bell, p. 264.

and this has a double meaning; on the one hand it means that the sight of the thing makes us *objective*, that is to say, that in contemplating it we are no longer conscious of ourselves as individuals, but as pure will-less subjects of knowledge; and on the other hand it means that we recognize in the object, not the particular thing, but an Idea; and this can only happen, so far as our contemplation of it is not subordinated to the principle of sufficient reason, does not follow the relation of the object to anything outside it (which is always ultimately connected with relations to our own will), but rests in the object itself. . . . Since, on the one hand, every given thing may be observed in a purely objective manner and apart from all relations; and since, on the other hand, the will manifests itself in everything at some grade of its objectivity, so that everything is the expression of an Idea; it follows that everything is also *beautiful*. . . .

Sometimes the possession of special beauty in an object lies in the fact that the Idea itself which appeals to us in it is a high grade of the objectivity of will, and therefore very significant and expressive. Therefore it is that man is more beautiful than all other objects, and the revelation of his nature is the highest aim of art.[1] Human form and expression are the most important objects of plastic art, and human action the most important object of poetry. Yet each thing has its own peculiar beauty, not only every organism which expresses itself in the unity of an individual being, but also everything unorganized and formless, and even every manufactured article. For all these reveal the Ideas through which the will objectifies itself at its lowest grades, they give, as it were, the deepest resounding bass-notes of nature. Gravity, rigidity, fluidity, light, and so forth, are the Ideas which express themselves in rocks, in buildings, in waters.[2] . . .

42. In aesthetic contemplation (in the real, or through the medium of art) of the beauty of nature in the

[1] Cf. Hegel on classical art, p. 169.   [2] Cf. Hegel on symbolic art, p. 168.

inorganic and vegetable worlds, or in works of architecture, the pleasure of pure will-less knowing will predominate, because the Ideas which are here apprehended are only low grades of the objectivity of will, and are therefore not manifestations of deep significance and rich content. On the other hand, if animals and man are the objects of aesthetic contemplation or representation, the pleasure will consist rather in the comprehension of these Ideas, which are the most distinct revelation of will; for they exhibit the greatest multiplicity of forms, the greatest richness and deep significance of phenomena, and reveal to us most completely the nature of will, whether in its violence, its terribleness, its satisfaction or its aberration (the latter in tragic situations), or finally in its change and self-surrender, which is the peculiar theme of Christian painting; as the Idea of the will enlightened by full knowledge is the object of historical painting in general, and of the drama. . .

45. We all recognize human beauty when we see it, but in the true artist this takes place with such clearness that he shows it as he has never seen it, and surpasses nature in his representation; this is only possible because *we ourselves are* the will whose adequate objectification at its highest grade is here to be judged and discovered. Thus alone have we in fact an anticipation of that which nature (which is just the will that constitutes our own being) strives to express. . . .

52. Music is as *direct* an objectification and copy of the whole *will* as the world itself, nay, even as the Ideas, whose multiplied manifestation constitutes the world of individual things. Music is thus by no means like the other arts, the copy of the Ideas, but the *copy of the will itself*, whose objectivity the Ideas are. This is why the effect of music is so much more powerful and penetrating than that of the other arts,[1] for they speak only of shadows, but it speaks of the thing itself. Since, however, it is the same will which objectifies itself both in the Ideas and in

[1] Cf. Aristotle, *Problems*, p. 35.

music, though in quite different ways, there must be, not indeed a direct likeness, but yet a parallel, an analogy, between music and the Ideas whose manifestation in multiplicity and incompleteness is the visible world. . . .

It does not, therefore, express this or that particular and definite joy, this or that sorrow, or pain, or horror, or delight, or merriment, or peace of mind; but joy, sorrow, pain, horror, delight, merriment, peace of mind *themselves* to a certain extent in the abstract, their essential nature, without accessories, and therefore without their motives. Yet we completely understand them in this extracted quintessence. Hence it arises that our imagination is so easily excited by music, and now seeks to give form to that invisible yet actively moved spirit-world which speaks to us directly, and clothe it with flesh and blood, i.e. to embody it in an analogous example.[1] . . .

The pleasure we receive from all beauty, the consolation which art affords, the enthusiasm of the artist, which enables him to forget the cares of life,—the latter an advantage of the man of genius over other men, which alone repays him for the suffering that increases in proportion to the clearness of consciousness, and for the desolate loneliness among men of a different race,—all this rests on the fact that the in-itself of life, the will, existence itself, is, as we shall see farther on, a constant sorrow, partly miserable, partly terrible; while, on the contrary, as idea alone, purely contemplated, or copied by art, free from pain, it presents to us a drama full of significance. This purely knowable side of the world, and the copy of it in any art, is the element of the artist. He is chained to the contemplation of the play, the objectification of will; he remains beside it, does not get tired of contemplating it and representing it in copies; and meanwhile he bears himself the cost of the production of that play, i.e. he himself is the will which objectifies itself, and remains in constant suffering. That pure, true, and deep knowledge of the inner nature of the

[1] Cf. Hanslick, p. 181.

world becomes now for him an end in itself: he stops there. Therefore it does not become to him a quieter of the will, as, we shall see in the next book, it does in the case of the saint who has attained to resignation: it does not deliver him for ever from life, but only at moments, and is therefore not for him a path out of life, but only an occasional consolation in it, till his power, increased by this contemplation and at last tired of the play, lays hold of the real.[1] . . .

Supplement, Chapter 29. The Ideas reveal not the thing in itself, but only the objective character of things, thus still only the phenomenon; and we would not even understand this character if the inner nature of things were not otherwise known to us at least obscurely and in feeling. This nature itself cannot be understood from the Ideas, nor in general through any merely *objective* knowledge; therefore it would remain an eternal secret if we were not able to approach it from an entirely different side. Only because every knowing being is also an individual, and thereby a part of nature, does the approach to the inner being of nature stand open to him in his own self-consciousness, where, as we have found, it makes itself known in the most immediate manner as will. . . .

PERCY BYSSHE SHELLEY
1792–1822
A Defence of Poetry
Written 1821;[2] published 1840

Man is an instrument over which a series of external and internal impressions are driven, like the alternations of an ever-changing wind over an Aeolian lyre, which

[1] Cp. Dennis, p. 60.

[2] This was a reply to his friend Peacock's *Four Ages of Poetry*. The first or iron age was barbarous; the golden was marked by the passion of Homer and Shakespeare, the silver by the polish of Pope; the romantic revival is brazen and must inevitably yield to the age of reason. The resemblances here to Hegel are obvious.

move it by their motion to ever-changing melody. But there is a principle within the human being, and perhaps within all sentient beings, which acts otherwise than in a lyre, and produces not melody alone, but harmony, by an internal adjustment of the sounds or motions thus excited to the impressions which excite them. It is as if the lyre could accommodate its chords to the motions of that which strikes them, in a determined proportion of sound; even as the musician can accommodate his voice to the sound of the lyre. A child at play by itself will express its delight by its voice and motions: and every inflexion of tone and every gesture will bear exact relation to a corresponding antitype in the pleasurable impressions which awakened it; it will be the reflected image of that impression; and as the lyre trembles and sounds after the wind has died away, so the child seeks, by prolonging in its voice and motions the duration of the effect, to prolong also a consciousness of the cause. . . . In the infancy of society every author is necessarily a poet, because language itself is poetry; and to be a poet is to apprehend the true and the beautiful, in a word, the good which exists in the relation, subsisting, first between existence and perception, and secondly between perception and expression. . . .

And this springs from the nature itself of language, which is a more direct representation of the actions and passions of our internal being, and is susceptible of more various and delicate combinations, than colour, form, or motion, and is more plastic and obedient to the control of that faculty of which it is the creation. For language is arbitrarily produced by the imagination and has relation to thoughts alone, but all other materials, instruments and conditions of art have relations among each other, which limit and interpose between conception and expression. . . . Sounds as well as thoughts have relation both between each other and towards that which they represent, and a perception of the order of those relations has always been found connected with a perception of the order of the relations of thought. Hence the language of poets has ever affected a certain uniform and harmonious recurrence of sound, without which it were not poetry, and which is scarcely less indispensable to the communication of its influence, than the words themselves, without reference to that peculiar order. Hence the vanity of translation; it were as wise to cast a violet into a crucible that you might discover the formal principle of its colour and odour, as seek to transfuse from one language into another the creations of a poet.[1] . . .

Ethical science arranges the elements which poetry has created, and propounds schemes and proposes examples of civil and domestic life: nor is it for want of admirable doctrines that men hate, and despise, and censure, and deceive, and subjugate one another. But poetry acts in another and diviner manner. It awakens and enlarges the mind itself by rendering it the receptacle of a thousand unapprehended combinations of thought. Poetry lifts the veil from the hidden beauty of the world. . . .

A man, to be greatly good, must imagine intensely and comprehensively; he must put himself in the place of another and of many others; the pains and pleasures of his species must become his own. The great instrument of moral good is the imagination; and poetry administers to the effect by acting upon the cause. . . . Poetry strengthens the faculty which is the organ of the moral nature of man, in the same manner as exercise strengthens a limb. A poet therefore would do ill to embody his own conceptions of right and wrong, which are usually those of his place and time, in his poetical creations, which participate in neither. By this assumption of the inferior office of interpreting the effect, in which perhaps after all he might acquit himself but imperfectly, he would resign a glory in the participation of the cause. There was little danger that Homer, or any of the eternal poets, should have so far misunderstood themselves as to have abdicated this throne of their widest dominion. Those

[1] Cf. Bradley, p. 224.

in whom the poetical faculty, though great, is less intense, as Euripides, Lucan, Tasso, Spenser, have frequently affected a moral aim, and the effect of their poetry is diminished in exact proportion to the degree in which they compel us to advert to this purpose. . . . In the drama of the highest order there is little food for censure or hatred; it teaches rather self-knowledge and self-respect.

JOHANN FRIEDRICH HERBART
1776–1841
Practical Philosophy[1] (1808)
Works, ed. Hartenstein, vol. viii.

12. That taste is fickle we may presume is a conclusion only from experience; and mainly from the experience of the varying judgements on very *complex* objects such as products of art or nature taken as wholes. . . . We may hope, on the other hand, to discover the causes of this fickleness so soon as those *primary judgements* are distinctly exhibited which are, indeed, implied by the total aesthetic effect of complex works but not separately revealed. . . .

The danger is that we lose ourselves too much in the impression which beauty makes on us, allow ourselves to be occupied too fully with the emotions commonly connected with it. Love and enthusiasm, as opposed to the cool judgement of the connoisseur, have this effect, and so still more has the shifting of fancy from one sphere of taste to another. Many people fall into poetry on the appearance of a beautiful landscape, and into sentimentality when they hear music; or they take music for a kind of painting, painting for poetry, poetry for the highest sculpture, and sculpture for a kind of aesthetic philosophy.[2] Such people should be prescribed a cold douche in the ridicule of the masters of the particular arts until they wake to the peculiar beauty of each kind,

[1] Herbart holds that moral approval is a kind of taste. The correlative of taste is objective value.   [2] Cf. Bradley, p. 227.

and see the landscape in the landscape, enjoy the concert at the concert, the values and shades in painting, and the entanglements of situations, feelings, and characters in poetry.[1] . . . When, then, does the pure judgement of taste arise? Is there or can there be such a thing? . . Can there or should there be a pure work of art, which does not also move, charm, entertain us?[2] . . .

Desire seeks the future, taste determines about what lies before it, for which reason it is only desire that can properly be *satisfied;* what answers to taste is rather compliance or conformity with its requirements. . . .

15. Just as it is easy to understand what must be *given* to desire in order to satisfy it, . . . so it would be strange if taste, though it requires nothing to be given it, should be supposed itself to *give* something, and by its mere judgement, as it were of its own power, to confer something upon an object whose idea is already complete.[3] . . . Was such an addition already stored in the mind? Was the distaste for an ugly thing kept in stock merely to be fetched out, when the thing presented itself, in order to be taken into account with it? If we inclined to such a strange notion, presumably the distaste for the thing would at least *coincide with the apprehension* of it and not subsequently arise without our knowing why or whence. And then the judgement would not be separated or distinguished from its object, any more than, in pleasure and pain, what we feel can be apprehended as distinct from the feeling of it. . . .

17. We thus reach two antitheses on which to ground the conditions governing all objects of taste. On the one hand, in a judgement of taste the object must be apprehended as already realized and involving no sense of strain,[4] whereas desire involves strain and contrast. On the other hand, the object of a judgement of taste must be susceptible of a purely theoretical apprehension apart from the judgement, that is to say, without approval or

---

[1] Cf. Bradley, p. 218, Santayana, p. 203. [2] Cf. Gentile.
[3] Cf. Kant, § 58, p. 123, and Perry, p. 298. [4] *Hemmung.*

distaste, merely as an object of knowledge, *about which*
the judgement is made.[1] This distinguishes it from the
pleasant and unpleasant, which can only be apprehended
in the actual feeling. So arises the question: how can an
object to which approval or distaste *attaches* present itself
without such addition as something indifferent? Clearly
the indifferent object lacks something in order to become
the object of approval or distaste. . . . The object of taste
must be composed of the indifferent and some addition.
But then the addition, as part of the compound object,
would be itself an object; and we should have to apply
to it what we established before, that the object of taste
must be susceptible of purely theoretical apprehension
as something indifferent. The conclusion is that *each*
element of the approved or distasteful whole is, in isolation, indifferent; in a word, the *material* is indifferent,
but the *form* comes under the aesthetic judgement. The
simplest instances are here the best. [18] What, for instance, in music is a third or fifth or any interval of
definite musical value? Obviously neither of the *single*
tones, whose relation composes the interval, has by itself,
in the least degree, that character which attaches to it
when they sound *together*.[2] Consequently taste is not a
faculty strictly of *conferring* approval or disapproval;
rather, those judgements which are commonly conceived
under the name of taste, to distinguish them as a class
from other mental manifestations, are the results of the
perfect apprehension [19] of relations formed by a complexity of elements. . . . These elements must not be
idly juxtaposed in a mere collection, but must interpenetrate each other as a colour and a tone, or a tone and
a mood, scarcely can; whereas tone and tone, colour and
colour, mood and mood, apprehended in a single act of
thought, actually so modify one another that approval
or distaste (of a peculiar kind for each peculiar relation)
arises in the apprehension.[2] . . .

[1] Cf. Santayana, § 11, p. 198, and Ross, p. 316.
[2] Cf. Plotinus, p. 44, Moore, p. 246.

Aesthetic philosophy, as the establishment of *aesthetic principles*, would properly be bound not to define or to demonstrate or to deduce, nor even to distinguish species of art or argue about existing works, but rather to *put us in possession of all* the single relations, however many they be, which in a complete apprehension of anything produce approval or distaste. . . . [20] Might we venture to say that the musical discipline which bears the strange name of figured bass is the only real example so far existing of genuine aesthetic?

Introduction to Philosophy (lectures 1813–37)

Works, ed. Hartenstein, vol. i.

III. i. § 85. Every work of nature or art which is beautiful lifts us above our ordinary level, and breaks the accustomed course of psychic mechanism. If it is asked how this is done, the easiest answer is: through the stirring up of emotions. These are either depressing or exciting, with numberless varieties in both classes, but always fleeting;—a character that distinguishes them from the aesthetic judgement, which is permanently attached to its object.[1] It is true that in most aesthetic objects we can trace evidence that their effect began with arousing some kind of emotion.[1] . . . This is the surest way for them to impress us; and the best way of quieting the emotion and *purging* our souls of it is to return to the underlying aesthetic judgement. . . . Between excitement and depression lies an impassive seriousness.[2] And there are aesthetic objects which hardly condescend to the trick of working on our emotions. Stern[2] virtue, a solemn[2] vaulting, a solemn chorale, a Doric column, even chaste, straightforward narration, and a calm landscape, begin their effect upon sensitive people simply with the aesthetic judgement, which then very likely occasions emotions, but allows them to subside and actually quiets them, without being modified by them. We cannot de-

[1] Cf. Ross, p. 316.   [2] *Ernst.*

mand that this should always happen; art can too
seldom affect men, as we find them, in this way.

II. § 89. All the single elements which general aesthetic
has to indicate are relations; the perfectly simple is
indifferent, neither pleasing nor distasteful.[1] . . .

III. § 100. What is harmonious in mingled tones or
colours depends upon the blending of ideas before
resistance,[2] or upon the tendency towards it. Spatial and
temporal beauty, on the other hand, presuppose space or
time and consequently the blending of distinct elements.[3]

Encyclopaedia of Philosophy (1831)
Works, ed. Hartenstein, vol. ii.

I. ix. 70. To appreciate music we must have some
practice in the apprehension of intervals and harmonies.
To poetry every man brings his knowledge of language,
but also of the various relations of life, of men's characters,
and of the things we perceive. Even statues and pictures
would remain unmeaning unless gestures and all the
bodily expression of mind were familiar to the daily
experiences of us all. Every work of art without exception
must have much read into it; its effect comes far more
from the beholder than to him. . . . Much in works of
art depends upon *unconscious association*,[4] which is quite
different from mere perception and from aesthetic impressions which rest on perception alone. . . .

71. To appraise the *essential* value of a work of art rightly,
we must set aside the effect of association so far as it does
not actually condition the apprehension of the work. It is
only a particular application of this maxim that *imitation*
can never be set up as a principle of aesthetic. . . .

72. People visit picture galleries with catalogues, and
operas with librettos; if they can get none, they complain
of not understanding the pictures or the music. And for

---

[1] Cf. Plotinus, I. vi. 1, p. 44.

[2] *Verschmelzung vor der Hemmung.* Cf. *Psychologie als Wissenschaft*, §§ 70–2, 100,
105, 114. The doctrine is, briefly, that ideas (Vorstellungen) tend to blend, but
resist this tendency in proportion to various kinds of difference between them.

[3] *abgestufte Verschmelzung*; cf. Hegel, pp. 173–4.   [4] *Apperception.*

like reasons poetry is often accompanied by a commentary.[1] Works of art are expected to have a meaning . . . and the artists are glad to oblige. . . . But music is *music* and to be beautiful need mean nothing.[2] . . . Even good musicians still repeat the maxim that music should express feelings; as though the feelings aroused by it, to express which it *may* accordingly be used, were the basis of those rules of double and single counterpoint in which its true essence lies.[3] What did the old masters mean to *express* who developed the possible forms of the fugue, or those still older whose industry differentiated the possible orders of column?[4] Nothing. Their thoughts did not travel beyond their arts but penetrated deeply into their essence. . . . We need not grudge such emotion as a work can arouse by its own proper aesthetic relations . . . but when an art tries to represent something outside itself, it should content itself with the portrait-painter's celebrity. We may even add that the excitement of strong emotion dulls sensibility, and in the end makes us forget *what* precisely it is that arouses the emotion.[4] We get enough of tears and laughter without the expense of art. . . .

73. Like the musician, the architect, in designing a building, interlaces pattern with pattern, of which each by itself constitutes a whole, yet finds its natural place in the other. Such a form nature has already introduced in the contours of the human face; . . . and she does the same in miniature for beautifully shaped flowers. Corresponding to this spatial counterpoint, we find the requirements of contrapuntal form satisfied by poetry, when every significant character goes its way and develops itself appropriately under the condition that these individual histories unite themselves in a whole. In painting, each figure, however artistically grouped, must have its own correct drawing; the eye must be able to distinguish or compose them with freedom and, indeed, pleasure, aided by the contrast of colours. . . .

[1] Cf. Bradley, p. 215. [2] Cf. Stevenson, p. 197.
[3] Cf. Hegel, p. 174, Hanslick, p. 181. [4] Cf. Bell p. 265, Prall, p. 311.

75. To ask unmeaning questions about the functions of sense, imagination, understanding, and feeling in the apprehension of beauty is to obscure the truth with fables. We must disentangle the pattern of perceptions which the work of art has interwoven, study them apart and in combination, until we discover the elements and conditions of beauty. It must be confessed that in no art is this so easy as in music, where we have only to read the parts. . . .

Sculpture, simple as it seems, extends in space a work of art which geometry can never fully analyse. . . . Yet the psychological grounds for spatial beauty should be ascertainable from the mechanics of mind, with the aid of geometry and psychology, sufficiently to determine so far as necessary the aesthetic value of those contours with which we are acquainted.

76. Poetry is an easier subject for analysis. But, to begin with, we must exclude the whole lyrical element, in which the poet becomes rather a *singer*, who sings not by the rules of our composition, but like a bird who imparts his overflowing passion. However powerfully such a flow of life may move the genial hearer, it is not so much art as nature; the subjective stimulants of sympathy lie outside the realm of objective beauty, which is valid for all men at all times. With the lyric we can dismiss everything in poetry that is merely speech, in spite of the truly aesthetic elements of rhythm and euphony which it may contain. . . . We have then excluded all that can be ascribed to either intellectual or emotional sympathy. What then remains in poetry? Only the purely objective, what the poet can communicate without communicating himself.[1] . . . Only pure drama and pure epic remain, . . . character, action, situation.

80. The poet does not despise the emotion or feeling which may result from the partiality of his audience and the sympathy it gives to some characters and witholds from others. Such feelings are, indeed, not aesthetic

[1] Contrast Gentile.

judgements, and the moving is not the beautiful. But the audience need not be mere critics. They are concrete men whom criticism should not despise nor grudge them their natural feelings. If it did, the lyrical element in poetry and music would lose its very heart, which consists in the communication of feeling, though neither poetry nor music is *merely* lyrical.

JOHN STUART MILL
1806–73
Poetry and its Varieties (1833)

Poetry, which is the delineation of the deeper and more secret workings of human emotion, is interesting only to those to whom it recalls what they have felt, or whose imagination it stirs up to conceive what they could feel, or what they might have been able to feel had their outward circumstances been different. . . . The truth of poetry is to paint the human soul truly. . . . Poetry and eloquence are both alike the expression or utterance of feeling. But, if we may be excused the antithesis, we should say that eloquence is *heard*, poetry is *over*heard. Eloquence supposes an audience; the peculiarity of poetry appears to us to lie in the poet's utter unconsciousness of a listener. Poetry is feeling, confessing itself to itself in moments of solitude, and embodying itself in symbols, which are the nearest possible representations of the feeling in the exact shape in which it exists in the poet's mind.

GEORG WILHELM FRIEDRICH HEGEL
1770–1831

Kant as a student of science had been stimulated by Hume's scepticism to show that our claims to attain truth in pure science are justified. In order to do this, he had restricted those claims to the phenomenal world. Ultimate, unconditioned reality was beyond their sphere. But within the sphere of experience Kant believed that he had refuted scepticism. The method by which he attempted to do this was by arguing that if we have any experience at all, as we have, the possibility of our having it depends on our already employing the principles of pure science. To question the possibility of scientific knowledge, then, was to question something by acceptance of which alone could we even ask a question or be aware of anything about which questions could be asked. Experience all hangs together, and, whatever its relation to absolute truth about unconditioned reality, it stands or falls together. You cannot, as the empiricists supposed, accept one element of it which they called particular facts and reject all the rest as delusions arising out of the facts. To be aware of the alleged facts you must already be employing the alleged delusions. But beyond the world of experience lies the ultimate reality only accessible to 'faith.' Hegel, with other 'absolute idealists', denied the distinction between experience and ultimate reality, or rather asserted that this distinction, like every other, arises within reality and within experience. His ambition was to do for the whole of reality what Kant claimed to have done for experience: to show that it all hangs together. Reality is rational; therefore, its necessity can be apprehended. There is no chance or brute fact. Everything that is can be seen to be rationally involved in everything else. And the pattern of the connexion, according to Hegel, was the synthesis of opposites. Of two opposites neither could be or be understood without the other; since they can only be together, they can only be fully understood when they are understood together as united in a Whole. Hegel's readiness to apply this 'triadic synthesis' alike to abstract universals (Being, Not-being, Becoming) and to historical events (Greek civilization, the Roman Empire, the modern world) influences his Aesthetic. Beauty is a synthesis of the abstract concept and the material which is 'given' in sense. Romantic art is the synthesis of Symbolic and Classical. Philosophy is the synthesis of art and religion. Since the experience of beauty certainly exists, it must, on Hegel's philosophy, be intelligible. And that means for him that it must be possible to apprehend how the existence of beauty and of every species of beauty is necessarily involved in the being of anything at all.

Because the reason, which is explicitly developed in our thought, is also latent in the sensible world, every stage of human consciousness is able to find a natural means of expression in some organization of sensible things. In other words sense is implicit reason; when we experience beauty we see through the illusion of their diversity.

Aesthetics [1]

Published 1835

Introduction, i. The beauty of art is a beauty that has not only been born of the mind or spirit but born again of it.[2] . . .

Everything that is beautiful is only really beautiful as partaking in something higher [namely mind] and being produced thereby. In this sense natural beauty manifests itself as only a reflection of the beauty which properly belongs to the mind,—as an imperfect and incomplete manifestation whose essential reality[3] is contained in the mind. . . .

Very serious purposes have been ascribed to art, and it has been recommended as a matchmaker between sense and reason or duty and inclination, and as able to reconcile those elements which clash in so harsh a conflict. To which one may reply that,—however respectable the purposes thus ascribed to art,—reason and duty are not the gainers by the efforts of such a go-between; since, by the essential purity of their nature, they are incapable of being so compromised, they cannot suffer anything less pure than themselves. Further, art itself is not thus made any more worthy of scientific treatment, for it is made to serve two masters; serious aims, no doubt, on the one hand, but, on the other, laziness and frivolity. In short, if this were art's service, instead of being an end, art could only appear a means. And, to consider the nature of such service, it would still be a contemptible character in art that, if it is really to serve serious ends and produce important results, its only means for doing so is illusion. For beauty lives in seeming.[4] . . .

[1] Hegel's *Aesthetik* has been translated by Osmaston (1920) and the *Introduction* by Bosanquet (1886, and *History of Aesthetic*, 1892, Appendix).
[2] Cf. Bosanquet, p. 190.   [3] *ihrer Substanz nach*.   [4] Cf. Plato, *Hippias*, p. 9.

Only when it has attained its appropriate freedom is fine art really art; it cannot fulfil its highest function till it has established itself in the same sphere with religion and philosophy and has become simply one of the ways of expressing, or presenting to consciousness, the divine, the deepest interests of man, the most comprehensive spiritual truths.[1] . . . This character art shares with philosophy and religion, but there is this difference: that art expresses even what is highest by sensuous form, and so brings it nearer to natural appearances, to our senses and feeling. . . .

iii. The universal and absolute need from which art, in its general character, springs, originates in the fact that man is a *thinking* consciousness; that is, that he makes explicit to himself, by means of his own nature,[2] what he is and what the world is. Natural things are simply there, and that is the end of it;[3] man, being a mind, gives himself a double existence, since he not only, like natural things, is, but also realizes his own existence,[4] perceives himself, has ideas of himself, thinks himself; and only by this active realization of himself is he a mind. Man attains this self-consciousness in a twofold way. First *theoretically*, so far as he has to bring his inmost self before consciousness—every movement of the human heart, every storm that sways it. In general he has to contemplate himself, to picture himself, to fix before himself what thought discovers as his essential character; he has to recognize only himself both in all that is called up in him and in all that he assimilates from without. Secondly man realizes himself through *practical* activity, since he has the impulse to express[5] himself, and so again to recognize himself, in things that are at first simply presented to him as externally existent. He attains this end by altering external things and impressing on them the stamp of his own inner nature, so that he rediscovers his

---

[1] Cf. Kant, § 59, p. 123, Bradley, p. 288.   [2] *aus sich selbst für sich macht.*
[3] *sind nur unmittelbar und einmal.*
[4] *für sich ist.* I think the ambiguity of 'realize' is in Hegel. Cf. Nettleship, p. 188.   [5] *hervorzubringen.*

own character in them. Man does this in order that he may profit by his freedom to break down the stubborn indifference of the external world to himself, and may enjoy in the countenance of nature only an outward embodiment of himself. . . .

The material or sensible element in a work of art only has any claim to its place so far as it exists for the mind of man; not in virtue of its own materiality.[1] . . . The interest in art is distinguished from the practical interest of desire by the fact that it leaves its objects alone in their independence, while desire adapts them, or even destroys them, for its own purposes. Conversely, artistic contemplation differs from the theoretical contemplation of the scientific intelligence in cherishing an interest for the objects in their individuality; it does not busy itself in reducing them to universal thoughts and conceptions. Hence it follows that, though the sensuous material must indeed be present in a work of art, it need only appear as a superficial semblance of matter. . . . The demand for realism as such is not fundamental or primary in art. So, although the representation of external nature is an essential element in art, actual nature does not prescribe the rule; nor is imitation of outward appearances for their own sake the end of art. So we have still to ask: What, then, is the subject-matter of the arts and with what end must it be presented? Here there at once rises to the mind the common view that it is the function and purpose of art to stir our senses, our feeling, our emotions with everything which can find a place in the human soul. Art must realize for us the famous saying *Nihil humani a me alienum puto*.[2] . . . Art does indeed possess this formal character of being able to beautify every possible subject-matter by engaging our contemplation and our feelings. . . . But the very heterogeneity of this subject prevents us from resting content with this merely formal characteristic of art. The rationality which permeates this motley chaos challenges us to recognize the emergence and actual

[1] Cf. Plato, *Hippias*, p. 7.　　　　[2] *sic.* Terence, *Heaut. Tim.* i. i.

attainment of some all-embracing purpose in these contradictory elements. . . . A very little reflection, then, suggests to us the consideration that the end of art lies in its
capacity and function of mitigating the passions.[1] . . . And
even if art confined itself to the task of presenting images
of the passions to our contemplation, though it should
thereby flatter them, yet even in that there is already a
kind of mitigation. For by that means man at least
becomes aware of what before he merely was. Now for
the first time man contemplates his impulses and in-
stincts; and whereas formerly they hurried him along
without reflection, he now sees them externalized, and
begins, so soon as they are presented to him as objects, to
achieve freedom from them. Thus it may often happen
to an artist, overtaken by grief, that he can mitigate the
intensity of his private feeling by the expression[2] of it.
Some comfort is to be found even in tears. The man who
at first was utterly concentrated and sunk in grief, at
least thus externalizes, in however physical a way, what
before was pent within him. Far greater is the relief by
expression[3] of inner feeling in words, forms, tones, and
shapes. . . .

But this definition of art, that it should guide and
educate our crude passions, remained purely formal and
general, so that a further question had to be asked about
the specific nature and essential aim of this education. . . .

If the end of art is confined to didactic utility, then its
other side, that of delight, entertainment, satisfaction, is
implied to be unessential and to have its justification[4]
only in the profit of the lesson which it accompanies. . . .

If we still continue to speak of an end, we must, to
begin with, guard against the perverse interpretation of
our question about the *end* as being really one about the
use. . . . Against this we must maintain that art has the
function of revealing truth in the form of sensuous artistic
shapes and of presenting to us the reconciliation of the

---

[1] Cf. Aristotle, *Poetics*, p. 33.   [2] *Darstellung.*   [3] *aussprechen.*
[4] *Substanz.*

contradiction [between sense and reason, between what is and what ought to be, between desire and duty].[1] Consequently it contains its end in itself, in this very revelation and presentation. . . .

Division of the Subject. Since we have spoken of art as issuing from the absolute spiritual reality,[2] and have assigned as its end the sensuous presentation of that absolute itself, we must now proceed with our summary to show, at least in outline, how the particular divisions of art[3] originate from this notion of artistic beauty in general as being the representation of absolute reality. For this purpose we must try to give some general idea of this notion. As already said, the subject-matter of art is the spiritual reality[4] and its form is the sensuous, plastic image. Art has to reconcile these two sides in an independent whole of mutually necessary parts. (1) The first condition for this is that the subject-matter to be represented in art should be intrinsically capable of such representation. Otherwise we only get an artificial combination, where some subject-matter which is naturally incapable of sensuous plastic expression[5] is forced into that form, and an essentially prosaic material struggles for an apt expression to which it is fundamentally unsuited. (2) The second condition, which follows from the first, is that the subject-matter of art shall not be essentially abstract. . . . (3) Thirdly, if a genuine[6] and therefore concrete subject-matter is to receive an adequate sensuous form, the latter must be a no less fully concrete and individual thing. This concreteness of the two elements in art, the subject and the presentation, is just the point in which they can harmonize and interpenetrate. The natural human body, for instance, is a concrete object of sense which is capable of expressing

---

[1] Cf. Muratori, p. 61, and Kant, § 59, p. 123.

[2] *Idee.* It is perhaps impossible to translate this word as used by Hegel. It means the whole of reality, but reality as intelligible, and only intelligible as being a phase of that of which intelligence is another phase.

[3] *Theile.*   [4] *Idee.*   [5] *Bildlichkeit und äussere Erscheinung.*

[6] *wahrhaft.*

adequately the concrete mind or spirit. We must reject the idea that it is only a coincidence when some natural object is used as a significant form.[1] Art adopts such form not just because it is to hand nor because nothing else is to hand; the definiteness of subject-matter implies the possibility of external actualization, in fact of sensuous expression. On the other hand, in order that this should be possible, this concrete object of sense in which an essentially spiritual subject-matter figures itself, is in its turn essentially spiritualized. The outward form by which the subject-matter becomes object of perception or imagination has no purpose except its appeal to our heart and mind.[2] . . . Although the sensuous shape bestowed by art is not, from this point of view, accidental, on the other hand it is not the highest method of apprehending the concrete spiritual reality. Thought is higher than any sensuously concrete representation. Relatively, thought is abstract; but in order to be true and rational it must not be one-sided but concrete thought. . . . The Greek gods, as contrasted with the Christian God, exemplify the difference between a subject-matter whose adequate form is sensuous artistic representation and one whose very nature essentially demands a form which is higher and more spiritual. The Greek god is no abstraction but an individual, to whom a bodily form is not alien; the Christian God likewise is concrete personality, but personality purely spiritual, that must be known as spirit and in spirit. He is present to us therefore essentially by inward knowledge[3] and not by external natural form, which can only represent him imperfectly and not in the full depth of our conception of him. But it is the function of art to present ultimate reality to our immediate perception in sensuous shape and not in the form of thought or pure spirit merely. And the value of this representation depends on the correspondence and unity between

---

[1] *wahre Gestalt.* Cf. Bell, p. 264.

[2] Cf. Kant, *Zweckmässigkeit ohne Zweck*, p. 118, and Schelling, p. 136.

[3] *sein Element des Daseins ist das innere Wissen.* Cf. Dennis, p. 60.

these two elements. Consequently the greatness and excellence of art in achieving its ideal will depend upon the degree of intimacy with which this form and subject-matter are fused and united.

Our scientific survey, then, must found its classification of art upon the degree of truth attained; that is, upon the degree to which mind has achieved a plastic form adequate to its ideal. For before mind attains a true conception of its absolute essence it must pass through a series of stages, a series which can be deduced from that conception. And to these stages in the development of a subject-matter which mind thus supplies to itself there answers an exactly corresponding series of types of art, in which the mind, by its artistic activity, becomes aware of itself. This evolution of the artistic spirit has itself from its own nature two sides. First, there is a universal spiritual development, wherein the series of different conceptions of the universe, different ways of regarding God, man, and nature as a whole, express themselves artistically.[1] Secondly, these inner developments of art have to find for themselves actual external realizations in sensuous media; and these make up the necessary distinctions of art, that is to say, the particular arts.[2] The distinction of different types[1] of art being a distinction in the universal nature of mind, it is impossible for any one type to be confined to a single medium,[3] and each sensuous medium also can be variously applied.[1] But since the sensuous medium, as well as the mind, is potentially rational,[4] each sensuous medium has an especially close and subtle correspondence with one of the different spiritual types of art.[5] . . .

Any subject-matter whatever can, so far as its own nature goes, be adequately represented, but it cannot merely thereby lay claim to ideal artistic beauty. The

---

[1] e.g. in primitive, classical, and Christian art.
[2] e.g. architecture, sculpture, painting, &c.
[3] e.g. colour, tones, marble.
[4] *an sich, wie der Geist, den Begriff zu seiner inneren Seele hat.*
[5] e.g. marble as used in sculpture to the classical spirit.

very representation of such a chance subject will, indeed, appear defective when compared with the ideal. Here may opportunely be suggested, what can only be proved later, that imperfection in a work of art need not always be attributed merely to lack of skill in the artist,[1] but that imperfection of form may arise from imperfection of subject. For instance, the idols and artistic representations of divinity among the Chinese, Indians, and Egyptians remained formless, or achieved only a false and vicious definiteness of form, never true beauty, because their mythological ideas, which were the mental subject-matter of this art, were still vague or falsely definite, and not the true subject matter of art.[2] . . .

So now that we have discussed artistic beauty in its essential nature, we must observe how the realm of beauty differentiates itself into diverse species. This affords us, as the second part of our treatise, the doctrine of the types of art.

A. These forms owe their birth to the various ways of conceiving the ultimate reality [which is to be their subject-matter]; from these varieties arise the differences of form in which they are expressed. Types of art, then, are nothing but the various relations of subject-matter to form, relations which arise out of the very nature of spiritual reality. . . . We have to consider three such relations.

(a) At first the ultimate reality which is conceived as the subject-matter of artistic presentation is something itself vague and indistinct, or endowed with false and inappropriate distinctness. It is indistinct as not being yet endowed with that individuality which is a condition of artistic beauty;[3] this abstractness and one-sidedness leave the outward manifestation arbitrary and incomplete. This first form of art is rather a mere straining after embodiment than a capacity for actual representation.[4] No true form has yet been found for the spiritual reality itself, these are only wrestlings and strivings towards one.

---

[1] Cf. Hulme, p. 274.   [2] *der in sich selbst absolute Inhalt.*
[3] *das Ideal.*   [4] Cf. Kant, § 59, p. 123.

This type of art may be generally described as the *Symbolic*. Here the abstract conception of spiritual reality finds an alien embodiment in natural sensible matter, with which artistic representation starts and to which it remains, at this stage, confined. Natural objects of perception are at first left as they are, but invested with a significance as embodiments of absolute spiritual reality, in virtue of which embodiment they are given the function of expressing it, and have to be interpreted as if they actually presented it to our senses. This implies, no doubt, that natural objects really have an element in virtue of which they are capable of representing a universal meaning. But as complete adequacy is not yet possible, the relation between the two can only be limited and artificial, as when, for instance, strength is indicated by a lion.

Another consequence of this artificial relation between the spiritual reality and the natural object is to make us aware of the gulf between them. When the spiritual reality, which has no other physical thing to express it, expatiates in all these shapes, and seeks to express itself in them with that impatience of limitation or definition which still belongs to it, it finds none of them adequate to itself. So it proceeds to exaggerate the shapes and appearances of nature to an unlimited monstrosity like its own. . . .

Owing to this inadequacy of the two sides to each other, the relation of the spiritual reality to its objectification becomes one of contrast; for the former, as something inward, despises any such externalization. As being the inward universal import of this host of inadequate forms, it elevates itself above them all as *Sublime*. In this sublimity, natural objects and the human form and its experiences are no doubt accepted and tolerated as they are; but they are recognized as inadequate to a meaning which is exalted above all things in heaven or earth.[1]

[1] Cf. Browning, *Fra Lippo Lippi*:

> A fine way to paint soul, by painting body
> So ill, the eye can't stop there, must go further
> And can't fare worse.

and cf. Nettleship, p. 188, and Tolstoy, p. 194.

These features determine the general character of the primitive artistic pantheism of the East, which either embodies the deepest meaning in the most trivial objects or violently distorts natural appearances to express its theory of life. Hence this form of art either becomes bizarre, grotesque, and tasteless, or contemptuously contrasts the infinite, though abstract, freedom of what is spiritually real [1] with the ephemeral nothingness of all actual appearances. In this way the import can never be fully embodied in the expression; and in spite of every effort and struggle, the inadequacy of the form to the spiritual reality [2] remains insuperable. This may be taken as the first type of art, the Symbolic with its yearning, and its turbid, enigmatic sublimity.

(β) In the second type, which we will call the *Classical*, the defect which beset the symbolic on both its sides is overcome. Symbolic imagery [3] is imperfect because on the one side ultimate reality is only thought of with artificial [4] definitions or quite indefinitely; and on the other, for that very reason, the union of import and imagery must remain imperfect and, itself, merely abstract. The classical type of art, as the correction of this double failure, is the natural [5] and adequate embodiment of the spiritual reality [6] in the form peculiarly and essentially [7] appropriate to it, so that the two unite in a perfect and natural harmony. [8] So in the classical type for the first time we get the production and apprehension of the perfect ideal, now realized in fact. . . .

The peculiarity of the subject-matter of classical art is that it is itself concrete reality, that is to say concrete mind; for only mind is truly individual or self-contained. We have then to look among natural things for one which naturally corresponds to the essential character of mind. . . . Now if ultimate reality as mind and, indeed, mind

---

[1] *Substanz.*   [2] *Idee.*   [3] *Gestalt.*   [4] *abstrakt.*   [5] *frei.*
[6] *Idee.*   [7] *ihrem Begriff nach.*
[8] Cf. Browning, *Rabbi Ben Ezra*: 'Nor soul helps flesh more, now, than flesh helps soul.'

definitely individualized, is to manifest itself in temporal appearances, it has as its natural form the human shape. Personification and anthropomorphism have been freely blamed as a degradation of the spiritual; but art, if it is to make mind apprehensible to sense, must rise to such anthropomorphism, for it is only in its body that mind is adequately manifest to the senses. . . .

The forms of the human body in classical art are treated no longer as mere objects presented to the senses, but only as the presentation and natural image of mind; for which reason they must be freed from all the deficiencies of what is merely material and from the accidental limitations of natural appearance. But just as the imagery must be thus purified if it is to express within its four corners a subject-matter suitable to it, so, too, its spiritual subject-matter must be of a kind which can be fully expressed in the natural human form, and which does not surpass the possibilities of sensuous bodily expression. Only so can the harmony of imagery and import be complete. Consequently mind is at this stage immediately limited to the particular human mind, as opposed to what is, without qualification, absolute and eternal, which can only express itself or announce its presence as pure spirituality. This limitation is fatal to classical art in its turn and necessitates the transition to a third and higher type, the Romantic.

(γ) The *Romantic* type of art rises above the complete identification of ultimate reality with its external manifestation, and returns, though at a higher level, to that distinction and opposition of the two sides which symbolic art had failed to overcome. Classical art in fact reached the perfection of sensuous presentation, and if it has any defect it is a defect inherent in art, a limitation in its very nature. This defect arises because art in general presents mind, whose essence is infinite concrete universality, as an object in sensuous concrete form, and classical art presents the complete fusion of spiritual and sensuous as a harmony. But mind cannot be represented in its true essence by any such fusion.[1] . . . Christianity represents God not as an individual separate spirit but as absolute in spirit and in truth. Consequently it sacrifices sensuous, spatial presentation and finds a more inward and spiritual way of embodying its meaning. . . . Similarly romantic art is the passing of art beyond its proper nature, though still retaining the form of art and working within its limits. . . . Such art, in conformity with its new subject-matter, addresses itself no longer to mere sensuous perception but to something more subjective and inward, which can identify itself more intimately with such a subject-matter:—to the inner soul and feeling. . . . The inner life is the subject of romantic art and has to be represented as such. . . . It celebrates its triumph over the body and manifests that triumph in bodily things themselves, so that the sensuous appearance is degraded and despised.[2]

Yet this form of art, like all others, needs some sensuous form of expression. Because mind has retired into itself and withdrawn from direct unity with the external world, the material sensuous form is treated, as it was in symbolic art, as something unessential and superficial. . . .

We find once more, then, the characteristics of symbolic art, mutual indifference, inadequacy, and separation between the spiritual meaning and the images; but with an essential difference. In symbolic art the defective conception of ultimate reality involved a defectiveness of imaging it. In romantic art this reality has to be presented as mind and soul made perfect, and consequently disdains any intimate union with external things. . . .

B. The third division of our subject, assuming the notion of the ideal and of the universal types of art established in the first two, has to trace out their realization in definite sensuous materials. . . .

Each type of art attains its specific character in a specific sensible material and realizes itself completely in the technique appropriate to that material. Yet these types

---

[1] Cf. Browning, *Old Pictures in Florence*, xix.   [2] Cf. Ruskin, p. 176.

being differentiations of *all* art, cannot be confined to realizing themselves each in a particular art, but are found actualizing themselves, though not so characteristically, in other arts also. Conversely, each particular art belongs properly to one of the general types of art and produces works appropriate thereto, yet each also, in its own way, illustrates all the types of art. . . .

(*a*) The material of *architecture* is just physical matter as a heavy mechanical mass, and its forms are merely the forms of inorganic nature arranged symmetrically by the abstract relations of understanding. In such material and forms the ideal cannot, as concrete mind,[1] be realized, and so the work produced stands over against the spiritual meaning[2] as something external to it, not permeated by it, but only in an artificial[3] relation to it. Consequently the symbolic type of art is the fundamental principle of architecture. . . . The import of architecture can be more or less clearly embodied in its material and forms, according as this import, which is the aim of the work, is more or less developed and distinct, and free from obscurity and superficiality. Architecture can even go so far in this direction as to create an adequate artistic embodiment of this import in its forms and material, but then it has passed its natural limits and is tending to the stage of sculpture, which is the grade above it. . . .

(*b*) In *sculpture*, the inner life of mind, which architecture could only dimly indicate, actually embodies itself in the sensuous form and its physical material, and the two sides so inform each other that neither overweights its fellow. Consequently the fundamental principle of this art is the classical type. Here the sensuous form expresses nothing except spirit as such, and conversely no spiritual import is completely expressible by sculpture which cannot be completely presented to our intuition in bodily form. In sculpture the mind should stand before us in undifferentiated unity, as untroubled and not divided against itself; what breathes life into the form is spiritual individuality.

[1] *Geistigkeit.*   [2] *Idee.*   [3] *abstracter.*

(*c*) A yet higher import than that expressed by sculpture is mind not only in its ultimate[1] reality, but as it actually manifests itself differentiated in individual spirits or souls. Here we have no longer the serene repose of a god, . . . but every kind of subjective emotion and activity in the passions, actions, and experiences of living men. In short the wide realm of human feeling, will, and failure is made the subject of artistic representation. To suit such a subject the sensuous element in art has to appear as similarly differentiated[2] and also as itself akin to the experience of our own minds.[2] Colours, sounds, and sounds used merely as signs of perceptions and ideas, afford such materials, and so we get *painting, music,* and *poetry* as the ways of embodying such an import. . . . These arts get their principle from the romantic type of art. It is a group of arts, not one, that is adequate to manifest most appropriately the romantic type, because that type is the least abstract.

(i) The next art after sculpture is *painting.* . . . Every feeling, idea, and aim that can arise in man's heart and everything that he can realize in action compose the varied subject-matter of painting. The whole realm of individual fact from the highest reach of soul to the most insignificant fact of nature has its place here; not even unconscious[3] nature is excluded in its various scenes and aspects so long as some hint of mind relates it to our thought and feeling.

(ii) The second art which goes to realize the romantic type, along with and in contrast to painting, is *music.* The

---

[1] *absolutes.*

[2] Hegel's argument is here suspiciously obscure. I suppose he means to suggest that uncoloured sculpture is inadequate to express the varieties of experience because (1) marble is homogeneous, whereas there are many colours, notes, words; (2) the appreciation of a statue is less intellectual. A picture has to be interpreted in three dimensions, a succession of notes or words remembered and integrated, the meaning and suggestion of words understood and imagined. The implication would seem to be that sculpture is less *like* a train of feeling than is a picture, a melody, or a poem, because its parts differ in spatial position and not in quality. Cf. Plotinus, p. 44, Herbart, *Introduction,* p. 155. [3] *endliche.* Evidently landscape and still life.

material it works with, though still sensuous, is yet more
differentiated and mental.[1] Painting acknowledges and
expressly counterfeits the spatial coexistence of unorgani-
cally connected parts. But music spiritualizes the sensuous by transcending this extension of parts in an
undivided unity.[2] . . . In musical tones the whole scale
of our feelings and passions, not yet defined in their
object, can echo and reverberate.[3] So, just as sculpture
stood between the extremes of architecture and the
romantic arts, so music forms the central point of these
romantic arts, midway between the one-sided materialism[4]
of painting and the one-sided intellectuality of poetry.
Like architecture, music sets over against subjective
feelings its own intelligible measurable relations.[5] . . .

(iii) The characteristic of *poetry* is its power of subduing
the sensuous element, against which music and painting
had already rebelled, to mind and ideas. Sound, the only
sensuous material it retains, is now no longer feeling *in*
sound, but a symbol without value of its own, and a
symbol no longer of indefinite feelings with their gradu-
ated shades, but of completely concrete ideas.[3] So sound
becomes words. . . . The sensuous element which in music
was inseparably fused with the spiritual[6] is here consciously distinguished from what it imports, . . . so that

[1] Cf. the last footnote but one.

[2] I cannot be sure whether Hegel means (1) that, in a picture the colours,
though harmonizing, remain clearly distinct alongside one another, but in
a chord (for example) the notes are almost indistinguishably blended,
being neither successive nor adjacent (cf. Herbart, *Introduction*, p. 155), or
(2) that a succession of musical sounds is somehow more mental than the
contiguity of colours, or at least requires a more obvious exercise of memory
for its apprehension, since of the harmonizing elements one is present and
others—which yet modify our apprehension of what is present—are past.
It might have been easier to decide between these interpretations had
Hegel said more about dancing. But I am not clear what the argument, on
either interpretation, proves. Perhaps he is meaning what Plato meant by
suggesting that, whereas painting imitates 'things', music 'imitates' states of
mind; and perhaps what Schopenhauer meant by saying that the other arts
represent the 'Ideas' (or essential characters of nature) but music the
Will itself. Cf. pp. 35, 146.

[3] Cf. Hanslick, p. 181.

[4] *räumliche Sinnlichkeit.*

[5] Cf. Herbart, p. 156, and Pater, p. 187.

[6] *Innerlichkeit.*

the sound may be replaced by mere letters, the visible and the audible alike being degraded to mere indications of spirit. So, properly speaking, the material with which poetry works is poetical ideas or images.[1] And since imagination is common to all the arts, poetry enters into them all and has a place of its own in each. Poetry is the universal art of the mind, no longer of mind confined for its self-realization to external sensuous materials, but free to expatiate in the imaginary space and time of its own ideas and feelings. But it is at this very stage that art transcends itself. It sacrifices the reconciliation and union of sensuous things with mind and passes from the poetry of imagination to the prose of thought.[2]

JOHN RUSKIN

1819–1900

Modern Painters (1843–1860)

[Vital Beauty.]

III, I, xii. § 4. The pleasure afforded by every organic form is in proportion to its appearance of healthy vital energy. . . . (§ 5) When we are told that the leaves of a plant are occupied in decomposing carbonic acid, and preparing oxygen for us, we begin to look upon it with some such indifference as upon a gasometer. It has become a machine; some of our sense of its happiness is gone; its emanation of inherent life is no longer pure. The bending trunk, waving to and fro in the wind above the waterfall, is beautiful because it is happy, though it is perfectly useless to us. The same trunk, hewn down, and thrown across the stream, has lost its beauty. It serves as a bridge,—it has become useful; and its beauty is gone, or what it retains is purely typical, dependent on its lines and colours, not on its functions. Saw it into planks, and though now adapted to become permanently useful, its

---

[1] Cf. Bradley, p. 217.   [2] Cf. Bacon, p. 56.

beauty is lost for ever, or to be regained only when decay
and ruin shall have withdrawn it again from use, and
left it to receive from the hand of nature the velvet moss
and varied lichen, which may again suggest ideas of
inherent happiness, and tint its mouldering sides with
hues of life.[1] . . . (§ 7) Whenever we dissect the animal
frame, or conceive it as dissected, and substitute in our
thoughts the neatness of mechanical contrivance for the
pleasure of the animal; the moment we reduce enjoyment
to ingenuity, and volition to leverage, that instant all
sense of beauty ceases . . .

[Vital Beauty in Man.]

xiv. § 4. The visible operation of the mind upon the
body may be classed under three heads.

First, the operation of the intellectual powers upon the
features, in the fine cutting and chiselling of them, and
removal from them of signs of sensuality and sloth, by
which they are blunted and deadened; and substitution
of energy and intensity for vacancy and insipidity (by
which wants alone the faces of many fair women are
utterly spoiled and rendered valueless); and by the
keenness given to the eye and fine moulding and development to the brow. . . . (§ 5) Secondly, the operation of
the moral feelings conjointly with the intellectual powers
on both the features and form. . . . (§ 7) The third point
to be considered with respect to the corporeal expression
of mental character is, that there is a certain period of
the soul-culture when it begins to interfere with some of
the characters of typical beauty belonging to the bodily
frame, the stirring of the intellect wearing down the
flesh, and the moral enthusiasm burning its way out to
heaven, through the emaciation of the earthen vessel;
and that there is, in this indication of subduing of the
mortal by the immortal part, an ideal glory of perhaps
a purer and higher range than that of the more perfect
material form. We conceive, I think, more nobly of the

[1] Cf. Price, p. 125.

weak presence of Paul, than of the fair and ruddy countenance of David.[1]

III, 2, ii. *Of Imagination Associative*, § 6. If, therefore, the
combination made is to be harmonious, the artist must
induce in each of its component parts (suppose two only,
for simplicity's sake), such imperfection as that the other
shall put it right. If one of them be perfect by itself, the
other will be an excrescence. Both must be faulty when
separate, and each corrected by the presence of the other.[2]
If he can accomplish this, the result will be beautiful;
it will be a whole, an organized body with dependent
members;—he is an inventor. If not, let his separate
features be as beautiful, as apposite, or as resemblant as
they may, they form no whole. They are two members
glued together. He is only a carpenter and joiner.

§ 7. Now the conceivable imperfections of any single
feature are infinite. It is impossible, therefore, to fix upon
a form of imperfection in the one, and try with this all the
forms of imperfection of the other until one fits; but the
two imperfections must be co-relatively and simultaneously conceived. This is imagination, properly so called.

IV, x, § 8. Not long ago, as I was leaving one of the towns
of Switzerland, early in the morning, I saw in the clouds
behind the houses an Alp which I did not know, a grander
Alp than any I knew, nobler than the Schreckhorn or the
Mönch; terminated, as it seemed, on one side by a pre-
cipice of almost unimaginable height; on the other,
sloping away for leagues in one field of lustrous ice, clear
and fair and blue, flashing here and there into silver
under the morning sun. For a moment I received a
sensation of as much sublimity as any natural object could
possibly excite; the next moment, I saw that my unknown
Alp was the glass roof of one of the workshops of the town
rising above its nearer houses and rendered aerial and
indistinct by some pure blue wood smoke which rose from
intervening chimneys.

---

[1] Cf. Hegel, p. 171, on Classical and Romantic Art.
[2] Cf. Plotinus, p. 44, Richards, p. 282.

It is evident, that so far as the mere delight of the eye was concerned, the glass roof was here equal, or at least equal for a moment, to the Alp. Whether the power of the object over the heart was to be small or great, depended altogether upon what it was understood for,[1] upon its being taken possession of and apprehended in its full nature, either as a granite mountain or a group of panes of glass; and thus, always, the real majesty of the appearance of the thing to us, depends upon the degree in which we ourselves possess the power of understanding it,—that penetrating, possession-taking power of the imagination, which has been long ago defined as the very life of the man, considered as a *seeing* creature. . . . Examine the nature of your own emotion (if you feel it) at the sight of an Alp, and you find all the brightness of that emotion hanging, like dew on gossamer, on a curious web of subtle fancy and imperfect knowledge. First, you have a vague idea of its size, coupled with wonder at the work of the great Builder of its walls and foundations, then an apprehension of its eternity, a pathetic sense of its perpetualness, and your own transientness, as of the grass upon its sides; then, and in this very sadness, a sense of strange companionship with past generations in seeing what they saw.[2] They did not see the clouds that are floating over your head: nor the cottage wall on the other side of the field; nor the road by which you are travelling. But they saw *that*. The wall of granite in the heavens was the same to them as to you. They have ceased to look upon it; you will soon cease to look also, and the granite wall will be for others. Then, mingled with these more solemn imaginations, come the understandings of the gifts and glories of the Alps, the fancying forth of all the fountains that well from its rocky walls, and strong rivers that are born out of its ice, and of all the pleasant valleys that wind between its cliffs, and all the châlets that gleam among its clouds, and happy farmsteads couched upon its pastures; while together with the thoughts of these,

[1] Cf. Bell, p. 265.   [2] Cf. Tolstoy, xvi, p. 194.

rise strange sympathies with all the unknown of human
life, and happiness, and death, signified by that narrow
white flame of the everlasting snow, seen so far in the
morning sky. . . .

[The Pathetic Fallacy.]

IV, xii, § 4. Examine the point in question,—namely,
the difference between the ordinary, proper, and true
appearances of things to us; and the extraordinary, or false
appearances, when we are under the influence of emotion,
or contemplative fancy; false appearances, I say, as being
entirely unconnected with any real power or character
in the object, and only imputed to it by us. . . . So long as
we see that the *feeling* is true, we pardon, or are even pleased
by, the confessed fallacy of sight which it induces: we are
pleased, for instance, with those lines of Kingsley's,

> They rowed her in across the rolling foam—
> The cruel, crawling foam

not because they fallaciously describe foam but because
they faithfully describe sorrow. But the moment the
mind of the speaker becomes cold, that moment every
such expression becomes untrue, as being for ever untrue
in the external facts. And there is no greater baseness in
literature than the habit of using these metaphorical
expressions in cool blood.[1]

IV, xvii. A curiously balanced condition of the powers
of mind is necessary to induce full admiration of any
natural scene. Let those powers be themselves inert, and
the mind vacant of knowledge, and destitute of sensibility;
and the external object becomes little more to us than it
is to birds and insects; we fall into the temper of the
clown. On the other hand, let the reasoning powers be
shrewd in excess, the knowledge vast, or sensibility intense,
and it will go hard but that the visible object will suggest
so much that it shall be soon itself forgotten, or become,
at the utmost, merely a kind of keynote to the course of
purposeful thought.

[1] Cf. Muratori, p. 64, Mitchell, p. 259.

The Seven Lamps of Architecture (1849)

v, i. The creations of Architecture . . . depend, for their dignity and pleasurableness in the utmost degree, upon the vivid expression of the intellectual life which has been concerned in their production.

EDUARD HANSLICK

The Beautiful in Music (1825–1904)

First edition 1854; fifth 1876; translation, Cohen, 1891

i. On the one hand, it is said that the *aim* and *object* of music is to excite emotions, i.e. pleasurable emotions; on the other hand, the emotions are said to be the *subject-matter* which musical works are intended to illustrate.

Both propositions are alike in this, that one is as false as the other. . . .

(1) There is no *causal nexus* between a musical composition and the feelings it may excite, as the latter vary with our experience and impressibility. . . . The *musical* merit of the many compositions which at one time made so deep an impression, and the aesthetic enjoyment which their originality and *beauty* still yield, are not altered in the least by this dissimilar effect on the feelings at different periods.

ii. (2) According to this theory, sound and its ingenious combinations are but the material and medium of expression, by which the composer represents love, courage, piety and delight. . . . The beautiful melody and the skilful harmony as such do not charm us, but only what they imply. . . . But definite feelings and emotions are unsusceptible of being embodied in music. . . . The feeling of hope is inseparable from the conception of a happier state which is to come, and which we compare with the actual state. The feeling of sadness involves the notion of a past state of happiness. These are perfectly definite ideas or conceptions; . . . to reduce these to a material form is altogether beyond the power of music. A certain class of *ideas*, however, is quite susceptible of being adequately expressed by means which unquestionably belong to the sphere of music proper. This class comprises all ideas which, consistently with the organ to which they appeal, are associated with audible changes of strength, motion and ratio: the ideas of intensity waxing and diminishing; of motion hastening and lingering; of ingeniously complex and simple progression, &c. The aesthetic expression of music may be described by terms such as graceful, gentle, violent, vigorous, elegant, fresh; all these ideas being expressible by corresponding modifications of sound. We may, therefore, use these adjectives as directly describing *musical* phenomena. . . . The ideas which a composer expresses are mainly and primarily of a *purely musical* nature. . . .

What part of the feelings, then, can music represent, if not the subject involved in them?

Only their *dynamic* properties. It may reproduce the motion accompanying psychical action according to its momentum: speed, slowness, strength, weakness, increasing and decreasing intensity. But motion is only one of the concomitants of feeling, not the feeling itself.[1] . . . Whatever else there is in music that apparently pictures states of feeling, is *symbolical*. Sounds, like colours, are originally associated in our minds with certain symbolical meanings, which produce their effects independently of and antecedently to any design of art.

iii. In music there is both meaning and logical sequence, but in a *musical* sense; it is a language we speak and understand, but which we are unable to translate.

vii. In music, no distinction can be made between substance and form, as it has no form independently of the substance. . . . What then is to be called its *subject*? The group of sounds? Undoubtedly; but they have a form already. And what is the *form*? The group of sounds again; but here they are a form already filled in.[2]

[1] Cf. Schopenhauer, p. 147, and Hegel, p. 174.   [2] Cf. Bradley, p. 221.

HERBERT SPENCER

1820–1903

Principles of Psychology (1870–2)

Summarized by F. H. Collins with a preface by H. Spencer, 1889

VIII. IX. *The Aesthetic Sentiments.* 533. The activities we call play[1] are united with the aesthetic activities, by the trait that neither subserve, in any direct way, the processes conducive to life. Whence arises the play impulse? And how comes that supplementary activity of the higher faculties which the Fine Arts imply?

534. As we ascend to animals of high types we find that time and strength are not wholly absorbed in providing for immediate needs. Now, every one of the mental powers being subject to the law that its organ, when dormant for an interval longer than ordinary, becomes unusually ready to act, it happens that a simulation of its activities is easily fallen into, when circumstances offer it, in place of the real activities.[2] Hence play of all kinds —hence the tendency to superfluous and useless exercise of faculties that have been quiescent. Hence, too, the fact that these uncalled-for exertions are most displayed by those faculties which take the most prominent part in the creature's life.

535. The general nature and position of the aesthetic sentiments will be made more clearly comprehensible by observing how the aesthetic character of a feeling is habitually associated with separateness from life-serving functions. In scarcely any degree do we ascribe the aesthetic character to sensations of taste. These gratifications are but rarely separated from life-serving functions. While, conversely, there arises a wide scope for pleasure, derivable from superfluous actions of the auditory faculty,

---

[1] Spencer says that the conception of art as play was suggested to him by reading some German author, doubtless Schiller. Cf. pp. 125–6.

[2] Cf. Burke, IV. vii, p. 93.

which are much dissociated from life-serving functions. That the aesthetic consciousness is essentially one in which the actions themselves, apart from ends, form the object-matter, is shown by the conspicuous fact that many aesthetic feelings arise from contemplation of the attributes and deeds of other persons, real or ideal.

536. The primitive source of aesthetic pleasure in simple sensations, is that character in the combination which makes it such as to exercise the faculties affected in the most complete ways, with the fewest drawbacks from excess of exercise. Joined to this, comes a secondary source of pleasure—the diffusion of a normal stimulus in large amount, awakening a glow of agreeable feeling, faint and undefinable. And a third source of pleasure is the partial revival, by this discharge, of the various special gratifications connected in experience with combinations of the kind presented.

537. The same general and special truths hold in the combinations of sensations that awaken ideas and feelings of beauty. Movements of the body pleasurable to self, and associated with the consciousness of gracefulness (as in skating), are movements of a kind that bring many muscles into moderate harmonious action and strain none. There are reasons for suspecting that beautiful arrangements of forms, are those which effectually exercise the largest numbers of the structural elements concerned in perception, while overtaxing the fewest of them. Similarly with the complex visual wholes presented by actual objects, or by the pictorial representation of objects, with all their lights and shades and colours.

538. We pass into that higher region where the states of consciousness are exclusively re-representative, in taking count of the remoter mental states aroused by landscapes and by music. The feelings of beauty yielded by the literature of the imagination are remotely re-representative.

539. Subject always to the cardinal requirement that the aesthetic feeling is not one immediately aiding any

life-serving function, the highest aesthetic feeling is one having the greatest volume, produced by due exercise of the greatest number of powers without undue exercise of any; or is one resulting from the full but not excessive exercise of the most complex emotional faculty. The height of the feeling is proportionate to the remoteness from simple sensation; to its complexity, as containing an immense variety of those elements of which emotions are composed; and as being a faint reproduction of the enormous aggregate of such elements massed together in the course of evolution.

540. Finally, the aesthetic activities in general may be expected to play an increasing part in human life as evolution advances. Greater economization of energy, resulting from superiority of organization, will have in the future effects like those it has had in the past. A growing surplus of energy will bring a growing proportion of the aesthetic activities and gratifications; and while the forms of art will be such as yield pleasurable exercise to the simpler faculties, they will in a greater degree than now appeal to the higher emotions.

FRIEDRICH NIETZSCHE

1844–1900

Nietzsche started from the philosophy of Schopenhauer. He accepted the distinction of music from the other arts. But whereas the irrational and immoral will to live was for Schopenhauer the object of a cold disgust, it filled Nietzsche with a mystical ecstasy. This alone was real; our individual lives and our reason and morality were illusions whose unsatisfying character could merely be concealed by plastic or narrative art. Greek tragedy, which presented, indeed, a narrative in the plastic poses of actors but also with the emotional stimulus of dancing and music and metre, seemed to him the perfect union of both forms of art. Music for Nietzsche is preeminently the art of emotion. All others are essentially formal. Nietzsche's relation to Schopenhauer is somewhat analogous to the alleged development of a primitive Buddhism which only looked for annihilation into one which looked for a blissful absorption.

The Birth of Tragedy (1871)

i. The existence of the world is only justified as aesthetic appearance.

16. In opposition to all those who are engaged in deducing the arts from one single principle as the indispensable life-spring of all their works, I fix my eyes on the two art-divinities of Greece, Apollo and Dionysus, in whom I recognize the living and concrete representatives of two worlds of art differing in their deepest essence and in their highest aims. Apollo stands before me as the Genius of enlightenment and of the principle of individuality, through whom alone atonement can really be attained in illusion, while at the joyous cry of Dionysus the bars of individuality are burst and the way is opened to the wombs of being, to the innermost heart of things. . . . Music is to be judged by quite other aesthetical principles than are the plastic arts, and especially not by the category of beauty; though a false aesthetic, adopted by a misguided and degenerate art, has come to demand from music an effect like that of plastic works of art, whose proper ideal is beauty—namely the awaking of our satisfaction in beautiful forms.

The metaphysical delight in tragedy is a translation of the instinctive, unconscious wisdom of Dionysus into the language of pictorial form. The hero, the highest manifestation of the Will, is brought to naught for our satisfaction, because he is, after all, only appearance, and the eternal life of the Will is not touched by his destruction. 'We believe in eternal life', cries tragedy; while music is the immediate idea of that life. Plastic art has a very different aim. Here Apollo overcomes the misery of the individual by the brilliant glorification of the eternity of appearance, here beauty triumphs over the inherent misery of life, and the pain in nature's countenance is, in a sense, dissimulated. In Dionysiac art and its tragic symbolism nature herself with her own undisguised voice speaks to us: 'Be as I am! I, beneath the perpetual change of appearances; I the eternally creative, ever urging into existence; I the mother of all things, ever satisfying myself in this apparent change!'

21. The mysterious relationship of Apollo and Dionysus in tragedy might be symbolized as a brotherhood of the two divinities. Dionysus speaks with the tongue of Apollo, but Apollo in the end with the tongue of Dionysus, whereby is achieved the highest aim of tragedy and of all art.[1]

WALTER PATER

1839–94

Appreciations, Style (1888)

Just in proportion as the writer's aim, consciously or unconsciously, comes to be the transcribing, not of the world, nor of mere fact, but of his sense of it, he becomes an artist, his work *fine* art; and good art (as I hope ultimately to show) in proportion to the truth of his presentment of that sense; as in those humbler or plainer functions of literature also, truth—truth to bare fact, there,— is the essence of such artistic quality as they may have. Truth! there can be no merit, no craft at all, without that. And further, all beauty is in the long run only *fineness* of truth, or what we call expression, the finer accommodation of speech to that vision within. . . .

Literary art, that is, like all art which is in any way imitative or reproductive of fact,—form, or colour, or incident,—is the representation of such fact as connected with soul, of a specific personality, in its preferences, its volition and power.

Such is the matter of imaginative or artistic literature— this transcript, not of mere fact, but of fact in its infinite

[1] Cf. Aristotle, *Poetics*, iv, xvii, pp. 31, 33.

variety, as modified by human preference in all its
infinitely varied forms. . . .

If music be the ideal of all art whatever, precisely because
in music it is impossible to distinguish the form from
the substance or matter, the subject from the expression,
then, literature, by finding its specific excellence in the
absolute correspondence of the term to its import, will
be but fulfilling the condition of all artistic quality in
things everywhere, of all good art. Good art, but not
necessarily great art; the distinction between great art
and good art depending immediately, as regards literature at all events, not on its form but on the matter. . . .

Given the conditions I have tried to explain as con-
stituting good art;—then, if it be devoted further to
the increase of men's happiness, to the redemption of the
oppressed, or the enlargement of our sympathies with each
other, or to such presentment of new or old truth about
ourselves and our relation to the world as may ennoble
and fortify us in our sojourn here, or immediately, as with
Dante, to the glory of God, it will be also great art;[1] if, over
and above those qualities I summed up as mind and soul
—that colour and mystic perfume, and that reasonable

---

[1] Cf. Pater, *The Renaissance*, 'Conclusion': 'We have an interval, and then our
place knows us no more. Some spend this interval in listlessness, some in high
passions; the wisest [at least among 'the children of this world,'] in art and
song. For our one chance *lies* (is) in expanding that interval, in getting as
many pulsations as possible into the given time. *Great* (High) passions [may]
give *us* (one) this quickened sense of life, ecstasy and sorrow of love, [the
various forms of enthusiastic activity, disinterested or otherwise, which come
naturally to many of us.] Only be sure it is passion —that it does yield you
this fruit of a quickened, multiplied consciousness. Of *such* (this) wisdom, the
poetic passion, the desire of beauty, the love of art for *its own* (art's) sake, has
most. For art comes to you *proposing* (professing) frankly to give nothing but
the highest quality to your moments as they pass, and simply for those
moments' sake.'
The words which I have put into square brackets did not appear in the first
edition (published 1873, dated 1868), nor did the words italicized, in
whose place the words in round brackets originally stood. The whole
'Conclusion' disappeared from the second edition, 1877, as 'it might possibly
mislead some of those young men into whose hands it might fall.' It was
subsequently reprinted 'with some slight changes which bring it closer to
(its) original meaning.' Some of these changes explain the doctrine of *Style*.

structure, it has something of the soul of humanity in it, and finds its logical, its architectural place, in the great structure of human life.

RICHARD LEWIS NETTLESHIP
1846–92

Philosophical Remains, Lectures on Logic (1888)

iii. Language (of which word-language is only one form) is anything by which man expresses or 'means' something. . . . Certain sounds or sights have come to suggest, firstly, certain other sounds, sights, smells and the like; and, secondly, certain further images and thoughts, with ever-growing complexity. . . . Language is thus always being made. We are unfortunately apt to speak as if it were a fixed set of symbols which we have simply to use; but the use of language is really a recreating of it. . . . An individual highly organized in a certain direction may be habitually conscious through other symbols than speech, e.g. through music. . . . A feeling affects certain nerves, and through them certain muscles, and so issues in a sound. This sound would generally be called the 'expression' of the feeling. The phrase is, however, misleading, because it separates the feeling from its expression in sound, and suggests that we first have the feeling and then express it. It would be truer to say that the expression *is* the completed feeling; for the feeling is not fully felt till it is expressed, and in being expressed it is still felt, but in a different way. What the act of expression does is to fix and distinguish it finally; it then, and then only, becomes *a* determinate feeling.[1] In the same way the consciousness which we express when we have found the 'right word' is not the same as our consciousness before we found it; so that it is not strictly correct to call the word the expression of what we meant before we found it.

[1] Cf. Hegel, pp. 161, 168, Croce, p. 243, and Ducasse, p. 315.

This remains true of more developed forms of expression; and, following it out, we may say that what is absolutely unexpressed and inexpressible is nothing. We can only describe it potentially and by anticipation. It cannot enter into human life until it has become articulate in *some* way, though not necessarily in words. . . . When then we say that we cannot find words for our meaning, unless this implies that our consciousness is too un-developed to be expressed,[1] it indicates the fact that the words at our command are so fixed in meaning that they would have to be recreated to express our present con-sciousness, or (to vary the phrase) that this consciousness is potentially more than will go into the known forms of expression. . . . Any particular act of naming is preceded by un-named or differently named consciousness; but the consciousness which is now named is *this* consciousness, which reaches its specific character in the act of being named. . . . What has happened to the consciousness, the thing, in being named? In the first place we have given it a more permanent position in our experience, and have made it more easily recognizable. Secondly, each time it is recognized, it takes a fresh meaning, gets *more* 'distinct'. It stands out more distinctly from a certain background of consciousness, of which it is a modification. . . .

'Communication' implies two beings, otherwise different, which meet or identify themselves in a certain respect, the 'medium' of communication. Applying this to language, we must observe that the two beings need not be two different people. There is no real difference between language, as a means of communication with self, and language as a means of communication with others. . . . If language is 'conventional' or dependent on a mutual understanding (κατὰ συνθήκην), this applies as much to the understanding between the self in one con-dition and the self in another as to the understanding between myself and another.

[1] Cf. Hegel on Symbolic Art, p. 168.

BERNARD BOSANQUET

1848–1923

A History of Aesthetic (1892)

i. All beauty is in perception or imagination. When we distinguish Nature from Art as a province of the beautiful, we do not mean to suggest that things have beauty independently of human perception, as for example in reactions upon one another such as those of gravitation or solidity. We must therefore be taken to include tacitly in our conception of natural beauty some normal or average capacity of aesthetic appreciation. But, if so, it is plain that 'nature' in this relation differs from 'art' principally in degree, both being in the medium of human perception or imagination, but the one consisting in the transient and ordinary presentation or idea of the average mind, the other in the fixed and heightened intuitions of genius which can record and interpret.[1] . . . Nature for aesthetic theory means that province of beauty in which every man is his own artist. . . .

Among the ancients the fundamental theory of the beautiful was connected with the notion of rhythm, symmetry, harmony of parts; in short with the general formula of unity in variety. Among the moderns we find that more emphasis is laid on the idea of significance, expressiveness, the utterance of all that life contains; in general, that is to say, on the conception of the characteristic. If these two elements are reduced to a common denomination, there suggests itself as a comprehensive definition of the beautiful, 'That which has characteristic or individual expressiveness for sense-perception or imagination, subject to the conditions of abstract or general expressiveness in the same medium.'[2]

[1] Cf. Hegel, p. 160.
[2] Cf. Aristotle, *Poetics*, p. 31, Schelling, p. 135, and Bradley, p. 223.

Three Lectures on Aesthetic (1915)

i. The aesthetic attitude is that in which we have a feeling which is so embodied in an object that it will stand still to be looked at, and in principle, to be looked at by everybody . . . 'Feeling expressed for expression's sake.'

iii. If there could be an expression of unexpressiveness, you would, in one sense, have in it the very highest achievements of the sublime and the humorous.

LYOV NIKOLAYEVITCH TOLSTOY

1828–1910

What is Art? (1896)

Translated by Aylmer Maude, 1905

iv. In the subjective aspect, we call beauty that which supplies us with a particular kind of pleasure.

In the objective aspect, we call beauty something absolutely perfect, and we acknowledge it to be so only because we receive, from the manifestation of this absolute perfection, a certain kind of pleasure; so that this objective definition is nothing but the subjective conception differently expressed. In reality both conceptions of beauty amount to one and the same thing, namely, the reception by us of a certain kind of pleasure, i.e. in all 'beauty' that which pleases us without evoking in us desire. . . .

People will come to understand the meaning of art only when they cease to consider that the aim of that activity is beauty, i.e. pleasure. . . .

v. To evoke in oneself a feeling one has experienced, and having evoked it in oneself, then, by means of movements, lines, colours, sounds, or forms expressed in words, so to transmit that feeling that others may experience the same feeling—this is the activity of art.[1] . . . It is a means of union among men, joining them together in the same

[1] Cf. Santayana, p. 204, Ducasse, p. 313.

feelings, and indispensable for the life and progress towards well-being of individuals and of humanity.[1] . . .

vi. If feelings bring men nearer the ideal their religion
indicates, if they are in harmony with it and do not contradict it, they are good; if they estrange men from it
and oppose it, they are bad. . . . Therefore, among all
nations, art which transmitted feelings considered to be
good by this general religious sense was recognized as
being good and was encouraged; but art which transmitted feelings considered to be bad by this general
religious conception, was recognized as being bad, and
was rejected. . . .

vii. From the time that people of the upper classes lost
faith in Church Christianity, beauty (i.e. the pleasure
received from art) became their standard of good and
bad art. . . .

viii. Such feelings as form the chief subjects of present-
day art—say, for instance, honour, patriotism and
amorousness, evoke in a working man only bewilder-
ment and contempt, or indignation. . . . But if art is an
important matter, a spiritual blessing, essential for all men
('like religion,' as the devotees of art are fond of saying),
then it should be accessible to every one. And if, as in our
day, it is not accessible to all men, then one of two things:
either art is not the vital matter it is represented to be,
or that art which we call art is not the real thing. . . .

ix. An art-product is only then a genuine art-product
when it brings a new feeling (however insignificant) into
the current of human life. . . . The variety of fresh
feelings flowing from religious perception is endless, and
they are all new, for religious perception is nothing else
than the first indication of that which is coming into
existence, namely the new relation of man to the world
around him.

x. To say that a work of art is good, but incomprehensible to the majority of men, is the same as saying of

[1] For the distinction of art as expression and beauty as pleasure cf. Véron,
L'Esthétique (1878).

some kind of food that it is very good but that most people can't eat it. . . . Art is differentiated from activity of the understanding, which demands preparation and a certain sequence of knowledge (so that one cannot learn trigonometry before knowing geometry), by the fact that it acts on people independently of their state of development and education. . . . A good and lofty work of art may be incomprehensible, but not to simple unperverted peasant labourers (all that is highest is understood by them); it may be, and often is, unintelligible to erudite perverted people destitute of religion. . . .

xi. The chief characteristic of a work of art is completeness, oneness, the inseparable unity of form and contents expressing the feeling the artist has experienced. . . . Many conditions must be fulfilled to enable a man to produce a real work of art. It is necessary that he should stand on the level of the highest life-conception of his time, that he should experience feeling, and have the desire and capacity to transmit it, and that he should, moreover, have a talent for some one of the forms of art. . . .

xii. An artist's work cannot be interpreted. Had it been possible to explain in words what he wished to convey, the artist would have expressed himself in words.[1] . . . We are only infected with an artist's state of mind when he finds those infinitely minute shades in which a work of art consists, and only to the extent to which he finds them. . . .

xv. The receiver of a true artistic impression is so united to the artist that he feels as if the work were his own and not some one else's—as if what it expresses were just what he had long been wishing to express. A real work of art destroys, in the consciousness of the receiver, the separation between himself and the artist, nor that alone, but also between himself and all whose minds receive the work of art. In this freeing of our personality from its separation and isolation, in this uniting of it with others, lies the chief characteristic and the great attractive force of art.[2] . . .

---

[1] Cf. Shelley and Bradley on translation, pp. 150, 224.
[2] Cf. Gentile, p. 329.

The stronger the infection the better is the art, as art, speaking now apart from its subject-matter, i.e. not considering the quality of the feeling it transmits. And the degree of the infectiousness of art depends on three conditions:

(1) On the greater or lesser individuality of the feeling transmitted;[1] (2) on the greater or lesser clearness with which the feeling is transmitted; (3) on the sincerity of the artist, i.e. on the greater or lesser force with which the artist himself feels the emotion he transmits. . . . This third condition—sincerity—is the most important of the three. . . .

xvi. How in art are we to decide what is good and what is bad in subject-matter? . . .

The subject-matter of Christian art is such feeling as can unite men with God and with one another. . . .The Christian union of man (in contradiction to the partial, exclusive union of only some men) is that which unites all without exception. . . . Only two kinds of feeling do unite all men: first, feelings flowing from the perception of our sonship to God and of the brotherhood of man; and next, the simple feelings of common life, accessible to every one without exception—such as the feeling of merriment, of pity, of cheerfulness, of tranquillity; . . . both alike produce one and the same effect—the loving union of man with man. . . . Each is glad that another feels what he feels; glad of the communion established, not only between him and all present, but also with all now living who will yet share the same impression; and more than that, he feels the mysterious gladness of a communion which, reaching beyond the grave, unites us with all men of the past who have been moved by the same feelings, and with all men of the future who will yet be touched by them. And this effect is produced both by the religious art which transmits feelings of love to God and one's neighbour, and by universal art transmitting the very simplest feelings common to all men.[2] . . .

---

[1] Cf. Hegel on symbolic art, p. 168.
[2] Cf. Ruskin, p. 178.

I fear it will be urged against me that having denied that the conception of beauty can supply a standard for works of art, I contradict myself by acknowledging ornaments to be works of good art. The reproach is unjust, for the subject-matter of all kinds of ornamentation consists not in the beauty, but in the feeling (of admiration of, and delight in, the combination of lines and colours) which the artist has experienced and with which he infects the spectator. . . . So that there are only two kinds of good Christian art: all the rest of art not comprised in these two divisions should be acknowledged to be bad art, deserving not to be encouraged but to be driven out, denied, and despised, as being art not uniting but dividing people. Such, in literary art, are all novels and poems which transmit Church or patriotic feelings, and also exclusive feelings pertaining only to the class of the idle rich; such as aristocratic honour, satiety, spleen, pessimism, and refined and vicious feelings flowing from sex-love—quite incomprehensible to the great majority of mankind. . . .

Every reasonable and moral man would again decide the question as Plato decided it for his *Republic*,[1] and as all the Church Christian and Mahommedan teachers of mankind decided it, i.e. would say, 'Rather let there be no art at all than continue the depraving art, or simulation of art, which now exists.' . . .

The destiny of art in our time is to transmit from the realm of reason to the realm of feeling the truth that well-being for men consists in being united together; and to set up, in place of the existing reign of force, that kingdom of God, i.e. of love, which we all recognize to be the highest aim of human life. Possibly, in the future, science may reveal to art yet newer and higher ideals, which art may realize; but in our time the destiny of art is clear and definite. The task for Christian art is to establish brotherly union among men.

[1] Cf. p. 18.

OSCAR FINGALL O'FLAHERTIE WILLS WILDE
1856–1900[1]

The Picture of Dorian Gray, Preface (1891)

The artist is the creator of beautiful things.

To reveal art and conceal the artist is art's aim.[2]

The critic is he who can translate into another manner or a new material his impression of beautiful things.

The highest, as the lowest, form of criticism is a mode of autobiography.

Those who find ugly meanings in beautiful things are corrupt without being charming. This is a fault.

Those who find beautiful meanings in beautiful things are the cultivated. For these there is hope.

They are the elect to whom beautiful things mean only Beauty.

There is no such thing as a moral or an immoral book. Books are well written or badly written. That is all.

The nineteenth-century dislike of Realism is the rage of Caliban seeing his own face in a glass.

The nineteenth-century dislike of Romanticism is the rage of Caliban, not seeing his own face in a glass.

The moral and immoral life of man forms part of the subject-matter of the artist, but the morality of art consists in the perfect use of an imperfect medium.

No artist desires to prove anything. Even things that are true can be proved.

No artist has ethical sympathies. An ethical sympathy in an artist is an unpardonable mannerism of style.

No artist is ever morbid. The artist can express everything.

Thought and language are to the artist instruments of an art.

[1] Wilde lectured on *Aesthetic Philosophy* in the United States in 1882. Cf., too, the same author's *Decay of Lying* (1889) and *The Critic as Artist* (1891), where the same ideas are expounded less succinctly and with due acknowledgments.

[2] Cf. Alexander, p. 271.

Vice and virtue are to the artist materials for an art.

From the point of view of form, the type of all the arts is the art of the musician. From the point of view of feeling, the actor's craft is the type.

All art is at once surface and symbol.[1]

Those who go beneath the surface do so at their peril.

Those who read the symbol do so at their peril.

It is the spectator, and not life, that art really mirrors.

Diversity of opinion about a work of art shows that the work is new, complex, and vital.

When critics disagree the artist is in accord with himself.

We can forgive a man for making a useful thing as long as he does not admire it. The only excuse for making a useless thing is that one admires it intensely.

All art is quite useless.[2]

ROBERT ALAN MOWBRAY STEVENSON

1847–1900

Velasquez (1895–1900)

iv. Every shade of the complicated emotion[3] in a symphony by Beethoven depends entirely upon technique—that is to say, upon the relations established among notes which are by themselves empty of all significance. The materials of other arts are more or less embarrassed in application by some enforced dependence on life. Words, since they serve as fixed counters or symbols, cannot be wholly wrenched from a determined meaning and suggestion; architecture satisfies a need of common life as well as an aesthetic craving, and painting not only weaves a purely decorative pattern, but also pretends to imitate the appearance of the world. None of these arts tranquilly pursue the beauties intrinsic to their medium.[4] . . . Our faith in any art reposes, however, upon the belief

---

[1] Cf. Prall, p. 311.   [2] Cf. Ruskin, p. 175.
[3] Cf. Herbart, p. 156.   [4] Cf. Schelling, p. 136.

that its material, even if unavoidably adulterated with foreign significations, is nevertheless as capable as the sounds of music of expressing character in virtue of artistic arrangement. Otherwise, no medium of expression but the symphony should deserve the name of art. . . . Plainly, then, there are two interests to be reconciled in a picture, the facts and impressions of nature on one hand, and, on the other, the beauties and exigencies of the framed pictorial world. A *modus vivendi* must be established between the imitative and the decorative, and the compact between these two may be called the convention of the art of painting.

GEORGE SANTAYANA
1863–

The Sense of Beauty (1896)

[Beauty is subjective and irrational, it is pleasure objectified.]

2. There is no value apart from some appreciation of it. . . . Values spring from the immediate and inexplicable reaction of vital impulse, and from the irrational part of our nature. The rational part is by its essence relative: it leads us from data to conclusions. . . . 9. It is unmeaning to say that what is beautiful to one man *ought* to be beautiful to another. . . . 10. If we say that other men should see the beauties we see, it is because we think these beauties *are in the object*, like its colour, proportion, or size. . . . But this notion is radically absurd and contradictory. . . . 11. *Beauty is pleasure regarded as the quality of a thing.*[1] . . . 13. The whole sentimental side of our aesthetic sensibility—without which it would be perceptive and mathematical rather than aesthetic—is due to our sexual organization remotely stirred. . . . If the stimulus does not appear as a definite image, the values evoked are dispersed over the world, and we are said to have become lovers of nature, and to have discovered the beauty and meaning of

[1] Cf. Herbart, *Practical Philosophy*, p. 153, Croce, p. 235.

things.[1] 15. Smell and taste, like hearing, have the great disadvantage of not being intrinsically spatial: they are therefore not fitted to serve for the representation of nature. . . . The objectification of musical forms is due to their fixity and complexity: like words they are thought of as existing in a social medium. . . .

[1. Sensuous charm.]

17. Sight is perception *par excellence*, since we become most easily aware of objects through visual agency. . . . Form, which is almost a synonym for beauty, is for us usually something visible: it is a synthesis of the seen. But prior to the effect of form, which arises in the constructive imagination, comes the effect of colour; this is purely sensuous, and no better intrinsically than the effects of any other sense: but being more involved in the perception of objects than are the rest, it becomes more readily an element of beauty. . . .

[2. Form is organization apt for being perceived.]

19. Where there is a sensuous delight, like that of colour, and the impression of the object is in its elements agreeable, we have to look no farther for an explanation of the charm we feel. Where there is expression, and an object indifferent to the senses is associated with other ideas that are interesting, the problem, although complex and varied, is in principle comparatively plain. But there is an intermediate effect that is more mysterious, and more specifically an effect of beauty. It is found where sensible elements, by themselves indifferent, are so united as to please in contemplation. . . . Beauty of form cannot be reduced to expression. . . . For if the object expressed by the form, and from which the form derives its value, had itself beauty of form, we should not advance. . . .22. The very process of perception is made delightful by the object's fitness to be perceived. . . . Symmetry is a principle of individuation and helps us to distinguish objects.[2]

[1] Cf. Plato, *Symposium*, p. 16.   [2] Cf. Kant, p. 122.

23. Form does not appeal to the unattentive; they get from objects only a vague sensation which may in them awaken extrinsic sensations.[1] . . . 25. [By the sky] every point in the retina is evenly excited, and the local signs of all are simultaneously felt. This equable tension, this balance and elasticity in the very absence of fixity, give the vague but powerful feeling that we wish to describe [as sublime]. . . .

39. The beautiful does not depend on the useful; it is constituted by the imagination in ignorance and contempt of practical advantage; but it is not independent of the necessary, for the necessary must also be the habitual and consequently the basis of the type, and of all its imaginative variations. . . . There is in the mere perceptibility of a thing a certain prophecy of its beauty; if it were not on the road to beauty, if it had no approach to fitness to our faculties of perception, the object would remain eternally unperceived. . . .

40. The non-imitative arts supply organisms different in kind from those which nature affords. If we seek the principle by which these objects are organized, we shall generally find that it likewise is utility.

[3. Expression. Our pleasure in the absent objectified in the present.]

48. The fluidity of the mind would make reflection impossible, did we not fix in words and other symbols certain abstract contents.[2] . . . The quality thus acquired by objects through association is what we call their expression. Whereas in form or material there is one object with its emotional effect, in expression there are two, and the emotional effect belongs to the character of the second or suggested one. Expression may thus make beautiful by suggestion things in themselves indifferent, or it may come to heighten the beauty which they already possess. Expression is not always distinguishable in con-

[1] Cf. Herbart, *Practical Philosophy*, p. 151, and Bell, p. 264.
[2] Cf. Alison, p. 106, Nettleship, p. 188, Bradley, p. 226, Croce, p. 243.

sciousness from the value of material or form, because we do not always have a distinguishable memory of the related idea which the expressiveness implies. . . . We [may] say explicitly: I value this trifle for its associations. And so long as this division continues, the worth of the thing is not aesthetic. But a little dimming of our memory will often make it so. . . . The value of the second term [=thing suggested] must be incorporated in the first. . . .

50. The value acquired by the expressive thing is often of an entirely different kind from that which the thing expressed possesses. The expression of physical pleasure, of passion, or even of pain, may constitute beauty. . . . The expressiveness of a smile is not discovered exactly through association of images. The child smiles (without knowing it) when he feels pleasure; and the nurse smiles back; his own pleasure is associated with her conduct, and her smile is therefore expressive of pleasure. . . . The circumstances expressive of happiness are not those that are favourable to it in reality, but those that are congruous with it in idea. The green of spring, the bloom of youth.[1] . . .

51. But as contemplation is actually a luxury in our lives, and things interest us chiefly on passionate and practical grounds, the accumulation of values too exclusively aesthetic produces in our mind an effect of closeness and artificiality. . . . We are more thankful for the presentation of the unlovely truth in a lovely form, than for the like presentation of an abstract beauty:[2] what is lost in the purity of the pleasure is gained in the stimulation of our attention, and in the relief of viewing with aesthetic detachment the same things that in practical life hold tyrannous dominion over our souls. . . . 55. There is no situation so terrible that it may not be relieved by the momentary pause of the mind to contemplate it aesthetically.[3] . . . This ministration makes, as it were, the piety of the Muses, who succour their mother, Life. . . .

---

[1] Cf. Mitchell, viii. § 6, p. 260. [2] Cf. Bradley, p. 212.
[3] Cf. Aristotle on purgation, p. 33.

We are not pleased by virtue of the suggested evils, but in spite of them.

57. Only by suffusing some sinister experience with this moral light, as a poet may do who carries that light within him, can we raise misfortune into tragedy and make it better for us to remember our lives than to forget them.[1] . . . Any violent passion, any overreaching pain, if it is not to make us think of a demonstration in pathology, and bring back the smell of ether, must be rendered in the most exalted style. Metre, rhythm, melody, the wildest flights of allusion, the highest reaches of fancy, are there in place.[2] . . . 58. Yet all these compensations would probably be unavailing but for another which the saddest things often have, the compensation of being true. . . . Many people, in whom the pursuit of knowledge and the indulgence in sentiment have left no room for the cultivation of the aesthetic sense, look in art rather for this expression of fact or passion than for the revelation of beauty.

[4. Sublimity and tragedy. Pleasure objectified in the contemplated self.]

59. But the heroic is an attitude of the will, by which the voices of the outer world are silenced, and a moral energy, flowing from within, is made to triumph over them. If we fail, therefore, to discover, by analysis of the object, anything which could make it sublime, we must not be surprised at our failure. . . . Among the ideas with which every object has relation there is one vaguest, most comprehensive, and most powerful one, namely the idea of self. . . . In the experience of momentary harmonies we have the basis of the enjoyment of beauty, and of all its mystical meanings. But there are always two ways of

[1] Cf. Richards, p. 282.

[2] Contrast Kant, § 23, p. 117, and Wordsworth, *Preface to Lyrical Ballads*: 'It is not, then, to be supposed that any one, who holds that sublime notion of Poetry which I have attempted to convey, will break in upon the sanctity and truth of his pictures by transitory and accidental ornaments . . . the necessity of which must manifestly depend upon the assumed meanness of his subject.' Cf. p. 129.

securing harmony: one is to unify all the given elements, and another is to reject and expunge all the elements that refuse to be unified. Unity by inclusion gives us the beautiful; unity by exclusion, opposition, and isolation gives us the sublime.[1] Both are pleasures: but the pleasure of the one is warm, passive, and pervasive; the pleasure of the other cold, imperious, and keen. The one identifies us with the world, the other raises us above it. There can be no difficulty in understanding how the expression of evil in the object may be the occasion of this heroic reaction in the soul. . . . The more intimate to himself the tragedy [the hero] is able to look back upon with calmness, the more sublime that calmness is, and the more divine the ecstasy in which he achieves it.

60. The immense is sublime as well as the terrible; and mere infinity of the object, like its hostile nature, can have the effect of making the mind recoil upon itself. Infinity, like hostility, removes us from things, and makes us conscious of our independence. . . . Let an infinite panorama be suddenly unfolded; the will is instantly paralysed, and the heart choked. It is impossible to desire everything at once. . . . The sublime is not the ugly, as some descriptions of it might lead us to suppose; it is the supremely, the intoxicatingly beautiful. It is the pleasure of contemplation reaching such an intensity that it begins to lose its objectivity, and to declare itself, what it always fundamentally was, an inward passion of the soul.[2] . . .

65. Tragedy and Comedy please in spite of this expressiveness [of pain] and not by virtue of it;[3] and except for the pleasures they give, they have no place among the fine arts. . . . The effort to be expressive has transgressed the conditions of pleasing art.[4] For the creative and imitative impulse is indiscriminate. It does not consider the eventual beauty of the effect, but only the blind instinct of self-expression.[5]

[1] Cf. Richards, p. 282.   [2] Cf. Schopenhauer, p. 146.
[3] Cf. Herbart, pp. 152, 156.   [4] Cf. Hegel on Romantic Art, p. 170.
[5] Cf. Aristotle, p. 31, Ducasse, p. 313.

67. The eye is quick, and seems to have been more docile to the education of life than the heart or the reason of man, and able sooner to adapt itself to the reality. Beauty therefore seems to be the clearest manifestation of perfection,[1] and the best evidence of its possibility. If perfection is, as it should be, the ultimate justification of being, we may understand the ground of the moral dignity of beauty. Beauty is a pledge of the possible conformity between the soul and nature, and consequently a ground of faith in the supremacy of the good.[2]

HENRI BERGSON
1859–
Laughter (1900)
Authorized translation by Brereton and Rothwell

I. I. The comic does not exist outside the pale of what is strictly *human*. A landscape may be beautiful, charming, and sublime, or insignificant and ugly; it will never be laughable. You may laugh at an animal, but only because you have detected in it some human attitude or expression. You may laugh at a hat, but what you are making fun of, in this case, is not the piece of felt or straw, but the shape that men have given it,—the human caprice whose mould it has assumed. . . .

Laughter has no greater foe than emotion. I do not mean that we could not laugh at a person who inspires us with pity, for instance, or even with affection, but in such a case we must, for the moment, put our affection out of court and impose silence upon our pity. In a society composed of pure intelligences there would probably be no more tears, though perhaps there would still be laughter. . . .

The comic will come into being, it appears, whenever a group of men concentrate their attention on one of their number, imposing silence on their emotions and calling into play nothing but their intelligence.

[1] Cf. Plato, *Phaedrus*, p. 16.   [2] Cf. Kant, p. 123.

4. The attitudes, gestures, and movements of the human body are laughable in exact proportion as that body reminds us of a mere machine. . . . Something mechanical encrusted on the living . . .

III. 1. Not only are we entitled to say that comedy gives us general types, but we might add that it is the *only* one of all the arts that aims at the general. . . .

What is the object of art? Could reality come into direct contact with sense and consciousness, could we enter into immediate communion with things and with ourselves, probably art would be useless, or rather we should all be artists, for then our soul would continually vibrate in perfect accord with nature. . . .

But what I see and hear of the outer world is purely and simply a selection made by my senses to serve as a light to my conduct; what I know of myself is what comes to the surface, what participates in my actions. My senses and my consciousness, therefore, give me no more than a practical simplification of reality.[1] In the vision they furnish me of myself and of things, the differences that are useless to man are obliterated, the resemblances that are useful to him are emphasized; ways are traced out for me in advance, along which my activity is to travel. These ways are the ways which all mankind has trod before me. Things have been classified with a view to the use I can derive from them. And it is this classification I perceive, far more clearly than the colour and the shape of things. Doubtless man is vastly superior to the lower animals in this respect. It is not very likely that the eye of a wolf makes any distinction between a kid and a lamb; both appear to the wolf as the same identical quarry, alike easy to pounce upon, alike good to devour. We, for our part, make a distinction between a goat and a sheep; but can we tell one goat from another, one sheep from another? The *individuality* of things or of beings escapes us, unless it is materially to our advantage to perceive it. Even when we do take note of it—as when we distinguish one man from another—it is not the individuality

[1] Cf. Stace, p. 302.

itself that the eye grasps, i.e. an entirely original harmony of forms and colours, but only one or two features
that will make practical recognition easier.

In short, we do not see the actual things themselves; in
most cases we confine ourselves to reading the labels
affixed to them. This tendency, the result of need, has
become even more pronounced under the influence of
speech; for words—with the exception of proper nouns—
all denote genera. The word, which only takes note of the
most ordinary function and commonplace aspect of the
thing, intervenes between it and ourselves, and would
conceal its form from our eyes, were that form not already
masked beneath the necessities that brought the word
into existence. Not only external objects, but even our
own mental states, are screened from us in their inmost,
their personal aspect, in the original life they possess.
When we feel love or hatred, when we are gay or sad, is
it really the feeling itself that reaches our consciousness
with those innumerable fleeting shades of meaning and
deep resounding echoes that make it something altogether
our own? . . .

From time to time, however, in a fit of absent-minded-
ness, nature raises up souls that are more detached from
life.[1] Not with that intentional, logical, systematical detachment—the result of reflection and philosophy—but
rather with a natural detachment, one innate in the
structure of sense or consciousness, which at once reveals
itself by a virginal manner, so to speak, of seeing, hearing,
or thinking . . .

One man applies himself to colours and forms, and since
he loves colour for colour and form for form, since he
perceives them for their sake and not for his own, it is
the inner life of things that he sees appearing through
their forms and colours. Little by little he insinuates it
into our own perception, baffled though we may be at
the outset. For a few moments at least, he diverts us from
the prejudices of form and colour that come between

[1] Cf. Schopenhauer, p. 141.

ourselves and reality. And thus he realizes the loftiest ambition of art, which here consists in revealing to us nature. Others, again, retire within themselves. Beneath the thousand rudimentary actions which are the outward and visible signs of an emotion, behind the commonplace, conventional expression that both reveals and conceals an individual mental state, it is the emotion, the original mood, to which they attain in its undefiled essence. And then, to induce us to make the same effort ourselves, they contrive to make us see something of what they have seen: by rhythmical arrangement of words, which thus become organized and animated with a life of their own, they tell us—or rather suggest— things that speech was not calculated to express. Others delve yet deeper still. Beneath these joys and sorrows which can, at a pinch, be translated into language, they grasp something that has nothing in common with language, certain rhythms of life and breath that are closer to man than his inmost feelings, being the living law —varying with each individual—of his enthusiasm and despair, his hopes and regrets. By setting free and emphasizing this music, they force it upon our attention; they compel us, willy-nilly, to fall in with it, like passers-by who join in a dance. And thus they impel us to set in motion, in the depths of our being, some secret chord which was only waiting to thrill. . . .

Art is certainly only a more direct vision of reality. But this purity of perception implies a break with utilitarian convention, an innate and specially localized disinterestedness of sense or consciousness, in short, a certain immateriality of life, which is what has always been called idealism.[1] So that we might say, without in any way playing upon the meaning of the words, that realism is in the work when idealism is in the soul, and that it is only through ideality that we can resume contact with reality. . . .

After seeing a stirring drama, what has just interested

[1] Cf. Bradley, p. 210, Richards, p. 277.

us is not so much what we have been told about others as
the glimpse we have caught of ourselves—a whole host of
ghostly feelings, emotions, and events that would fain have
come into real existence, but, fortunately for us, did not.
It also seems as if an appeal had been made within us to
certain ancestral memories belonging to a far-away past
—memories so deep-seated and so foreign to our present
life that this latter, for a moment, seems something unreal
and conventional, for which we shall have to serve a fresh
apprenticeship. So it is indeed a deeper reality that
drama draws up from beneath our superficial and utilitarian attainments, and this art has the same end in view
as all the others.

Hence it follows that art always aims at what is *individual*.
What the artist fixes on his canvas is something he has
seen at a certain spot, on a certain day, at a certain hour,
with a colouring that will never be seen again. . . .

What the dramatist unfolds before us is the life-history of
a soul, a living tissue of feelings and events—something,
in short, which has once happened and can never be
repeated. We may, indeed, give general names to these
feelings, but they cannot be the same thing in another
soul. They are *individualized*. Thereby, and thereby only,
do they belong to art; for generalities, symbols, or even
types form the current coin of our daily perception. . . .

Altogether different is the object of comedy. Here it is in
the work itself that the generality lies. Comedy depicts
characters we have already come across and shall meet with
again. It takes note of similarities. It aims at placing types
before our eyes. It even creates new types, if necessary. . . .

This essential difference between tragedy and comedy,
the former being concerned with individuals and the latter
with classes, is revealed in yet another way. It appears in
the first draft of the work. From the outset it is manifested
by two radically different methods of observation.

Though the assertion may seem paradoxical, a study of
other men is probably not necessary to the tragic poet. . . .

What interests us in the work of the poet is the glimpse

we get of certain profound moods or inner struggles. Now, this glimpse cannot be obtained from without. Our souls are impenetrable to one another. Certain signs of passion are all that we ever apperceive externally. These we interpret—though always, by the way, defectively— only by analogy with what we have ourselves experienced. So what we experience is the main point, and we cannot become thoroughly acquainted with anything but our own heart—supposing we ever get so far. Does this mean that the poet has experienced what he depicts, that he has gone through the various situations he makes his characters traverse, and lived the whole of their inner life? . . .

But then a distinction should perhaps be here made between the personality *we have* and all those we might have had. Our character is the result of a choice that is continually being renewed. There are points—at all events there seem to be—all along the way, where we may branch off, and we perceive many possible directions though we are unable to take more than one. To retrace one's steps, and follow to the end the faintly distinguishable directions, appears to be the essential element in poetic imagination.

ANDREW CECIL BRADLEY

1851–

Poetry for Poetry's Sake (1901)

Without aiming here at accuracy, we may say that an actual poem is the succession of experiences—sounds, images, thoughts, emotions—through which we pass when we are reading as poetically as we can.[1] Of course this imaginative experience—if I may use the phrase for brevity—differs with every reader and every time of reading: a poem exists in innumerable degrees. But that insurmountable fact lies in the nature of things and does not concern us now.

What then does the formula 'Poetry for poetry's sake'

[1] Cf. Gentile, p. 323.

tell us about this experience? It says, as I understand it, these things. First, this experience is an end in itself, is worth having on its own account, has an intrinsic value. Next, its *poetic* value is this intrinsic worth alone. Poetry may have also an ulterior value as a means to culture or religion; because it conveys instruction, or softens the passions, or furthers a good cause; because it brings the poet fame or money or a quiet conscience. So much the better: let it be valued for these reasons too. But its ulterior worth neither is nor can directly determine its poetic worth as a satisfying imaginative experience; and this is to be judged entirely from within. And to these two positions the formula would add, though not of necessity, a third. The consideration of ulterior ends, whether by the poet in the act of composing or by the reader in the act of experiencing, tends to lower poetic value. It does so because it tends to change the nature of poetry by taking it out of its own atmosphere. For its nature is to be not a part, nor yet a copy, of the real world (as we commonly understand that phrase), but to be a world by itself, independent, complete, autonomous; and to possess it fully you must enter that world, conform to its laws, and ignore for the time the beliefs, aims, and particular conditions which belong to you in the other world of reality.[1]

Of the more serious misapprehensions to which these statements may give rise I will glance only at one or two. The offensive consequences often drawn from the formula 'Art for Art' will be found to attach not to the doctrine that Art is an end in itself, but to the doctrine that Art is the whole or supreme end of human life. And as this latter doctrine, which seems to me absurd, is in any case quite different from the former, its consequences fall outside my subject. The formula 'Poetry is an end in itself' has nothing to say on the various questions of moral judgement which arise from the fact that poetry has its place in a many-sided life. For anything it says, the intrinsic value of poetry might be so small, and its ulterior

[1] Cf. Bergson, p. 207, Richards, pp. 277–8.

effects so mischievous, that it had better not exist. The
formula only tells us that we must not place in antithesis
poetry and human good, for poetry is one kind of human
good; and that we must not determine the intrinsic value
of this kind of good by direct reference to another. If we
do, we shall find ourselves maintaining what we did not
expect. If poetic value lies in the stimulation of religious
feelings, *Lead, kindly Light*[1] is no better a poem than many
a tasteless version of a Psalm: if in the excitement of
patriotism, why is *Scots, wha hae*[2] superior to *We don't want
to fight*? if in the mitigation of the passions, the Odes of
Sappho will win but little praise: if in instruction, Arm-
strong's *Art of preserving Health* should win much.

Again, our formula may be accused of cutting poetry
away from its connexion with life. And this accusation
raises so huge a problem that I must ask leave to be dogmatic as well as brief. There is plenty of connexion
between life and poetry, but it is, so to say, a connexion
underground. The two may be called different forms of
the same thing: one of them having (in the usual sense)
reality, but seldom fully satisfying imagination; while the
other offers something which satisfies imagination but has
not full 'reality.' They are parallel developments which
nowhere meet, or, if I may use loosely a word which will
be serviceable later, they are analogues. Hence we understand one by help of the other, and even, in a sense, care
for one because of the other; but hence also, poetry
neither is life, nor, strictly speaking, a copy of it. They
differ not only because one has more mass and the other
a more perfect shape, but because they have different
kinds of existence. The one touches us as beings occupying a given position in space and time, and having feelings, desires, and purposes due to that position: it appeals
to imagination, but appeals to much besides. What
meets us in poetry has not a position in the same series of
time and space, or, if it has or had such a position, it is
taken apart from much that belonged to it there; and

[1] Newman.   [2] Burns.

therefore it makes no direct appeal to those feelings, desires, and purposes, but speaks only to contemplative imagination—imagination the reverse of empty or emotionless, imagination saturated with the results of 'real' experience, but still contemplative. Thus, no doubt, one main reason why poetry has poetic value for us is that it presents to us in its own way something which we meet in another form in nature or life;[1] and yet the test of its poetic value for us lies simply in the question whether it satisfies our imagination; the rest of us, our knowledge or conscience, for example, judging it only so far as they appear transmuted in our imagination. So also Shakespeare's knowledge or his moral insight, Milton's greatness of soul, Shelley's 'hate of hate' and 'love of love,' and that desire to help men or make them happier which may have influenced a poet in hours of meditation—all these have, as such, no poetical worth: they have that worth only when, passing through the unity of the poet's being, they reappear as qualities of imagination, and then are indeed mighty powers in the world of poetry.

I come to a third misapprehension, and so to my main subject. This formula, it is said, empties poetry of its meaning: it is really a doctrine of form for form's sake. 'It is of no consequence what a poet says, so long as he says the thing well. The *what* is poetically indifferent: it is the *how* that counts. Matter, subject, content, substance, determines nothing; there is no subject with which poetry may not deal: the form, the treatment, is everything. Nay, more: not only is the matter indifferent, but it is the secret of Art to "eradicate[2] the matter by means of the form," '—phrases and statements like these meet us everywhere in current criticism of literature and the other arts. They are the stock-in-trade of writers who understand of them little more than the fact that somehow or other they are not 'bourgeois.' But we find them

[1] Cf. Santayana, § 51, p. 201.
[2] Cf. Schiller, xxii, p. 127, and Pater, *The Renaissance*, 'The School of Giorgione.'

also seriously used by writers whom we must respect, whether they are anonymous or not; something like one or another of them might be quoted, for example, from Professor Saintsbury, the late R. A. M. Stevenson,[1] Schiller, Goethe himself; and they are the watchwords of a school in the one country where Aesthetics has flourished. They come, as a rule, from men who either practise one of the arts, or, from study of it, are interested in its methods. The general reader—a being so general that I may say what I will of him—is outraged by them. He feels that he is being robbed of almost all that he cares for in a work of art. 'You are asking me,' he says, 'to look at the Dresden Madonna as if it were a Persian rug. You are telling me that the poetic value of *Hamlet* lies solely in its style and versification, and that my interest in the man and his fate is only an intellectual or moral interest. You allege that, if I want to enjoy the poetry of *Crossing the Bar*, I must not mind what Tennyson says there, but must consider solely his way of saying it. But in that case I can care no more for a poem than I do for a set of nonsense verses; and I do not believe that the authors of *Hamlet* and *Crossing the Bar* regarded their poems thus.'

These antitheses of subject, matter, substance on the one side, form, treatment, handling on the other, are the field through which I especially want, in this lecture, to indicate a way. It is a field of battle; and the battle is waged for no trivial cause; but the cries of the combatants are terribly ambiguous. Those phrases of the so-called formalist may each mean five or six different things. Taken in one sense they seem to me chiefly true; taken as the general reader not unnaturally takes them, they seem to me false and mischievous. It would be absurd to pretend that I can end in a few minutes a controversy which concerns the ultimate nature of Art, and leads perhaps to problems not yet soluble; but we can at least draw some plain distinctions which, in this controversy, are too often confused.

[1] Cf. *Velasquez*, p. 198.

In the first place, then, let us take 'subject' in one particular sense; let us understand by it that which we have in view when, looking at the title of an unread poem, we say that the poet has chosen this or that for his subject. The subject, in this sense, so far as I can discover, is generally something, real or imaginary, as it exists in the minds of fairly cultivated people. The subject of *Paradise Lost* would be the story of the Fall as that story exists in the general imagination of a Bible-reading people. The subject of Shelley's stanzas *To a Skylark* would be the ideas which arise in the mind of an educated person when, without knowing the poem, he hears the word 'skylark.' If the title of a poem conveys little or nothing to us, the 'subject' appears to be either what we should gather by investigating the title in a dictionary or other book of the kind, or else such a brief suggestion as might be offered by a person who had read the poem, and who said, for example, that the subject of *The Ancient Mariner* was a sailor who killed an albatross and suffered for his deed.

Now the subject, in this sense (and I intend to use the word in no other), is not, as such, inside the poem, but outside it. The contents of the stanzas *To a Skylark* are not the ideas suggested by the word 'skylark' to the average man; they belong to Shelley just as much as the language does. The subject, therefore, is not the matter *of* the poem at all; and its opposite is not the *form* of the poem, but the whole poem. The subject is one thing; the poem, matter and form alike, another thing. This being so, it is surely obvious that the poetic value cannot lie in the subject, but lies entirely in its opposite, the poem. How can the subject determine the value when on one and the same subject poems may be written of all degrees of merit and demerit; or when a perfect poem may be composed on a subject so slight as a pet sparrow,[1] and, if Macaulay[2] may be trusted, a nearly worthless poem on a subject so stupendous as the omnipresence of the Deity? The 'formalist' is here perfectly right. Nor is he insisting

[1] Catullus.   [2] *Robert Montgomery.*

on something unimportant. He is fighting against our tendency to take the work of art as a mere copy or re- minder of something already in our heads, or at the best as a suggestion of some idea as little removed as possible from the familiar. The sightseer who promenades a picture-gallery, remarking that this portrait is so like his cousin, or that landscape the very image of his birth- place, or who, after satisfying himself that one picture is about Elijah, passes on rejoicing to discover the subject, and nothing but the subject, of the next—what is he but an extreme example of this tendency? [1] Well, but the very same tendency vitiates much of our criticism, much criticism of Shakespeare, for example, which, with all its cleverness and partial truth, still shows that the critic never passed from his own mind into Shakespeare's; and it may be traced even in so fine a critic as Coleridge, as when he dwarfs the sublime struggle of Hamlet into the image of his own unhappy weakness. Hazlitt by no means escaped its influence. Only the third of that great trio, Lamb, appears almost always to have rendered the conception of the composer.

Again, it is surely true that we cannot determine before- hand what subjects are fit for Art, or name any subject on which a good poem might not possibly be written. To divide subjects into two groups, the beautiful or ele- vating, and the ugly or vicious, and to judge poems according as their subjects belong to one of these groups or the other, is to fall into the same pit, to confuse with our pre-conceptions the meaning of the poet. What the thing is in the poem he is to be judged by, not by the thing as it was before he touched it; and how can we venture to say beforehand that he cannot make a true poem out of something which to us was merely alluring or dull or revolting? The question whether, having done so, he ought to publish his poem; whether the thing in the poet's work will not be still confused by the incom- petent Puritan or the incompetent sensualist with the

[1] Cf. Herbart, *Encyclopaedia*, § 72, p. 156.

thing in *his* mind, does not touch this point; it is a further question, one of ethics, not of art. No doubt the upholders of 'Art for art's sake' will generally be in favour of the courageous course, of refusing to sacrifice the better or stronger part of the public to the weaker or worse; but their maxim in no way binds them to this view. Rossetti suppressed one of the best of his sonnets, a sonnet chosen for admiration by Tennyson, himself extremely sensitive about the moral effect of poetry; suppressed it, I believe, because it was called fleshly. One may regret Rossetti's judgement and at the same time respect his scrupulousness; but in any case he judged in his capacity of citizen, not in his capacity of artist.

So far then the 'formalist' appears to be right. But he goes too far, I think, if he maintains that the subject is indifferent and that all subjects are the same to poetry. And he does not prove his point by observing that a good poem might be written on a pin's head, and a bad one on the Fall of Man. That truth shows that the subject *settles* nothing, but not that it counts for nothing. The Fall of Man is really a more favourable subject than a pin's head. The Fall of Man, that is to say, offers opportunities of poetic effects wider in range and more penetrating in appeal. And the fact is that such a subject, as it exists in the general imagination, has some aesthetic value before the poet touches it. It is, as you may choose to call it, an inchoate poem or the débris of a poem. It is not an abstract idea or a bare isolated fact, but an assemblage of figures, scenes, actions, and events, which already appeal to emotional imagination; and it is already in some degree organized and formed. In spite of this a bad poet would make a bad poem on it; but then we should say he was unworthy of the subject. And we should not say this if he wrote a bad poem on a pin's head. Conversely, a good poem on a pin's head would almost certainly transform its subject far more than a good poem on the Fall of Man. It might revolutionize its subject so completely that we should say, 'The subject may be a pin's head, but the substance of the poem has very little to do with it.'

This brings us to another and a different antithesis. Those figures, scenes, events, that form part of the subject called the Fall of Man, are not the substance of *Paradise Lost*; but in *Paradise Lost* there are figures, scenes, and events resembling them in some degree. These, with much more of the same kind, may be described as its substance, and may then be contrasted with the measured language of the poem, which will be called its form. Subject is the opposite not of form but of the whole poem. Substance is within the poem, and its opposite, form, is also within the poem. I am not criticizing this antithesis at present, but evidently it is quite different from the other. It is practically the distinction used in the old-fashioned criticism of epic and drama, and it flows down, not unsullied, from Aristotle. Addison,[1] for example, in examining *Paradise Lost* considers in order the fable, the characters, and the sentiments; these will be the substance: then he considers the language, that is, the style and numbers; this will be the form. In like manner, the substance or meaning of a lyric may be distinguished from the form.

Now I believe it will be found that a large part of the controversy we are dealing with arises from a confusion between these two distinctions of substance and form, and of subject and poem. The extreme formalist lays his whole weight on the form because he thinks its opposite is the mere subject. The general reader is angry, but makes the same mistake, and gives to the subject praises that rightly belong to the substance.[2] I will give an example of what I mean. I can only explain the following

[1] *Spectator*, 267, &c.

[2] What is here called 'substance' is what people generally mean when they use the word 'subject' and insist on the value of the subject. I am not arguing against this usage, or in favour of the usage which I have adopted for the sake of clearness. It does not matter which we employ, so long as we and others know what we mean. (I use 'substance' and 'content' indifferently.) (A. C. B.)

words of a good critic by supposing that for the moment he has fallen into this confusion: 'The mere matter of all poetry—to wit, the appearances of nature and the thoughts and feelings of men—being unalterable, it follows that the difference between poet and poet will depend upon the manner of each in applying language, metre, rhyme, cadence, and what not, to this invariable material.' [1] What has become here of the substance of *Paradise Lost*—the story, scenery, characters, sentiments as they are in the poem? They have vanished clean away. Nothing is left but the form on one side, and on the other not even the subject, but a supposed invariable material, the appearances of nature and the thoughts and feelings of men. Is it surprising that the whole value should then be found in the form?

So far we have assumed that this antithesis of substance and form is valid, and that it always has one meaning. In reality it has several, but we will leave it in its present shape, and pass to the question of its validity. And this question we are compelled to raise, because we have to deal with the two contentions that the poetic value lies wholly or mainly in the substance, and that it lies wholly or mainly in the form. Now these contentions, whether false or true, may seem at least to be clear; but we shall find, I think, that they are both of them false, or both of them nonsense: false if they concern anything outside the poem, nonsense if they apply to something in it. For what do they evidently imply? They imply that there are in a poem two parts, factors, or components, a substance and a form; and that you can conceive them distinctly and separately, so that when you are speaking of the one you are not speaking of the other. Otherwise how can you ask the question, In which of them does the value lie? But really in a poem, apart from defects, there are no such factors or components; and therefore it is strictly nonsense to ask in which of them the value lies. And on the other hand, if the substance and the form

[1] Cf. Herbart, *Practical Philosophy*, p. 152.

referred to are not in the poem, then both the contentions are false, for its poetic value lies in itself.

What I mean is neither new nor mysterious; and it will
be clear, I believe, to any one who reads poetry poetically
and who closely examines his experience. When you are
reading a poem, I would ask—not analysing it, and much
less criticizing it, but allowing it, as it proceeds, to make
its full impression on you through the exertion of your
recreating imagination—do you then apprehend and
enjoy as one thing a certain meaning or substance, and
as another thing certain articulate sounds, and do you
somehow compound these two? Surely you do not, any
more than you apprehend apart, when you see some one
smile, those lines in the face which express a feeling, and
the feeling that the lines express. Just as there the lines
and their meaning are to you one thing, not two, so in
poetry the meaning and the sounds are one: there is, if I
may put it so, a resonant meaning, or a meaning reso-
nance. If you read the line, 'The sun is warm, the sky is
clear,' you do not experience separately the image of a
warm sun and clear sky, on the one side, and certain
unintelligible rhythmical sounds on the other; nor yet do
you experience them together, side by side; but you
experience the one *in* the other. And in like manner
when you are really reading *Hamlet*, the action and the
characters are not something which you conceive apart
from the words; you apprehend them from point to
point *in* the words, and the words as expressions of them.
Afterwards, no doubt, when you are out of the poetic
experience but remember it, you may by analysis decompose this unity, and attend to a substance more or less
isolated, and a form more or less isolated. But these are
things in your analytic head, not in the poem, which is
poetic experience. And if you want to have the poem again,
you cannot find it by adding together these two products of
decomposition; you can only find it by passing back into
poetic experience. And then what you recover is no
aggregate of factors, it is a unity in which you can no more

separate a substance and a form than you can separate
living blood and the life in the blood. This unity has, if
you like, various 'aspects' or 'sides', but they are not
factors or parts; if you try to examine one, you find it is
also the other. Call them substance and form if you
please, but these are not the reciprocally exclusive substance and form to which the two contentions *must* refer.
They do not 'agree', for they are not apart: they are one
thing from different points of view, and in that sense
identical. And this identity of content and form, you will
say, is no accident; it is of the essence of poetry in so far
as it is poetry, and of all art in so far as it is art. Just as
there is in music not sound on one side and a meaning on
the other, but expressive sound, and if you ask what is
the meaning you can only answer by pointing to the
sounds; just as in painting there is not a meaning *plus*
paint, but a meaning *in* paint, or significant paint, and
no man can really express the meaning in any other way
than in paint and in *this* paint; so in a poem the true content and the true form neither exist nor can be imagined
apart. When then you are asked whether the value of a
poem lies in a substance got by decomposing the poem,
and present, as such, only in reflective analysis, or whether
the value lies in a form arrived at and existing in the
same way, you will answer, 'It lies neither in one, nor in
the other, nor in any addition of them, but in the poem,
where they are not.'[1]

We have then, first, an antithesis of subject and poem.
This is clear and valid; and the question in which of them
does the value lie is intelligible; and its answer is, *In the
poem*. We have next a distinction of substance and form.
If the substance means ideas, images, and the like taken
alone, and the form means the measured language taken
by itself, this is a possible distinction, but it is a distinction of things not in the poem, and the value lies *in neither
of them*. If substance and form mean anything *in* the
poem, then each is involved in the other, and the ques-

[1] Cf. Moore, p. 252.

tion in which of them the value lies has no sense. No doubt you may say, speaking loosely, that in this poet or poem the aspect of substance is the more noticeable, and in that the aspect of form; and you may pursue interesting discussions on this basis, though no principle or ultimate question of value is touched by them.[1] And apart from that question, of course, I am not denying the usefulness and necessity of the distinction. We cannot dispense with it. To consider separately the action or the characters of a play, and separately its style or versification, is both legitimate and valuable, so long as we remember what we are doing. But the true critic in speaking of these apart does not really think of them apart; the whole, the poetic experience, of which they are but aspects, is always in his mind; and he is always aiming at a richer, truer, more intense repetition of that experience. On the other hand, when the question of principle, of poetic value, is raised, these aspects *must* fall apart into components, separately conceivable; and then there arise two heresies, equally false, that the value lies in one of two things, both of which are outside the poem, and therefore where its value cannot lie.

On the heresy of the separable substance a few additional words will suffice. This heresy is seldom formulated, but perhaps some unconscious holder of it may object: 'Surely the action and the characters of *Hamlet* are in the play; and surely I can retain these, though I have forgotten all the words. I admit that I do not possess the whole poem, but I possess a part, and the most important part.' And I would answer: 'If we are not concerned with any question of principle, I accept all that you say except the last words, which do raise such a question. Speaking loosely, I agree that the action and characters, as you perhaps conceive them, together with a great deal more, are in the poem. Even then, however, you must not claim to possess all of this kind that is in the poem; for in forgetting the words you must have lost innumerable details of the action and the characters. And,

[1] Cf. Ducasse, p. 313.

when the question of value is raised, I must insist that the action and characters, as you conceive them, are not in *Hamlet* at all. If they are, point them out. You cannot do it. What you find at any moment of that succession of experiences called *Hamlet* is words. In these words, to speak loosely again, the action and characters (more of them than you can conceive apart) are focused; but your experience is not a combination of them, as ideas, on the one side, with certain sounds on the other; it is an experience of something in which the two are indissolubly fused. If you deny this, to be sure I can make no answer, or can only answer that I have reason to believe that you cannot read poetically, or else are misinterpreting your experience. But if you do not deny this, then you will admit that the action and characters of the poem, as you separately imagine them, are no part of it, but a product of it in your reflective imagination, a faint analogue of one aspect of it taken in detachment from the whole. Well, I do not dispute, I would even insist, that, in the case of so long a poem as *Hamlet*, it may be necessary from time to time to interrupt the poetic experience, in order to enrich it by forming such a product and dwelling on it. Nor, in a wide sense of "poetic", do I question the poetic value of this product, as you think of it apart from the poem. It resembles our recollections of the heroes of history or legend, who move about in our imaginations, "forms more real than living man", and are worth much to us though we do not remember anything they said. Our ideas and images of the "substance" of a poem have this poetic value, and more, if they are at all adequate. But they cannot determine the poetic value of the poem, for (not to speak of the competing claims of the "form") nothing that is outside the poem can do that, and they, as such, are outside it.'[1]

Let us turn to the so-called form—style and versification.

---

[1] These remarks will hold good, *mutatis mutandis*, if by 'substance' is understood the 'moral' or the 'idea' of a poem, although perhaps in one instance out of five thousand this may be found in so many words in the poem. (A. C. B.)

There is no such thing as mere form in poetry. All form is expression. Style may have indeed a certain aesthetic worth in partial abstraction from the particular matter it conveys, as in a well-built sentence you may take pleasure in the build almost apart from the meaning. Even so, style is expressive—presents to sense, for example, the order, ease, and rapidity with which ideas move in the writer's mind—but it is not expressive of the meaning of that particular sentence. And it is possible, interrupting poetic experience, to decompose it and abstract for comparatively separate consideration this nearly formal element of style.[1] But the aesthetic value of style so taken is not considerable;[2] you could not read with pleasure for an hour a composition which had no other merit. And in poetic experience you never apprehend this value by itself; the style is here expressive also of a particular meaning, or rather is one aspect of that unity whose other aspect is meaning. So that what you apprehend may be called indifferently an expressed meaning or a significant form. Perhaps on this point I may in Oxford appeal to authority, that of Matthew Arnold and Walter Pater,[3] the latter at any rate an authority whom the formalist will not despise. What is the gist of Pater's teaching about style, if it is not that in the end the one virtue of style is truth or adequacy; that the word, phrase, sentence, should express perfectly the writer's perception, feeling, image, or thought; so that, as we read a descriptive phrase of Keats's, we exclaim, 'That is the thing itself'; so that, to quote Arnold, the words are 'symbols equivalent with the thing symbolized', or, in our technical language, a form identical with its content? Hence in true poetry it is, in strictness, impossible to express the meaning in any but its own words, or to change the words without changing the meaning. A translation of such poetry is not really the old meaning in a fresh dress; it is

---

[1] Cf. Bosanquet, p. 190.
[2] On the other hand, the absence, or worse than absence, of style, in this sense, is a serious matter. (A. C. B.).   [3] Cf. p. 186.

a new product, something like the poem, though, if one
chooses to say so, more like it in the aspect of meaning
than in the aspect of form.[1]

No one who understands poetry, it seems to me, would
dispute this, were it not that, falling away from his experience, or misled by theory, he takes the word 'meaning' in a sense almost ludicrously inapplicable to poetry.
People say, for instance, 'steed' and 'horse' have the
same meaning; and in bad poetry they have, but not in
poetry that *is* poetry.

> 'Bring forth the horse!' The horse was brought:
> In truth he was a noble steed!

says Byron in *Mazeppa*.[2] If the two words mean the same
here, transpose them:

> 'Bring forth the steed!' The steed was brought:
> In truth he was a noble horse!

and ask again if they mean the same. Or let me take a
line certainly very free from 'poetic diction':

> To be or not to be, that is the question.

You may say that this means the same as 'What is just
now occupying my attention is the comparative dis-
advantages of continuing to live or putting an end to
myself.' And for practical purposes—the purpose, for
example, of a coroner—it does. But as the second version
altogether misrepresents the speaker at that moment of
his existence, while the first does represent him, how can
they for any but a practical or logical purpose be said to
have the same sense? Hamlet was well able to 'unpack
his heart with words', but he will not unpack it with our
paraphrases.

These considerations apply equally to versification. If
I take the famous line which describes how the souls of
the dead stood waiting by the river, imploring a passage
from Charon:

> Tendebantque manus ripae ulterioris amore,[3]

and if I translate it, 'and were stretching forth their

[1] Cf. Shelley, p. 150.   [2] ix.   [3] Aen. VI. 314.

hands in longing for the further bank', the charm of the
original has fled. Why has it fled? Partly (but we have
dealt with that) because I have substituted for five words,
and those the words of Virgil, twelve words, and those
my own. In some measure because I have turned into
rhythmless prose a line of verse which, as mere sound, has
unusual beauty. But much more because in doing so I
have also changed the *meaning* of Virgil's line. What
that meaning is *I* cannot say: Virgil has said it. But I can
see this much, that the translation conveys a far less vivid
picture of the outstretched hands and of their remaining
outstretched, and a far less poignant sense of the distance
of the shore and the longing of the souls. And it does so
partly because this picture and this sense are conveyed
not only by the obvious meaning of the words, but
through the long-drawn sound of 'tendebantque', through
the time occupied by the five syllables and therefore by
the idea of 'ulterioris', and through the identity of the
long sound 'or' in the penultimate syllables of 'ulterioris
amore'—all this, and much more, apprehended not in
this analytical fashion, nor as *added* to the beauty of mere
sound and to the obvious meaning, but in unity with them
and so as expressive of the poetic meaning of the whole.

It is always so in fine poetry. The value of versification,
when it is indissolubly fused with meaning, can hardly be
exaggerated. The gift for feeling it, even more perhaps
than the gift for feeling the value of style, is the *specific*
gift for poetry, as distinguished from other arts. But
versification, taken, as far as possible, all by itself, has
a very different worth. Some aesthetic worth it has; how
much, you may experience by reading poetry in a language of which you do not understand a syllable. The
pleasure is quite appreciable, but it is not great; nor in
actual poetic experience do you meet with it, as such, at
all. For, I repeat, it is not *added* to the pleasure of the
meaning when you read poetry that you do understand:
by some mystery the music is then the music *of* the meaning, and the two are one. However fond of versification

you might be, you would tire very soon of reading verses in Chinese; and before long of reading Virgil and Dante if you were ignorant of their languages. But take the music as it is *in* the poem, and there is a marvellous change. Now

> It gives a very echo to the seat
> Where Love is throned;[1]

or 'carries far into your heart', almost like music itself, the sound

> Of old, unhappy, far-off things
> And battles long ago.

What then is to be said of the following sentence of the critic quoted before:[2] 'But when any one who knows what poetry is reads—

> Our noisy years seem moments in the being
> Of the eternal silence,

he sees that, quite independently of the meaning, . . . there is one note added to the articulate music of the world—a note that never will leave off resounding till the eternal silence itself gulfs it'? I must think that the writer is deceiving himself. For I could quite understand his enthusiasm, if it were an enthusiasm for the music of the meaning; but as for the music, 'quite independently of the meaning', so far as I can hear it thus (and I doubt if any one who knows English can quite do so), I find it gives some pleasure, but only a trifling pleasure. And indeed I venture to doubt whether, considered as mere sound, the words are at all exceptionally beautiful, as Virgil's line certainly is. . . .

Pure poetry is not the decoration of a preconceived and clearly defined matter: it springs from the creative impulse of a vague imaginative mass pressing for development and definition. If the poet already knew exactly[3] what he meant to say, why should he write the poem?

[1] *Twelfth Night*, II. iv.

[2] Saintsbury, *History of English Prosody*, iii. pp. 74–7; Wordsworth, *Immortality*, ix.

[3] Cf. Nettleship, p. 188, Santayana, p. 200, Bergson, p. 207, Ducasse, p. 315.

The poem would in fact already be written. For only its completion can reveal, even to him, exactly what he wanted. When he began and while he was at work, he did not possess his meaning; it possessed him. It was not a fully formed soul asking for a body: it was an inchoate soul in the inchoate body of perhaps two or three vague ideas and a few scattered phrases. The growing of this body into its full stature and perfect shape was the same thing as the gradual self-definition of the meaning. And this is the reason why such poems strike us as creations, not manufactures, and have the magical effect which mere decoration cannot produce. This is also the reason why, if we insist on asking for the meaning of such a poem, we can only be answered 'It means itself.'

And so at last I may explain why I have troubled myself and you with what may seem an arid controversy about mere words. It is not so. These heresies which would make poetry a compound of two factors—a matter common to it with the merest prose, *plus* a poetic form, as the one heresy says: a poetical substance *plus* a negligible form, as the other says—are not only untrue, they are injurious to the dignity of poetry. In an age already inclined to shrink from those higher realms where poetry touches religion and philosophy, the formalist heresy encourages men to taste poetry as they would a fine wine, which has indeed an aesthetic value, but a small one. And then the natural man, finding an empty form, hurls into it the matter of cheap pathos,[1] rancid sentiment, vulgar humour, bare lust, ravenous vanity—everything which, in Schiller's phrase,[2] the form should extirpate, but which no mere form can extirpate. And the other heresy—which is indeed rather a practice than a creed—encourages us in the habit so dear to us of putting our own thoughts or fancies into the place of the poet's creation. What he meant by *Hamlet*, or the *Ode to a Nightingale*, or *Abt Vogler*, we say, is this or that which we knew already; and so we

---

[1] Cf. Herbart, *Practical Philosophy*, p. 151.
[2] Not that to Schiller 'form' meant mere style and versification. (A. C. B.)

lose what he had to tell us. But he meant what he said, and said what he meant.

Poetry in this matter is not, as good critics of painting and music often affirm, different from the other arts; in all of them the content is one thing with the form. What Beethoven meant by his symphony, or Turner by his picture, was not something which you can name, but the picture and the symphony. Meaning they have, but *what* meaning can be said in no language but their own: and we know this, though some strange delusion makes us think the meaning has less worth because we cannot put it into words. Well, it is just the same with poetry. But because poetry is words, we vainly fancy that some other words than its own will express its meaning. And they will do so no more—or, if you like to speak loosely, only a little more—than words will express the meaning of the Dresden Madonna. Something a little like it they may indeed express. And we may find analogues of the meaning of poetry outside it, which may help us to appropriate it. The other arts, the best ideas of philosophy or religion, much that nature and life offer us or force upon us, are akin to it. But they are only akin. Nor is it the expression of them. Poetry does not present to imagination our highest [1] knowledge or belief, and much less our dreams and opinions; but it, content and form in unity, embodies in its own irreplaceable way something which embodies itself also in other irreplaceable ways, such as philosophy or religion. And just as each of these gives a satisfaction which the other cannot possibly give, so we find in poetry, which cannot satisfy the needs they meet, that which by their natures they cannot afford us. But we shall not find it fully if we look for something else.

And now, when all is said, the question will still recur, though now in quite another sense, What does poetry mean? This unique expression, which cannot be replaced by any other, still seems to be trying to express something beyond itself. And this, we feel, is also what

[1] Cf. Hegel, p. 161.

the other arts, and religion, and philosophy are trying to express: and that is what impels us to seek in vain to translate the one into the other. About the best poetry, and not only the best, there floats an atmosphere of infinite suggestion. The poet speaks to us of one thing, but in this one thing there seems to lurk the secret of all. He said what he meant, but his meaning seems to beckon away beyond itself, or rather to expand into something boundless which is only focused in it; something also which, we feel, would satisfy not only the imagination, but the whole of us; that something within us, and without, which everywhere

> makes us seem
> To patch up fragments of a dream,
> Part of which comes true, and part
> Beats and trembles in the heart.[1]

Those who are susceptible to this effect of poetry find it not only, perhaps not most, in the ideals which she has sometimes described, but in a child's song by Christina Rossetti about a mere crown of wind-flowers, and in tragedies like *Lear*, where the sun seems to have set for ever. They hear this spirit murmuring its undertone through the *Aeneid*, and catch its voice in the song of Keats's nightingale, and its light upon the figures on the Urn, and it pierces them no less in Shelley's hopeless lament, *O world, O life, O time*, than in the rapturous ecstasy of his *Life of Life*. This all-embracing perfection cannot be expressed in poetic words or words of any kind, nor yet in music or in colour, but the suggestion of it is in much poetry, if not all, and poetry has in this suggestion, this 'meaning', a great part of its value. We do it wrong, and we defeat our own purposes when we try to bend it to them:

> We do it wrong, being so majestical,
> To offer it the show of violence;
> For it is as the air invulnerable,
> And our vain blows malicious mockery.[2]

---

[1] Shelley, *Is it that in some brighter sphere?*   [2] *Hamlet*, i. i.

It is a spirit. It comes we know not whence. It will not speak at our bidding, nor answer in our language. It is not our servant; it is our master.

The Sublime (1903)[1]

It will not do, then, to lay it down that the sublime is the beautiful which has immeasurable, incomparable, or infinite greatness. But I suggest that, after the explanations given, we may conveniently use the adjective 'unmeasured', so long as we remember that this means one thing where we do not measure at all, and another thing where we try to measure and fail. And, this being so, it seems that we may say that *all* sublimity, and not only that in which the idea of infinite greatness or of the Infinite emerges, is an image of infinity; for in all, through a certain check or limitation and the overcoming of it, we reach the perception or the imaginative idea of something which, on the one hand, has a positive nature, and, on the other, is either *not* determined as finite or *is* determined as infinite. But we must not add that this makes the sublime superior to the 'beautiful'. For the 'beautiful' too, though in a different way, is an image of infinity. In 'beauty', as we said, that which appears in a sensuous form seems to rest in that form, to be wholly embodied in it; it shows no tendency to pass beyond it, and intimates no reserve of force that might strain or break it. So that the 'beautiful' thing is a whole complete in itself, and in moments when beauty fills our souls we know what Wordsworth meant when he said 'each thing seemed infinite', though each, being but one of many, must from another point of view, here suppressed, be finite. 'Beauty', then, we may perhaps say, is the image of the total presence of the Infinite within any limits it may choose to

---

[1] A bibliography of writings on *The Sublime* between Kant (1790) and 1888 will be found in Seidl, *Zur Geschichte des Erhabenheitsbegriffes seit Kant* (Leipzig, 1888). He gives some sixty names, in addition to those of historians, for this period, though he confines himself to the Germans. Some other references are given in my *Theory of Beauty*, ix. § 14.

assume; sublimity the image of its boundlessness, and of its rejection of any pretension to independence or absoluteness on the part of its finite forms; the one the image of its immanence, the other of its transcendence.

BENEDETTO CROCE
1866–

To some idealist, and therefore in the main sympathetic, readers of Hegel, his weakness seemed to lie in his treatment of the individual. To establish a rational and necessary connexion between universals seemed an ideal realizable if not realized by his methods. Hegel, in reply to the crude challenge to 'deduce' his critic's pen, replied that he had more important things to do. But perhaps he had not. He had attempted to 'deduce' individual persons and events of history: only those which eluded him were classed with the professor's pen as 'unimportant'.[1] Either every individual thing and event was capable of rationalization—and then in the very process it seemed to lose its individual character of immediate given fact—or by its very nature it was not. And then it would be incumbent on the idealist philosopher to 'deduce' this irrationality, to show more explicitly how the character of individual things as such necessarily precluded the hope of exhibiting a rational necessity for each one. Croce has been accused by his critics of mysticism, of reintroducing into philosophy, under the name of *intuition*, an irrational or alogical element.

For Hegel, beauty had been the embodiment of reason, reason not indeed abstract nor explicit, rather implicit and fused in sense. But since this fusion in sense was a less perfect mode of reason than its explicit emergence in a 'concrete' philosophy— was indeed a stage to be superseded both by the individual and the race—it was difficult to exhibit its wholly rational necessity. Croce attempts to restore independence to the individual, which he regards as the result or object of immediate intuition and as being alone and always beautiful. An individual is that which is immediately intuited without being thought or judged to be real or unreal, good or bad, useful or pernicious;

---

[1] *Philosophy of History* (Introduction).

and so long as this innocence of apprehension can be maintained we have the experience of beauty. Intuition is imagination; it is not knowledge, but provides the material upon which thought works to produce knowledge. But this aesthetic experience, though the most primitive *apprehension*, is not crude sensation. It is already a union of form and matter, though neither of these can be *apprehended* separately but only inferred. Croce infers that the matter to which intuition or imagination gives form—that which stimulates the aesthetic experience and which, through this experience, we come to know in the only way in which it is knowable—is the activities of our own will. Under will he includes desire and feeling.

Spirit, then, has two characteristics—to will and to know, neither of which would be possible without the other. For will can only be exercised in a known situation and conversely (since there is nothing outside spirit) there is primarily nothing to know but those blind states of attraction and repulsion called 'feeling' which are the primary manifestation of will. The ultimately unintelligible presupposition of all experience, then, is that the spirit's own volitional states should be intuited by it in the form of 'images'. It is hardly less mysterious how or why the spirit next proceeds, by the exercise of thought, to distinguish some among these images as 'true perceptions of reality' and others as 'mere imaginations'.

But whatever the difficulties, we recognize in Croce an attempt both to explain on idealist lines our experience of individuals not rationally seen to be necessary, and also, by the same means, to restore the autonomy of aesthetic experience, degraded by Hegel as imperfect rationality, and to give it an independent place among spiritual activities, prior, indeed, to rational experience and the basis of it, but not replaceable by it.

Whenever, then, we apprehend a pure individual image, without reasoning or judging about it, without raising even the question of reality or unreality, then, according to Croce, we have 'expressed' to ourselves or intuited a state of our own souls and have experienced beauty. Without accepting this whole metaphysic, it may be possible to agree that individuals, perceived or imagined, which express feeling are alone and always beautiful, and that feelings can only be apprehended—as distinct from being felt—when expressed in perceived or imagined individuals.

A Breviary of Aesthetics[1] (1913)

i. *What is Art?* 'What is art?' I reply, in the briefest and simplest terms, that art is vision or intuition. The artist produces an image or a dream; and those who appreciate his art turn their eyes in the direction he has indicated, look through the loophole which he has opened, and reproduce in themselves that image. 'Intuition', 'vision', 'contemplation', 'fancy', 'imagination', 'patterns', 'representations', and the like, are almost synonymous words, continually recurring in discussions about art, and all leading us to the same conception or system of conceptions:—a clear indication of universal agreement.

But this reply, that art is intuition, gets both its meaning and its value by all which it implicitly denies, by all that from which it distinguishes art. What then are the distinctions implicit in it? I will indicate the chief, or at least those which are most important to us in the present stage of thought.

First, the answer denies that art is a physical fact:[2] that it consists, for instance, in any definite colours or colour-relations, or bodily forms, or sounds or sound-relations; in any definite manifestations of heat or electricity, or, shortly, in anything that can be called physical. Even in popular thought we find signs of this 'physical' heresy. Like children who grasp a soap-bubble and try to grasp the rainbow, the human mind, in its love of beautiful things, naturally turns to look for their causes in nature, and tries to think, or believes it ought to think, that certain colours and shapes are beautiful and certain others ugly. The same attempt has been deliberately and methodically carried out more than once in the history of thought: from the artists and thinkers of Greece and of the Renais-

[1] Signor Croce, in generously allowing me to extract from his writings, asked that stress should be laid on the *Breviario*, as representing his maturer thought, rather than on the fuller and more fully argued *Estetica* (1901), and that it should be read in the light of his article on Aesthetics in the 14th edition of the *Encyclopædia Britannica* (1929). I have felt bound to comply. There is a translation of the *Breviario* by Ainslie (*Essentials of Aesthetic*, 1921).

[2] Cf. Plato, *Hippias*, p. 6, Plotinus, p. 49.

sance, who fixed 'canons' for bodily beauty, and specu-
lated on the discovery of geometrical or numerical relations in form and music, down to the aesthetic researchers
of the nineteenth century, such as Fechner,[1] and those
'observations' on the connexion of scientific facts with
art, which, in our own day, are naïvely reported to our
congresses of philosophy, psychology, and natural science.
The question 'Is Art a physical fact?' should properly be
put in a different form: 'Can art be analysed by physical
science?'[2] That certainly can be done, and in fact we
do it every time that we neglect the sense of a poem, and
sacrifice its enjoyment, in order to count the words of
which it is made up or to divide them into letters and
syllables; or whenever we neglect the beauty of a statue
in order to measure and weigh it—things as necessary for
the transport of statuary as the others were for setting up
a page of poetry, but quite useless to the votary of artistic
contemplation, for whom it is neither profitable nor law-
ful to neglect his proper object. Even in this second interpretation, then, art is not a physical fact. That is to say,
when we try to penetrate into its nature and its methods,
we are not helped by any scientific analysis.

A second distinction is implied in defining art as intuition. If art is intuition, and if intuition means 'theory'[3]
in the original sense of contemplation, then art cannot be
a utilitarian activity.[4] And since a utilitarian activity
is one which aims at securing a pleasure or removing a
pain, art in its essence can have nothing to do with utility,
pleasure, or pain, as such. The best that can be done
in support of the definition of art as what pleases, is to
maintain that it is not simply what pleases, but what
pleases in a particular way.[5] But such a qualification is
not a defence but an abandonment of the position;
since, if art is a particular kind of pleasure, its distinctive

---

[1] *Vorschule der Aesthetik* (1876); cf. Hogarth, p. 88, Mitchell, p. 261.
[2] *sia construibile fisicamente.*   [3] Italian *teoria*, Greek θεωρία.
[4] Cf. Plato, *Hippias*, p. 10.
[5] Cf. Plato, p. 14, Santayana, § 11, p. 198, Richards, p. 282, Dewey, p. 306.

character would depend not on its pleasantness but on what distinguishes it from other pleasant things. And so we should have to turn our investigations to this distinctive element, which is more or other than mere pleasure. But this doctrine, which defines art as pleasure, is technically known as Hedonistic Aesthetic, and has a long and complicated evolution in the history of aesthetics. It appeared first in the Graeco-Roman world, was prevalent in the eighteenth century, flourished again in the second half of the nineteenth, and is still popular, especially among beginners in aesthetic, who are chiefly struck by the fact that art arouses pleasure. The history of this doctrine has consisted in the putting forward in turn various classes of pleasure, or several classes together— for instance the pleasures of the higher senses, the pleasures of play, the pleasure of conscious power, sexual pleasure, and the like—or else in inserting elements extraneous to pleasure—the satisfaction of intellectual and moral needs, and so on.[1] And the evolution of the doctrine has been due precisely to its instability, to its attempt to digest the foreign elements which it had to introduce if it was in any way to agree with the facts of art. And thus it ended by destroying itself as a hedonistic theory and by unconsciously suggesting a new theory, or at least showing the necessity for one. And since every error is founded upon some truth (and the truth of the physical theory is, as we have seen, in the possibility of analysing art scientifically like other things), the hedonistic theory has its eternal basis of truth in its emphasis on the hedonistic accompaniment or pleasure which is common to the aesthetic activity and all other activities of the mind. This we have no intention of denying, however flatly we deny the identification of art with pleasure and distinguish them by defining it as intuition.

A third distinction effected by our theory of art as intuition is that between it and the moral activity.[2] By the

[1] See index under Pleasure, Senses (aesthetic), Play, Sex, Truth, Morality.
[2] Cf. Sidney, Tolstoy, pp. 54, 192.

latter we mean that type of practical activity, which, though necessarily concerned with what is useful, and with pleasure and pain, is not itself simply utilitarian or hedonistic, but occurs on a higher mental level. But intuition, as being contemplative, is opposed to any practical activity. Art, in fact, as was long ago observed, is not produced by an act of will; the good will which makes a good man does not make an artist. And since it is not produced by an act of will, art is exempt from moral distinctions, not by any privilege of immunity, but because moral distinctions simply do not apply. An artist may imaginatively represent an act worthy of moral praise or blame; but his representation, being imagination, is worthy of neither. Not only can no penal code condemn an imaginative representation to death or to prison, but no reasonable man can make it the object of a moral judgement. To judge immoral Dante's Francesca, or moral Shakespeare's Cordelia, whose functions are purely artistic and who are like notes of music from the soul of Dante or Shakespeare, would be no better than to judge a triangle wicked, or a square moral. Not but what the moralistic theory is, in its turn, represented in the history of aesthetic doctrines, and even to-day is not altogether dead, though pretty well discredited in popular thought. It is discredited not only by its intrinsic weakness, but to some extent by a certain moral weakness to which our time is prone, and which recommends to our sophisticated temperaments a refutation that ought to be based, as we base it, on purely rational grounds. An offspring of this moralistic doctrine is the end set before art of guiding to good and inspiring hatred of evil, of correcting and refining manners; as is also the demand made on artists to do their part in educating the masses, animating the warlike or nationalist spirit of a people, and spreading the ideals of sobriety and industry. None of which things can be done by art any more than by geometry, which is not thought the less respectable for that; nor does one see why art should be. That art cannot do these things seems to be suspected even by the moralistic philosophers, since they so readily make terms with her, and allow her to purvey pleasures, even if they are not moral, so long as they are not confessedly shameful, and counsel her to use for good ends her power of conquering men's minds with pleasure; to gild the pill and smear with sweetmeat the lip of the cup which holds the bitter draught.[1]   In short they bid her play the harlot (since her original sin cannot be rooted out), but all in the service of Holy Church and of morality—*meretrix ecclesiae.* Or again such theorists bethought them of using art for didactic ends, since science as well as virtue is arduous, and art might sweeten its harshness and charm us within the doors of the mansion of science; might indeed lead us thither, as through a garden of Armida, gaily and luxuriously, without our knowing what great profit we were receiving or what solemn regeneration was in store for us.[2]   Nowadays we cannot recall these theories without a smile, but we should not forget that in their time they were taken seriously and sprang from a serious effort to understand the nature of art and to conceive of it more worthily; and that there were believers (to confine ourselves to Italian literature) named Dante and Tasso, Parini and Alfieri, Manzoni and Mazzini. And this moralistic doctrine in its turn has been, and is, and ever will be profitable in virtue of its very contradictions; it has been, is, and will be an attempt, however misguided, to distinguish art from mere pleasure, with which it is often confused, and to give it a more worthy place.[3]   Moreover, like other doctrines, it has its element of truth. For, if art is outside the sphere of morality, the artist is not. As a man he comes under its laws and never escapes the duties of a man. His art itself, that art which is not and cannot be morality, he must consider as a mission, to be exercised as if it were a priesthood.

Finally—and this perhaps is the most important of the general distinctions which I must here enumerate—

---

[1] Cf. Sidney, p. 54, and Hegel, p. 163.   [2] Cf. Muratori, p. 60.
[3] Cf. Plato, *Hippias*, p. 11.

the definition of art as intuition denies to it the character
of conceptual knowledge.[1] Conceptual knowledge, in
its pure form of philosophy, is always realistic. That is
to say, it aims at distinguishing reality from unreality,
or at putting what is 'unreal' in its proper place by including it in the real world as an inadequate aspect of
reality. But intuition just means the absence of distinction
between reality and unreality;[2] it is the imaginary as a
mere mental picture, the pure idealism of imagination.
By contrasting the intuitive or sensuous with the conceptual or intelligent consciousness we aim at establishing
the independence of this more simple and elementary
form of consciousness, which has been compared to the
dream of the contemplative life, whose waking is philosophy. The man who, when faced by a work of art, asks
whether what the artist has expressed is metaphysically
or historically true or false, asks a meaningless question,
and makes a mistake like that of summoning to the bar of
morality the airy pictures of imagination. The question
is meaningless, because the distinction of truth and falsehood must concern a judgement or statement about
reality and cannot apply to the mere presence of an
image, to a mere subject without a predicate, of which
nothing is asserted, and which, therefore, does not enter
into a judgement. It is irrelevant to object that the very
individual character of the image depends upon a reference to the universal of which it is an instance. We are
not denying that the universal, like the spirit of God, is
omnipresent and breathes its life into all things. What we
deny is that in intuition as such the universal is logically
and explicitly thought. It is equally irrelevant to recall
the doctrine of the unity of the mind; for this is not
destroyed, but rather emphasized, by the clear distinction
between imagination and thought, since from this distinction arises the opposition in which concrete unity consists.[3]

[1] Cf. Muratori, p. 61.
[2] Cf. Vico, p. 73, Kant, § 2, p. 110, Moore, § 116, p. 249, Collingwood, p. 292.
[3] Cf. Gentile.

This character of art which distinguishes intuition from conception, art from philosophy and history,—that is to say, from both the assertion of the universal and the perception or narration of the event,—has also been called its ideality. And ideality is the very essence of art. No sooner are reflection and judgement developed out of this ideality than art fades and dies. It dies in the artist, who becomes a critic; and it dies in his audience, who become critics of life instead of his enchanted listeners.[1] . . .

In the philosophy of the nineteenth century, examples of identifying or confusing art with religion and philosophy are afforded by Schelling and Hegel; of its confusion with natural science by Taine;[2] of its confusion with historical and documentary research by the theories of the French 'verists'; of its confusion with mathematics by the Herbartian formalists. But it would be vain to look in these authors, or others that might be named, for clear instances of such errors. Error is always confused; if it were not, it would be the truth.

But, it may be asked, what place can there be in man's mind for a world of pure imagination, without philosophical, historic, religious, or scientific truth, without even moral or hedonistic value? What can be more futile than to dream with our eyes open, in a life that needs not only open eyes but open mind and active spirit? Mere imagination—we have no very flattering names for the man who lives upon that; we call him a dreamer, and, often as not, an idle dreamer. Dreaming is not very effective and not very interesting: can that be art? No doubt we can amuse ourselves with reading some rigmarole of adventures, where picture follows picture without rhyme or reason, but we do it when we are tired, when we have to kill time; we are well enough aware that such stuff is not art.

In truth, intuition is the creation of an image; not of a mass of incoherent images produced by calling up old

---

[1] Cf. Matthew Arnold's saying that poetry is criticism of life: *Essays in Criticism*, I. 'The Study of Poetry'.   [2] *L'Idéal dans l'Art*, and *Philosophie de l'Art* (1864).

images and letting them follow one another at random,
or at random combining them together—a man's head
with a horse's body—as in the childish game. It was to
express this difference between intuition and fantasy that
the ancient Poetics chiefly used the idea of Unity, re-
quiring that every work of art should be *simplex et unum*;[1]
or the allied idea of Unity in Variety, according to which
the manifold images should find a focus, and be absorbed
in one complex image. For the same purpose the aesthetic
of the nineteenth century invented the distinction, to be
found in many of its philosophers, between imagination,[2] the peculiarly artistic faculty, and fancy,[3] which is
inartistic. To pile up images, to select, to divide, to combine them, presupposes their creation and possession.
It is imagination which creates, while fancy is barren,
fit for mechanical combination, not for generating organic
life. . . .

Intuition is truly artistic, is truly intuition, and not
a chaotic mass of images, only when it is animated by a
vital principle native to itself. What then is this principle?

The answer may be said to emerge as the result of criticizing the greatest contest of conflicting tendencies ever
waged in the field of art, a conflict waged not only in the
age when it was most conspicuous, and to which it gave
its name: the conflict of Classicism and Romanticism.[4]
In general terms, such as we must use at present, and
apart from minor accidental differences, romanticism
demands from art above all things a spontaneous torrent
of emotion, love and hatred, anguish and triumph,
despair and rapture. It is contented, even delighted,
with vague and misty images, a suggestive and unequal
style, dim hints, approximation of phrase, violent turbid
outlines. Classicism, on the other hand, loves the serene
soul, the learned design, figures studied in their character

[1] Cf. Aristotle, *Poetics*, p. 32.   [2] *fantasia*.

[3] *immaginazione*. Since Coleridge the English usage of these terms has been
fixed as opposite to the Italian. Cf. Wordsworth, p. 130.

[4] Cf. Hegel, pp. 169–70, and Nietzsche, p. 185.

and precise in line; deliberation, balance, lucidity. It sets its face resolutely towards truth as romanticism did towards feeling. And a host of reasons can be found for maintaining either point of view and for confuting the other. For what, ask the romantics, is an art worth, for all its polished imagery, that does not speak to our hearts? And if it speak to our hearts what matter if its imagery lack polish? And their enemies will answer them: What is this emotional excitement worth, when the mind can find no lovely imagery to rest in? And if the imagery be lovely, what matters the lack of a passion attainable without the help of art, showered upon us by life often more freely than we could wish? [1]

But we see this distinction vanish, we become unable to utter the watchword of either school, so soon as we experience the weakness and futility of the defence of either of these inadequate points of view. We have only to turn our eyes away from the commonplaces of art produced by the romantic and classicizing schools, those alike which are convulsed with passion and those which are coldly conventional; we have only to fix them on the works no longer of imitators but of masters, not of mediocrity but of genius. Great artists and great work, or at least the great parts of it, can be called neither classicist nor romantic, neither passionate nor imitative; for they are both classical and romantic, emotional and life-like; they are sheer emotion absolutely identified with the most lucid imagery. Such notably were the works of Greek art and of Italian art and poetry. . . .

What gives unity and coherence to intuition is feeling.[2] Intuitions are truly such because they represent feeling, and only thence can they arise. It is not a thought but a feeling that gives to art the airy lightness of its symbolism. Art is an ideal within the four corners of an image. Here the aspiration and the imagery exist in and for each other. Epic and lyric or drama and lyric are scholastic distinc-

---

[1] Cf. Herbart, *Encyclopaedia*, p. 156.
[2] Cf. Alison, p. 105, Coleridge, p. 134.

tions of what cannot be separated. Art is always lyrical just because it is the epic and drama of the feelings. What we admire in genuine works of art is the perfect imaginative form in which a state of mind clothes itself; that is what we call the life, the unity, the fulness, the consistency of a work of art. What offends us in false or faulty work is the unresolved discord of different moods, their mere superimposition or confusion or their alternation, which gets but a superficial unity forced upon it by the author, who for this purpose makes use of some abstract idea or plan or of some unaesthetic passion. . . .

From this point of view it is instructive to consider the endless disputes over dramatic unity,[1] which from the external limitations of time and place was first reduced to the unity of 'action', and this finally to the unity of 'interest', just as interest might in its turn have been properly dissolved into the interest of the poet's mind, his personal aspiration or feeling. Instructive too, as we have seen, are the negative results of the great dispute between classicists and romantics; where we find refuted, on the one hand, the art of abstract feeling, which, by the violence of crude passion not mastered in contemplation, tries to distract us from its feeble imagery; and, on the other hand, the classicist art, which by superficial lucidity, pretentious correctness of design, and preciosity of phrase, would hide the absence of what alone could justify its ingenuity, an inspiring passion. A famous saying of an English critic,[2] which has now become a journalistic commonplace, asserts that 'all art constantly aspires towards the condition of music.' It might be said more exactly that all the arts are music, thus emphasizing that it is neither mechanical combination nor pedantic realism that can give birth to artistic imagery, but feeling only. Another saying, not less celebrated, by a quasi-philosopher[3] of Switzerland, which has had the same questionable fortune of popularity, makes the discovery that

---

[1] Aristotle, *Poetics*, v, viii. Cf. Butcher, *Aristotle's Theory of Poetry and Fine Art*, vii.
[2] Pater, *The Renaissance*, 'The School of Giorgione'.   [3] Amiel.

'every landscape is a mood'—a truism, not because the landscape is a landscape, but because it is art.

ii. *Prejudices about Art.* The feeling or mood is not a particular kind of import, it is the whole universe seen *sub specie intuitionis.* Expression and beauty are not two ideas but one, which may be called by either of these synonymous terms. Artistic imagination is always embodied but has no excrescences. It has always its appropriate clothing, but is not hung with extrinsic ornament.

New Essays in Aesthetics (1920)

An Eclectic Attempt in the History of the Formative Arts. The difficult point to keep clear is that the form is always expressive and yet the expression is always pure form; the artistic act turns passion into contemplation and thereby makes it a thing of beauty.[1] Inexpressive forms, beautiful in their own nature, forms purely plastic or picturesque, are things easy to talk about but in fact mere vocal sounds. To dispose figures in one way or another, to imagine in one way or another the bodies of men and animals, plants and everything else, to light a picture in this way or that, and so on; all these are the activity of imagination itself, at once necessary and free, issuing from a particular feeling and creating a particular image which is no longer that particular feeling because it is that and something more.[2] Not only 'a landscape is a mood', but every line, colour, or tone is the embodiment or reality of a 'mood'. . . . 'Eyes which see differently' are in fact the mind which feels and dreams and desires differently.

Aesthetics[3] (1901)

xiii. Physical beauty is usually divided into natural and artificial. Here we are faced by one of the greatest difficulties of aesthetic:—*Natural Beauty.* These words often indicate merely the satisfaction of our wants. When we call the country beautiful because the eye is rested by

[1] Cf. Wordsworth, *Preface*, p. 129.   [2] Cf. Nettleship, p. 188.
[3] There is a translation by Ainslie. The second edition only should be used.

verdure, the body is braced, and the warm sunshine caresses our limbs, we use the word in no aesthetic sense. But it is unquestionable that at other times the epithet 'beautiful', applied to natural scenes and objects, is purely aesthetic.

It has been noticed that to get aesthetic satisfaction from natural objects, we must neglect their actual or historical reality, and distinguish their pure appearance or manifestation from their actual existence, . . . that nature is only beautiful for the man who sees it *with the eyes of an artist*; that zoologists and botanists know nothing of beautiful animals or flowers, and that natural beauty is *revealed* to us. Without the aid of imagination, nothing in nature is beautiful; and with its aid, according to our disposition, the same thing is now expressive, now unmeaning, now expressive in one way, now in another, sad or joyful, sublime or ridiculous, . . . Man, faced with natural beauty, is exactly the mythical Narcissus at the pool.[1] . . . One artist is in raptures before a smiling landscape, another before a rag-and-bone shop: one before the face of a pretty girl and another before the squalid features of some old ruffian. The first will perhaps say that the rag-shop and the ruffian are disgusting, and the second that the smiling landscape and the pretty girl are boring. They may dispute endlessly; they will not agree till they have been treated with such a dose of aesthetics as will enable them to see that they are both right.

Pure Intuition and the Lyrical Character of Art
Published in *Problems of Aesthetics*, 1910

What we seek and enjoy in art, what makes our heart leap up and ravishes our admiration, is the life, the movement, the passion, the fire, the feeling of the artist; that alone gives us the supreme criterion for distinguishing works of true and false art, inspiration and failure. Passion and feeling cover a multitude of sins. If they are lacking, nothing can take their place.

[1] Cf. Plotinus V, viii. 2, p. 49, Alison, p. 105, Hegel, p. 160.

GEORGE EDWARD MOORE
1873–

Principia Ethica (1903)

114 (1). It is plain that in those instances of aesthetic appreciation, which we think most valuable, there is included, not merely a bare cognition of what is beautiful in the object, but also some kind of feeling or emotion. It is not sufficient that a man should merely see the beautiful qualities in a picture and know that they are beautiful, in order that we may give his state of mind the highest praise. We require that he should also *appreciate* the beauty of that which he sees and which he knows to be beautiful—that he should feel and see *its beauty*. And by these expressions we certainly mean that he should have an appropriate emotion towards the beautiful qualities which he cognizes. It is perhaps the case that all aesthetic emotions have some common quality; but it is certain that differences in the emotion seem to be appropriate to differences in the kind of beauty perceived: and by saying that different emotions are *appropriate* to different kinds of beauty, we mean that the whole which is formed by the consciousness of that kind of beauty *together with* the emotion appropriate to it, is better than if any other emotion had been felt in contemplating that particular beautiful object. Accordingly we have a large variety of different emotions, each of which is a necessary constituent in some state of consciousness which we judge to be good. All of these emotions are essential elements in great positive goods; they are *parts* of organic wholes, which have great intrinsic value. But it is important to observe that these wholes are organic, and that, hence, it does not follow that the emotion, *by itself*, would have any value whatsoever, nor yet that, if it were directed to a different object, the whole thus formed might not be positively bad. And, in fact, it seems to be the case that if we distinguish the emotional

element, in any aesthetic appreciation, from the cognitive element, which accompanies it and is, in fact, commonly thought of as a part of the emotion; and if we consider what value this emotional element would have, *existing by itself,* we can hardly think that it has any great value, even if it has any at all. Whereas, if the same emotion be directed to a different object, if, for instance, it is felt towards an object that is positively ugly, the whole state of consciousness is certainly often positively bad in a high degree.

115 (2). In the last paragraph I have pointed out the two facts, that the presence of some emotion is necessary to give any very high value to a state of aesthetic appreciation, and that, on the other hand, this same emotion, in itself, may have little or no value: it follows that these emotions give to the wholes of which they form a part a value far greater than that which they themselves possess. The same is obviously true of the cognitive element which must be combined with these emotions in order to form these highly valuable wholes;[1] and the present paragraph will attempt to define what is meant by this cognitive element, so far as to guard against a possible misunderstanding. When we talk of seeing a beautiful object, or, more generally, of the cognition or consciousness of a beautiful object, we may mean by these expressions something which forms no part of any valuable whole. There is an ambiguity in the use of the term 'object', which has probably been responsible for as many enormous errors in philosophy and psychology as any other single cause. This ambiguity may easily be detected by considering the proposition, which, though a contradiction in terms, is obviously true: That when a man sees a beautiful picture, he may see nothing beautiful whatever.[2]

---

[1] Cf. Ross, *The Right and the Good*, p. 71, where the Provost of Oriel, criticizing *Principia Ethica*, § 18, says: 'The true analysis of the consciousness of a beautiful object, it would seem, is not into consciousness plus the beautiful object, but into (a) its being an instance of consciousness in general, and (b) its being an instance of consciousness of something beautiful. And it seems to owe its whole value to the second of the facts named.' Cf. Herbart, p. 153.

[2] Cf. Berkeley, p. 76.

The ambiguity consists in the fact that, by the 'object' of vision (or cognition), may be meant *either* the qualities actually seen *or* all the qualities possessed by the thing seen.[1] Thus in our case: when it is said that the picture is beautiful, it is meant that it contains qualities which are beautiful; when it is said that the man sees the picture, it is meant that he sees a great number of the qualities contained in the picture; and when it is said that, nevertheless, he sees nothing beautiful, it is meant that he does *not* see those qualities of the picture which are beautiful. When, therefore, I speak of the cognition of a beautiful object, as an essential element in a valuable aesthetic appreciation, I must be understood to mean only the cognition of *the beautiful qualities* possessed by that object, and *not* the cognition of other qualities of the object possessing them. And this distinction must itself be carefully distinguished from the other distinction expressed above by the distinct terms 'seeing the beauty of a thing' and 'seeing its beautiful qualities'. By 'seeing the beauty of a thing' we commonly mean the having an emotion towards its beautiful qualities; whereas in the 'seeing of its beautiful qualities' we do not include any emotion. By the cognitive element, which is equally necessary with emotion to the existence of a valuable appreciation, I mean merely the actual cognition or consciousness of any or all of an object's *beautiful qualities*—that is to say any or all of those elements in the object which possess any positive beauty. That such a cognitive element is essential to a valuable whole may be easily seen, by asking: What value should we attribute to the proper emotion excited by hearing Beethoven's Fifth Symphony, if that emotion were entirely unaccompanied by any consciousness, either of the notes, or of the melodic and harmonic relations between them? And that the mere *hearing* of the Symphony, even accompanied by the appropriate emotion, is not sufficient, may be easily seen, if we consider what would be the state of a man, who should

---

[1] Cf. Alexander, p. 267, Ducasse, p. 312.

hear all the notes, but should *not* be aware of any of those melodic and harmonic relations, which are necessary to constitute the smallest beautiful elements in the Symphony.

116 (3). Connected with the distinction just made between 'object' in the sense of the qualities actually before the mind, and 'object' in the sense of the whole thing which possesses the qualities actually before the mind, is another distinction of the utmost importance for a correct analysis of the constituents necessary to a valuable whole. It is commonly and rightly thought that to see beauty in a thing which has no beauty is in some way inferior to seeing beauty in that which really has it. But under this single description of 'seeing beauty in that which has no beauty', two very different facts, and facts of very different value, may be included. We may mean *either* the attribution to an object of really beautiful qualities which it does not possess *or* the feeling towards qualities, which the object does possess but which are in reality not beautiful, an emotion which is appropriate only to qualities really beautiful. Both these facts are of very frequent occurrence; and in most instances of emotion both no doubt occur together: but they are obviously quite distinct, and the distinction is of the utmost importance for a correct estimate of values. The former may be called an error of judgement, and the latter an error of taste; but it is important to observe that the 'error of taste' commonly involves a false judgement *of value*; whereas the 'error of judgement' is merely a false judgement *of fact*.

Now the case which I have called an error of taste, namely, where the actual qualities we admire (whether possessed by the 'object' or not) are ugly, can in any case have no value, except such as may belong to the emotion *by itself*; and in most, if not in all, cases it is a considerable positive evil. In this sense, then, it is undoubtedly right to think that seeing beauty in a thing which has no beauty is inferior in value to seeing beauty where beauty really is. But the other case is much more difficult. In this case there is present all that I have hitherto mentioned as necessary to constitute a great positive good: there is a cognition of qualities really beautiful, together with an appropriate emotion towards these qualities. There can, therefore, be no doubt that we have here a great positive good. But there is present also something else; namely, a belief that these beautiful qualities exist, and that they exist in a certain relation to other things—namely, to some properties of the object to which we attribute these qualities: and further the object of this belief is false.[1] And we may ask, with regard to the whole thus constituted, whether the presence of the belief, and the fact that what is believed is false, make any difference to its value? We thus get three different cases of which it is very important to determine the relative values. Where both the cognition of beautiful qualities and the appropriate emotion are present we may *also* have either, (1) a belief in the existence of these qualities, of which the object, i.e. that they exist, is true: or (2) a mere cognition, without belief,[2] when it is (*a*) true, (*b*) false, that the object of the cognition, i.e. the beautiful qualities, exists: or (3) a belief in the existence of the beautiful qualities, when they do not exist. The importance of these cases arises from the fact that the second defines the pleasures of imagination,[2] including a great part of the appreciation of those works of art which are *representative*; whereas the first contrasts with these the appreciation of what is beautiful in Nature, and the human affections.[3] The third, on the other hand, is contrasted with both, in that it is chiefly exemplified in what is called misdirected affection; and it is possible also that the love of God, in the case of a believer, should fall under this head.

117. Now all these three cases, as I have said, have something in common, namely, that, in them all, we have a cognition of really beautiful qualities together with an appropriate emotion towards those qualities. I think, therefore, it cannot be doubted (nor is it com-

[1] Cf. Ross, p. 317.   [2] Cf. Croce, p. 238.   [3] Cf. Alexander, p. 269.

monly doubted) that all three include great positive goods; they are all things of which we feel convinced that they are worth having for their own sakes. And I think that the value of the second, in either of its two subdivisions, is precisely the same as the value of the element common to all three. In other words, in the case of purely imaginative appreciations we have merely the cognition of really beautiful qualities together with the appropriate emotion; and the question, whether the object cognized exists or not, seems here, where there is no belief either in its existence or in its non-existence, to make absolutely no difference to the value of the total state. But it seems to me that the two other cases do differ in intrinsic value both from this one and from one another, even though the object cognized and the appropriate emotion should be identical in all three cases. I think that the additional presence of a belief in the reality of the object makes the total state much better, if the belief is true; and worse, if the belief is false. In short, where there is belief, in the sense in which we *do* believe in the existence of Nature and horses, and do *not* believe in the existence of an ideal landscape and unicorns, the *truth* of what is believed does make a great difference to the value of the organic whole.

121 (4). It has been commonly supposed that the beautiful may be *defined* as that which produces certain effects upon our feelings; and the conclusion which follows from this—namely, that judgements of taste are merely *subjective*—that precisely the same thing may, according to circumstances, be *both* beautiful *and* not beautiful—has very frequently been drawn.[1] The conclusions of this chapter suggest a definition of beauty, which may partially explain and entirely remove the difficulties which have led to this error. It appears probable that the beautiful should be *defined* as that of which the admiring contemplation is good in itself.[2] That is to say: To assert that a thing is beautiful is to assert that the

[1] Cf. Xenophon, p. 2.　　　[2] Cf. Ross, p. 320.

cognition of it is an essential element in one of the intrinsically valuable wholes we have been discussing; so
that the question, whether it is *truly* beautiful or not,
depends upon the *objective* question whether the whole in
question is or is not truly good, and does not depend
upon the question whether it would or would not excite
particular feelings in particular persons. This definition
has the double recommendation that it accounts both
for the apparent connexion between goodness and beauty
and for the no less apparent difference between these two
conceptions. It appears, at first sight, to be a strange
coincidence, that there should be two *different* objective
predicates of value, 'good' and 'beautiful', which are
nevertheless so related to one another that whatever is
beautiful is also good. But, if our definition be correct,
the strangeness disappears; since it leaves only one
unanalysable predicate of value, namely 'good', while
'beautiful', though not identical with, is to be defined by
reference to this, being thus, at the same time, different
from and necessarily connected with it. In short, on this
view, to say that a thing is beautiful is to say, not indeed
that it is *itself* good, but that it is a necessary element in
something which is: to prove that a thing is truly beautiful is to prove that a whole, to which it bears a particular
relation as a part, is truly good.[1] And in this way we
should explain the immense predominance, among objects commonly considered beautiful, of *material* objects—
objects of the external senses; since these objects, though
themselves having, as has been said, little or no intrinsic
value, are yet essential constituents in the largest group
of wholes which have intrinsic value. These wholes
themselves may be, and are, also beautiful; but the comparative rarity, with which we regard them as themselves
objects of contemplation, seems sufficient to explain the
association of beauty with external objects.

And secondly (2) it is to be observed that beautiful
objects are themselves, for the most part, organic unities,

[1] Cf. Ross, p. 320.

in this sense, that they are wholes of great complexity, such that the contemplation of any part, by itself, may have no value, and yet that, unless the contemplation of the whole includes the contemplation of that part, it will lose in value. From this it follows that there can be no single criterion of beauty. It will never be true to say: 'This object owes its beauty *solely* to the presence of this characteristic'; nor yet that: 'Wherever this characteristic is present, the object must be beautiful.' All that can be true is that certain objects are beautiful *because* they have certain characteristics, in the sense that they would not be beautiful *unless* they had them. And it may be possible to find that certain characteristics are more or less universally present in all beautiful objects, and are, in this sense, more or less important conditions of beauty. But it is important to observe that the very qualities, which differentiate one beautiful object from all others, are, if the object be truly beautiful, as *essential* to its beauty, as those which it has in common with ever so many others. The object would no more have the beauty it has, without its specific qualities, than without those that are generic; and the generic qualities, *by themselves*, would fail, as completely, to give beauty, as those which are specific.[1]

THEODOR LIPPS

1851–1914

'Empathy', Inward Imitation, and Sense Feelings[2]

Archiv für die gesamte Psychologie, i (1903)

The sensible appearance of the beautiful object is the object of aesthetic satisfaction; but, just as surely, it is not the ground of that satisfaction. The ground is myself or the self, the same self who 'in respect of' or 'over against' the object feel myself pleased or delighted. But we must add that I may not only feel myself pleased or delighted, but also at the same time otherwise affected. It is clear

---

[1] Cf. Plato, p. 5.   [2] *Einfühlung, innere Nachahmung und Organempfindungen.*

that I feel myself, among other things, striving or willing, bestirring myself, or taking pains and, in such striving or contriving, I feel myself meeting or overcoming obstacles, or perhaps yielding to them. I feel myself attaining a goal, satisfying my striving and my will, I feel my efforts successful. In a word I feel various inner activities. And therein I feel myself strong, light, sure, resilient, perhaps proud and the like. Some such manner of feeling myself is always the ground of aesthetic satisfaction.

It can be seen that this ground stands properly midway between the object of aesthetic satisfaction and the self. It must first be remarked that the feelings described have not, like the satisfaction, the beautiful thing as their object. It is myself that I feel as powerfully active, free or proud, when I aesthetically contemplate the beautiful thing. And I do not so feel myself in relation to the thing or over against it, but in it. But just as little is the feeling of activity the object of my satisfaction, that is my pleasure, in the beautiful object. . . . This activity does not stand before me as an object. Just as I do not feel active over against the object but in it, so I do not feel pleasure over against my activity but in it. . . .

When I contemplate the strong, proud, free human figure that stands before me, I do not feel myself strong, proud, and free without qualification as I stand there in my own body in my own right; but I feel myself thus in the contemplated object and only in it. . . . Aesthetic satisfaction consists in this; that it is satisfaction in an object, which yet, just so far as it is an object of satisfaction, is not an object but myself; or it is satisfaction in a self which yet, just so far as it is aesthetically enjoyed, is not myself but something objective. This is what is meant by Empathy: that the distinction between the self and the object disappears or rather does not yet exist.[1] I see a man making powerful, free, light, perhaps courageous motions of some kind, which are objects of my full attention. I feel a sense of effort. I may carry this out

[1] Cf. Collingwood, p. 294.

in real imitative movements. If so, I feel myself active. I do not merely imagine but feel the endeavour, the resistance of obstacles, the overcoming, the achievement. But here are two possibilities. The imitation may be voluntary: I might wish to share the other's feeling of security and pride. But then I have passed quite out of the sphere of aesthetic feeling.[1] The immediate cause of my effort and activity is not the movement seen, but this wish, which is different both from the limbs I see and the self who contemplate.

First, let us suppose that the imitation is involuntary. This is likely in proportion as I am wrapped in contemplation of the seen movement. If I am entirely absorbed in contemplation of the movement, by that very fact I am entirely distracted from what I am doing, namely from the movements which I actually perform, and from all that is going on in my body; I am no longer conscious of this outward imitation. Still the sense of activity and effort persists in my consciousness . . . I still have the consciousness of inward imitation. But this inward imitation happens for my consciousness only in the thing I see. In a word, with my feeling of activity I am absolutely incorporated in the moving body. I am even spatially in its position, so far as the self has a spatial position; I am transported into it. So far as my consciousness goes I am absolutely identical with it. So far as I thus feel myself active in the observed object, I at the same time feel myself free, light, proud, in it. This is aesthetic imitation and also aesthetic empathy.

Here all emphasis must be laid on the 'identity' which exists for my consciousness. This must be taken quite strictly. In conscious imitation I see the movement on the one hand, and I know how the man who executes it feels himself in it. I have an *idea* of the activity which the other feels, and of his freedom and pride. On the other hand I directly experience *my* movement; I feel my activity, freedom, pride, &c.

[1] Cf. Plato, p. 27.

Contrariwise in the aesthetic imitation this opposition is absolutely overcome. The two are made one. The mere idea disappears and is replaced by my actual feeling. And so it comes about that I feel myself carrying out the movement in the other's movement.

In this aesthetic imitation we may seem to find a fact analogous to that of our own unimitative movement. The only difference seems to be that I now have the consciousness of experiencing and carrying out a movement which in fact, and for subsequent reflection, is another's. But this would be to overlook the essential difference. In both instances my inner activity, my effort and success, the experienced satisfaction of my effort, are all *mine*. But they are not in both instances the activities of the same self. In unimitative movement the activity belongs to my real self, my whole personality endowed, as it actually is, with all its sensations, ideas, thoughts, feelings, and especially with the motive or inner occasion from which the movement springs. In aesthetic imitation, on the other hand, the self is an ideal self. But this must not be misunderstood. This ideal self too is real, but it is not the practical self. It is the contemplative self which only exists in the lingering contemplation of the object. . . .

So far we have treated aesthetic imitation as being outward as well as inward, as though we actually made the movements we were watching. But this outward completion of the movement may not emerge. . . . The chief feature of aesthetic imitation is that it aims at activity of the self. In this instinctive tendency to self-activity is its ultimate ground. But it also lies in the nature of the impulse to this imitation that the effort for such self-activity can be satisfied in a mere perception of the movement, which relaxes the effort of imitation. So this effort seeks no further satisfaction, and in particular it does not seek satisfaction in experiences of the sense-organs of our own bodies. . . .

Feelings due to my bodily states disappear from my

consciousness in proportion as I am lost in contemplation of the aesthetic object, since it is an object to which my bodily states do not belong.[1]

The beauty of an object is always the beauty of that object and never the pleasantness of anything else which is not the beautiful object nor belonging to it. I mean particularly that it is impossible that pleasure in the condition of my body—which is something other than the contemplated object and perhaps far removed from it in space—should be felt by me as a pleasure in that object.

A further consideration of 'Empathy'
Archiv. iv (1905)

It is a very different thing to say that a gesture seems to me the expression of pride or grief (or, better, that it actually expresses to me or to my consciousness pride or grief) and to say that when I perceive the gesture the idea of pride or grief is associated with it. If I see a stone the idea of hardness, smoothness, &c., is associated with this perception. But I never therefore say that the stone I see or the stone as I see it 'expresses' hardness or smoothness. On the contrary, I say of what I perceive when I contemplate the stone, that it is hard or smooth. Conversely I do not say of the gesture that it is proud or sad, or if I say so, I know that I express myself inaccurately. I know it would be better to say it is a gesture *of* pride or grief. But this only means it is one which expresses pride or grief. . . . The relation between the gesture and what it expresses is symbolical . . . it is empathy.

What is connected with the perceived object merely by association in the usual sense, does not belong to the aesthetic object as such. The fact that Faust's trouble and despair affect us unpleasantly does not prevent our total experience of them from being pleasant, owing to the enrichment, extension, and elevation of mind which it contains. The real self does not . . . experience the troubles of Faust, . . . it is the contemplative or ideal self.

[1] Cf. Mitchell, p. 263.

We must not, however, forget the distinction between positive and negative empathy, to illustrate which I have put side by side the empathy with a gesture of noble pride and that with one of foolish vanity. The feeling embodied for me in the former makes an impression on me which is readily accepted. My whole being rebels against the suggestion that I should feel as the latter demands. . . . I am aware of the noble pride as an affirmation of vitality which I gladly embrace, of the foolish vanity as something repulsive because it is the negation of vitality.[1] But of neither have I merely an idea; both are experienced, the one as a free activity (though not wholly spontaneous, since it springs from the object and is stimulated by it), the other as an oppression.

The only condition under which the state of mind presented to me gives me pleasure is when I 'approve' it.[2] . . . When I 'approve' a past pleasure, I feel pleasure again, not at having had a pleasure in the past, but at what pleased me before. 'Approval' is the actual harmony of my present nature and activity with what I approve. Just so I must 'approve' the mental activities I apprehend in others (that is to say I must sympathize with them) if they are to please me.[3] . . .

There is a distinction between empathic feelings—those which I have 'in an object'—and those which I have about an object. . . . If I feel my effort in a column, my effort is that of the column,[4] and this is quite different from my effort, for instance, to erect or ruin the column. Or again, if I empathically feel my gaiety and cheerfulness in the blue sky, then the blue sky smiles. My gaiety is in it, belongs to it. This is quite different from smiling at or about something. . . .

Empathy implies that my apprehension of a sensible object immediately involves a tendency in me to a particular mental activity and that, owing to an instinct which in the last resort can be analysed no further, these

---

[1] Cf. Richards, p. 281.   [2] *billigen.*
[3] Cf. Ducasse, pp. 314, 316.   [4] Cf. Home, p. 94.

two, the apprehension and the definite mental activity, are one inseparable activity. . . . The consciousness of this relation is the consciousness of pleasure in an object and presupposes the apprehension of the object. It is Empathy.

SIR WILLIAM MITCHELL
1861–

Structure and Growth of the Mind (1907)

vii, 1. In reading an experience into other minds, and in our feeling it with them, we have the most obvious examples of two mental acts. . . . One of them is the individualizing of an object; the other is the being absorbed in it.[1] . . .

2. A fellow-feeling with lifeless things may seem a contradiction, but it fills the poetry of nature old and new. The trees of the field clap their hands, the little hills shout for joy, great mountains have a voice, break forth into singing, look abroad with silent brow; there are souls of lonely places, the moanings of the homeless sea, the sullen river and the woods waving and muttering. In poetry nature is constantly represented as the body of spirit, as

[1] These two acts comprise what is vaguely called 'inner imitation', especially by German writers on the sense of beauty. The term has now been given up for *Einfühlung*, a word coined expressly to mean (a) our reading a spirit into others and into things, and (b) our having fellow-feeling with them. In all early *Einfühlung* both factors are present; just as we do not feel a colour first as ours and then as the quality of a thing, so, as mentioned in the text above, we do not first find another's experience as ours and then transfer it to him. And always the first factor is present if the second is present. But frequently the first comes to be present without the second; we think an object to have an experience without ourselves living it with him. Hence the two factors have been distinguished, the first as *Einfühlung*—the reading an experience into an object; and the second as *Einsfühlung*—the feeling at one with it. When the question arose how much of ourselves we read into things, the word was naturally extended from reading an experience to reading a life, and then (most fully by Lipps, *Aesthetik*) to reading any individuality into things. With this extension *Einfühlung* corresponds to the first of the two acts mentioned in the text, viz. to individualizing. The second of the two— absorption in an object—includes *Einsfühlung*, but extends to our living in any object whether we individualize it or not; it is our experience of any object in which we are finding a purely intrinsic interest. (W. M.)

concentred in a life intense. To mingle with the universe and feel, not only with rattling thunders, self-poised stars, or the quiet of her sky, but with common plants, the silver-fall of springs, and other quite earthly things, and in the golden time, our time of learning, to fling arms of love round Nature and find her living, as Pygmalion found the statue, that is the language of the literature that we have to get by heart when we are young.[1] . . .

And, to the apparent contradiction of making lifeless things feel, we appear to add another; for in sympathizing with them we are sometimes said to give them our spirit, but as often we are said to enter into theirs. We speak of giving them the colour of our minds, of clothing them with sentiment, of charging them with emotion, of throwing a veil of mystery over them, and so giving them their beauty. On the other hand we certainly have to find, and not feign, the beauty in them, if it is real.[2] If their beauty or ugliness, their glory or meanness, is always or ever felt in a fellow-feeling with them, it must be with them as we find them, and directly, not by way of after-thought. A tree is in many ways like a man, erect and defiant, or bowing to trouble, gnarled and crippled with years, stretching out its branches like arms, but 'the branches and the stretching would not give a better aesthetic effect, but would be ludicrous, the more nearly they resembled the form of human arms and their movement.' 'Nor is a tree more beautiful because I make a dryad live in it, nor mountains because of nymphs or dwarfs; and the stick that a child treats as a living thing, dressing and undressing it, is not made more beautiful than it is in itself.'[3] . . .

7. We read things in our image though we regard them as lifeless and unconscious. For, as merely individual, each possesses and unites its qualities, and exercises its powers in a community of other things. The only way

---

[1] Cf. Wordsworth, *Preface*, pp. 128–9.
[2] Cf. Ruskin on the Pathetic Fallacy, p. 179.
[3] Lipps, *Aesthetik*, i. pp. 166, 168 (W. M.). Cf. Wordsworth, Sonnet xxxi.

in which we can set this property of theirs directly before us is to live it. As for merely thinking about it, we can do that in a thought which merely means it; but, in order to realize this meaning, we must think it out, and that is to live it, for, of course, our own is the only life that we feel. There is no opposition between the thought of this real nature of things as we experience them, and the thought of nature as the real or independent system by the discovery of which we can calculate and so far control them. Art takes the one fact, science the other, and so their faces are set in totally different directions. If we looked at nature as science aims at finally presenting it, we should never suppose that the divergence of the path of art from that of science must be in play, or a weak preference for the appearance instead of the reality of things; and we should not look on the mere understanding of things as an advance on their aesthetic and sympathetic understanding. . . . Science develops the notion of them as stimuli, art develops them as objects to experience.

viii, 6. Shapes and curves, as well as rhythms, are naturally gay or austere; and rhythms, like shapes, are smooth or rugged. These affective qualities of sound and sight are not borrowed from the associations in which we happen to have met them. We do not have to learn them, though their expressiveness develops with our experience. . . .

The object is not merely pleasant or unpleasant, stimulating or depressing, but beautiful or ugly. The voice, the colour, the day is felt as having a nature of its own, which is revealed and embodied in the sensible quality, viz. the timbre, the brilliance, or the gloom.[1] The nature that we thus find in the object is no other than that which we live when absorbed in it, and so it depends on our past experience how much we find in the timbre, the brilliance, and the gloom. They do not need to recall our days of passion, gladness, or misery, for then we should be leaving them for these; but it makes all the difference whether we see them with a mind that has felt much or little.[2] . . .

[1] Cf. Leon, p. 284.   [2] Cf. Santayana, § 50, p. 201.

7. Since they can express no nature but one that we can live, they express nothing that we do not read into them. But this is an explanation, and it comes to us with the same surprise that we have in finding that the very individuality and powers of things are in them after our image.[1] As there, the explanation does not alter our perceiving. For a thing to have aesthetic quality it must be felt beautiful or ugly in itself, just as its colour is felt to be in it and not in our eye. Its beauty or ugliness must be felt as expressing its own nature, but its nature as we live and experience it. We expect all the arts to have truth as well as to please, and those artists are right enough who claim to paint only what they see. But their copying is a revealing; it is nature as they see it; and it has taken them to see it, if their work has any distinction. There is no moral obligation that we should be true to real or actual nature, except where that is professed, as in portraiture; but an object of imagination has its own nature as an object to experience, and to this they must be true. . . .

xviii, 17 (ii). The explanation of aesthetic interest as motor and organic sensation can best be examined in a series of three simple views about our appreciation of visible form.

(a) It was perhaps a natural supposition that, as the eye follows a regular or a graceful outline, it describes the same regular or graceful curves; that we feel pleasure in this movement, or in the ease of it, and that we turn this pleasure into a quality of the object whose outlines we follow. But it has recently been discovered, by photographing the movements of the eye, that instead of describing the curve continuously, and as it is, the eye moves in a series of jerks from point to point on the curve, and that the lines between the points are straight rather than curved. 'If mere ease of ocular movement were the controlling principle in our enjoyment of forms, we should enjoy straight lines and angles rather than curves.' It is

[1] Cf. Collingwood, p. 295, Alexander, p. 270.

essential that the muscles moving our eyes do not force their awkward movements on our notice: 'they are mere scene-shifters'. In order to feel the beauty of the curve, we must be absorbed in it, and, if it is a single curve, we may, in order to this, trace it with our eyes. But, first, it is not this experience of the movement of our eyes that we feel to be beautiful, but the curve. This objection has always been met by saying that we deceive ourselves. But there is no answer to the new objection. The movements of our eyes do not describe graceful curves by any means; indeed, they do not describe the same curve twice when tracing the same object. And so, secondly, though we feel their movement, neither it, nor our feeling of it, can be the cause or the base of our aesthetic satisfaction in the object.

(*b*) Instead of eye-movements, our whole bodily attitude has been thought to account for our like and dislike of visible forms and attitudes. 'Here is a jar equally common in antiquity and in modern peasant ware. Looking at this jar one has a specific sense of a *whole*. One's bodily sensations are extraordinarily composed, balanced, correlated in their diversity. To begin with, the feet press on the ground while the eyes fix the base of the jar. Then one accompanies the *lift up*, so to speak, of the body of the jar by a *lift up* of one's own body; and one accompanies by a slight sense of downward pressure of the head the downward pressure of the widened rim on the jar's top. Meantime the jar's equal sides bring both lungs into equal play; the curve outwards of the jar's two sides is simultaneously followed by an *inspiration* as the eyes move up to the jar's widest point. Then expiration begins, and the lungs seem slowly to collapse as the curve inward is followed by the eyes, till, the narrow part of the neck being reached, the ocular following of the widened-out top provokes a short inspiration. Moreover, the shape of the jar provokes movements of balance, the left curve a shifting on to the left foot', and so on; in fact, 'the phenomenon of inner motor adjustment must be, in each

single case, exactly as complex, as co-ordinated, and as
individual a totality as the artistic form perceived is complex, co-ordinated, and individual.'[1] If this does not
mean that we have to make a jar of ourselves in order to
be absorbed in the jar before us, it means that we take the
nearest substitute; we take an invisible one, in order, I
suppose, that we may escape ridicule. Ridiculous though
the notion is, it only carries out thoroughly a theory that
may appear reasonable enough, if we recall our experience when absorbed in listening to a march, in
watching a tussle, or in looking at a statue of man or
beast, whose attitude is energetic, drooping, light, or
burdened. For, first, we cannot appreciate those things
if we have never marched or fought, and been energetic,
or the reverse. And, secondly, to take an actual posture
is the way to experience it most vividly; and, the more
vivid the imagining, the nearer it comes to our adopting
the posture. Hence, at first sight, it does not seem extravagant to say that, the more we are absorbed in the
object, the more we must copy its curves, its balance, and
movements, in our body; or, short of actually copying it,
the more we must innervate the necessary muscles to the
edge of action. But it would also follow, first, that no
ordinary person could appreciate even so simple an
aesthetic object as this jar; for he has not only to begin
with it as a whole, but, while adding details, he must
continue to be absorbed in the whole. And, secondly,
the changes in his breathing and in his posture, actual or
imagined, must be beyond or beneath his notice of them.
For, if they called his attention to themselves, they would
hinder and not help, far less actually be, his absorption
in the object. . . . Absorbed in a part, e.g. the curve of a
jar, we move our hand along it, or feel our hand as if
passing over it; but we lose nothing of it when we learn
to dispense with this, and become absorbed in the whole.

[1] Vernon Lee and Anstruther Thomson in *Contemporary Review*, vol. lxxii,
pp. 554, 681. The view is modified in *Quarterly Review*, April 1904, in favour
of Lipps's theory. Cf. also Vernon Lee, *The Beautiful*. Cf. Lipps, p. 256.

... It is not that we need be less absorbed in body the more we are absorbed in spirit, but simply that, as in all learning, our nervous system becomes relatively independent of peripheral stimulation and peripheral emphasis.

CLIVE BELL
1881–

Art (1913)

i. Lines and colours combined in a particular way, certain forms and relations of forms stir our aesthetic emotions. These relations and combinations of lines and colours, these aesthetically moving forms, I call 'Significant Form'; and 'Significant Form'[1] is the one quality common to all works of visual art. . . .

It is not what I call an aesthetic emotion that most of us feel generally for natural beauty. . . .

The representative element in a work of art may or may not be harmful; always it is irrelevant.[2] For, to appreciate a work of art, we need bring with us nothing from life, no knowledge of its ideas and affairs, no familiarity with its emotions.[3] . . . To appreciate a work of art we need bring with us nothing but a sense of form and colour and a knowledge of three-dimensional space. . . . It is the mark of great art that its appeal is universal and eternal.

iii. It seems to me possible, though by no means certain, that created form moves us so profoundly because it expresses the emotion of its creator. . . . If this be so, it will explain that curious but undeniable fact, that what I call material beauty (e.g. the wing of a butterfly) does not move most of us in at all the same way as a work of art moves us. It is beautiful form, but it is not significant form. It moves us, but it does not move us aesthetically. . . . For what, then, does the artist feel the emotion that he

---

[1] Cf. Prall, pp. 310–11.
[2] Cf. Hegel, p. 165, Bradley, p. 226, Fry, p. 267, Hulme, p. 275, Richards, p. 280, and Dewey, p. 307.   [3] Cf. Nietzsche, p. 185.

is supposed to express? Sometimes it certainly comes to him through material beauty. . . . Can it be that sometimes for the artist material beauty is somehow significant—that is, capable of provoking aesthetic emotion? And if the form that provokes aesthetic emotion be form that expresses something, can it be that material beauty is to him expressive? . . . It is for, or at any rate through, pure form that he feels his inspired emotion.

Now to see objects as pure forms is to see them as ends in themselves. For though, of course, forms are related to each other as parts of a whole, they are related on terms of equality; they are not means to anything except emotion. . . . Who has not, once at least in his life, had a sudden vision of landscape as pure form?[1] . . .

No one ever doubted that a Sung pot or a Romanesque church was as much an expression of emotion as any picture that ever was painted.[2]

But if an object considered as an end in itself moves us more profoundly (i.e. has greater significance) than the same object considered as a means to practical ends or as a thing related to human interests—and this undoubtedly is the case—we can only suppose that when we consider anything as an end in itself we become aware of that in it which is of greater moment than any qualities it may have acquired from keeping company with human beings. Instead of recognizing its accidental and conditioned importance, we become aware of its essential reality, of the God in everything, of the universal in the particular, of the all-pervading rhythm. . . . Whatever the world of aesthetic contemplation may be, it is not the world of human business and passion; in it the chatter and tumult of material existence is unheard, or heard only as the echo of some more ultimate harmony.

[1] Cf. Ruskin, p. 178.
[2] Cf. Plato, *Republic*, p. 18, and Herbart, *Encyclopaedia*, § 72, p. 156.

ROGER FRY
1866–

Vision and Design (1923)

ii. *An Essay in Aesthetics* (1909). The artist passes from the stage of merely gratifying our demand for sensuous order and variety to that where he arouses our emotions. I will call the various methods by which this is effected the emotional elements of design.

The first element is that of the rhythm of the line with which the forms are delineated. The drawn line is the record of a gesture, and that gesture is modified by the artist's feeling which is thus communicated to us directly.

The second element is mass. When an object is so represented that we recognize it as having inertia we feel its power of resisting movement, or communicating its own movement to other bodies, and our imaginative reaction to such an image is governed by our experience of mass in actual life.

The third element is space. The same-sized square on two pieces of paper can be made by very simple means to appear to represent either a cube two or three inches high, or a cube of hundreds of feet, and our reaction to it is proportionately changed.

The fourth element is that of light and shade. Our feelings towards the same object become totally different according as we see it strongly illuminated against a black background or dark against light.

A fifth element is that of colour. That this has a direct emotional effect is evident from such words as gay, dull, melancholy in relation to colour.

I would suggest the possibility of another element, though perhaps it is only a compound of mass and space: it is that of the inclination to the eye of a plane, whether it is impending over or leaning away from us. . . .

If we represent these various elements in simple diagrammatic terms, this effect upon the emotions is, it must be confessed, very weak.[1] Rhythm of line, for instance, is incomparably weaker in its stimulus of the muscular sense than is rhythm addressed to the ear in music, and such diagrams can at best arouse only faint ghostlike echoes of emotions of differing qualities; but when these emotional elements are combined with the presentation of natural appearances, above all with the appearance of the human body, we find that this effect is indefinitely heightened.[1] When we look, for instance, at Michelangelo's 'Jeremiah'.

Transformations (1926)

1. *Some Questions in Aesthetics.* Our reaction to works of art is a reaction to a relation and not to sensations or objects or persons or events. . . . Responses to sensation may be very rich and complex and tinged with emotion, but they are distinct (from this). . . . In the case of works of art the whole end and purpose is found in the exact quality of the emotional state.

SAMUEL ALEXANDER
1859–

Space, Time, and Deity (1920)

Book III, Chap. IX, D. *Beauty and Ugliness.* Perhaps the simplest way to understand beauty is to contrast the beautiful object on the one hand with a percept and on the other with an illusion. As contrasted with the percept, the beautiful is illusory, but it differs from illusion in that it is not erroneous. Considered from the point of view of cognition, the beautiful object[2] is illusory, for it does not as an external reality contain the characters it possesses for the aesthetic sense. I perceive the tree in front of me to have a reverse side though I see only the front; but the tree really has a reverse side, and if I change my position the back of it is now seen and the front is supplied in idea. The marble is seen cold, to revert to the

---

[1] Cf. Schiller, p. 126, Bell, p. 264, and Hulme, p. 275.   [2] Cf. Moore, p. 247.

trite example, but the cold which is only present in idea really belongs to the marble, and I may in turn feel it cold and with eyes shut represent its whiteness in idea. The painted tree on the other hand looks solid but is not, and no change of my position helps me to see its other side. The Hermes is a marble block of a certain form and is perceived in its real qualities of solidity and hardness, but the block does not possess the repose and playfulness and dignity that I read into it aesthetically. The words of a poem are not merely descriptive of their object, but suffused with suggestions of feeling and significance which a mere scientific description would not possess. The more perfect the artistry the more definitely does the work of art present in suggestion features which as a cognized object it has not. Mr. Berenson compares the two Madonnas that stand side by side in the Academy at Florence—the one by Cimabue, the other by Giotto.[1] The Cimabue Madonna is flat and looks flat, though otherwise beautiful. The Giotto is flat but looks three-dimensional, and so far is the more perfectly beautiful.

What is true of works of art is true of natural objects, with the necessary qualifications. In general the natural object is, when its beauty is appreciated, perceived incorrectly, or if it actually has the characters which we add to it, that is for aesthetic appreciation an accident, and is the source of a different and additional pleasure.[2] Like the artist in painting a landscape, we select from or add to nature in feeling its beauty. Literal fidelity is, or at least may be, fatal to beauty, for it is the means of securing not beauty but truth and satisfies our scientific rather than our aesthetic sense. If this is true for the mere onlooker, it is still more so for the painter or poet who renders the work of nature in an alien material which has its own prescriptions. Or we read our moods into the scene; or endow animate or even inanimate objects with our feelings; see daffodils for instance out-

[1] *Florentine Painters of the Renaissance* (New York and London, ed. 3), p. 13 (S. A.). [2] Cf. Moore, p. 249.

doing in glee the waves which dance beside them, or fancy a straight slender stem as springing from the ground, or liken with it as Odysseus did the youthful grace of a girl.

The cases of natural beauty which most obstinately resist this interpretation are the graceful movements of animals or the beauty of human faces, a large part of which arises from their expressiveness of life and character. You may see a face as majestic as that of the Zeus of Otricoli and the man may perchance possess that character; or the horse's arching of his neck may really proceed from the self-display we read into it in finding it beautiful. But in the first place we read the feeling or the character into these forms before we learn that the creatures in question possess them; and in the next place though a natural form may thus in reality happen to possess the supplement which we add from our minds, and may so far be unlike the work of art, yet the intellectual recognition that it does conform to the aesthetic appreciation is not itself aesthetic. This is best shown by the truth that the artistic representation may be more beautiful than the original, like the suggested movements of the winged Victory or of the figures in Botticelli's Spring. But also the knowledge that the natural object possesses the imputed characters—which is aesthetically indifferent—may even mar the aesthetical effect, for when we learn that a man is really as fine a character as he looks, our appreciation is apt to turn to moral instead of aesthetic admiration. In place of aesthetic contemplation we may have sympathy or practical respect. We may then safely follow the guidance of the beauty of art and declare that in natural objects beauty, so far as it is appreciated aesthetically, involves illusion.[1] . . .

Thus in the beautiful object, whether of art or nature, one part is contributed by the mind, and it is relatively a matter of indifference whether the mind in question is that of the person who creates the work of art or that of the mere spectator, who follows in the artist's

[1] Cf. Moore, p. 249.

traces. In the case of natural beauty, the spectator and the creator are one. The element contributed by the mind may vary from the mere addition of external properties, as in seeing the flat picture solid, e.g. in the bare aesthetic effect of the drawing of a cube or a truncated pyramid, up to distinctively human characters[1] of feeling or character, as in animating a statue with pride, or words or sounds with emotion as in a lyric or in music. Animation with life is intermediate between these extremes, for life though less than mental, and still for us something external which we contemplate, is yet on a higher level of external existence than solidity of form. It is only through what is thus added that the beautiful object has meaning or character or expressiveness.

I add that the expressiveness need not be something characteristic of man. The expressiveness of the work of art is to be itself, to be what it represents, to have the significance appropriate to it; for the painted animal or tree to seem alive and to grow or move according to its kind; for the drawn cube to look solid; for the pillar to seem (and to be) perfectly adjusted to support the weight it bears, and to bear it with ease. An ugly portico with stunted Doric columns gives the impression that the weight which the columns bear is crushing them; the tall columns of the Parthenon suggest that the roof is a light burden; the suggestion in neither case being true in fact. We may naturally enough render these impressions by investing the columns with life—springing up from the ground, and the like—but they belong really to the mechanical order. Thus the imputation of life and character enters into the expressiveness of the beautiful object, only when that object means life or character. They are but one species of expressiveness. Further in every case, no matter how much of mind or character is read into the thing by the mind for which it is beautiful, the expressiveness remains that of the thing and not that of the creating or appreciating mind itself.[2] In choice and

[1] ? imputations.   [2] Cf. Mitchell, p. 261.

treatment of his subject the artist impresses himself indeed upon his work, which so far expresses or reveals him. But to feel Shakespeare in *Hamlet* is not to appreciate *Hamlet* aesthetically but to judge it critically. In the expressiveness which he adds to his material from his very personality the artist depersonalizes the work of art.[1] Even in a beautiful lyric the passion ceases to be merely that of the artist. It is the paradox of beauty that its expressiveness belongs to the beautiful thing itself and yet would not be there except for the mind. Under the conditions of the material in which it is expressed, the beautiful owes some part of its meaning to the mind, and so far it owes to the mind not only its *percipi* as every perceived object does, but its *esse*. We have therefore all the greater need of caution in extending what is true of beauty to the objects of knowledge, whose *esse* is not *percipi*, but *esse*, independently of the mind which is compresent with them.

The beauty of the beautiful object lies in the congruence or coherence of its parts. According to the ancient doctrine it is the unity within that variety. Of these elements some are intrinsic to the beautiful thing, and some are imported from the mind and thereby belong to the thing; and it is a condition of the beauty that its external form must be such as to bear and compel that imputation. Disproportion or want of perspective, to take the simplest illustrations, may mar the beauty. Or the material may be inadequate to the effect, as when an architect builds in terra-cotta what requires stone for stateliness. In virtue of the harmonious blending within the beautiful of the two sets of elements, some existing in reality and some supplied by the mind, the unity in variety is also expressive or significant. The beautiful satisfies both the ancient and the modern criterion; and a new reality is generated in which mind and the non-mental have become organic to each other, not in the sense that the beautiful necessarily contains mind, though it may do

[1] Cf. Wilde, p. 196.

so, e.g. in a picture of a man, but that its expressiveness is due to the blending of elements supplied from two sources, and the external beautiful thing is beautiful only through this fitness of the externally real elements to their expressiveness. Like truth and goodness, beauty exists only as possessed by mind, but whereas in them mind and the external still sit loosely to each other, and in the one case the mind contemplates an external reality which owes to the mind its truth but not its reality, and in the other case the mind alters reality practically but the practical results do not owe their character to mind but only their goodness; in beauty external reality and mind penetrate each other, and the external thing receives its character of coherence from its connexion with mind.

Thus when Kant[1] declared that beauty was so judged because it set the understanding at work in harmony with the imagination, he spoke truly, but according to his fashion in subjective terms, and so far inadequately. Truly, because, whereas in perception of an external object the imaginative elements are but a part of the real object which is cognized, in beauty the supplementing imagination is independent of what is perceived and yet is blended with what is perceived into a new aesthetic whole. Inadequately, because the beauty or coherence between the elements supplied in sense and in imagination belongs to the aesthetic object, and the interplay of cognition and imagination describes only the condition of the mental process involved in the aesthetic appreciation and not the beauty of the aesthetic thing itself. Such an account considers beauty as a purely subjective character, whereas beauty belongs to the complex of mind and its object, or as I have so often expressed it, to the beautiful object as possessed by the mind. Since the beautiful object owes one part of its constituents to the actual participation of the mind, beauty is in this sense a tertiary 'quality' of the beautiful object, thus conceived.

[1] Cf. p. 113.

THOMAS ERNEST HULME

1883–1917

Speculations

Ed. H. Read, 1924[1]

A Critique of Satisfaction. The change of sensibility which has enabled us to regard Egyptian, Polynesian, and Negro work as *art* and not as archaeology has had a double effect. It has made us realize that what we took to be the necessary principles of aesthetic constitute in reality only a psychology of Renaissance and Classical art. At the same time it has made us realize the essential *unity* of these latter arts. For we see that they both rest on certain common presuppositions, of which we only become conscious when we see them *denied* by other arts (cf. the work of Riegl).[2]

Modern Art. You have these two different kinds of art, you have first the art which is natural to you, Greek art and modern art since the Renaissance. In these arts the lines are soft and vital. You have other arts like Egyptian, Indian, and Byzantine, where everything tends to be angular, where curves tend to be hard and geometrical, where the representation of the human body, for example, is often entirely non-vital, and distorted to fit into stiff lines and cubical shapes of various kinds.

What is the cause of the extraordinary difference between these geometrical arts and the arts we are accustomed to admire? Why do they show none of the qualities which we are accustomed to find in art?

We may at once put on one side the idea that the difference between archaic and later art is due to a difference of capacity, the idea that geometrical shapes are used because the artist had not the technical ability

---

[1] Hulme represents with convenient brevity the ideas which Worringer, Riegl, both of whom he cites, and Wölfflin support with historical and technical detail out of place here. As he did not live to edit his notes, I have ventured to transpose some extracts.

[2] *Stilfragen* and *Spätrömische Kunst-Industrie* (1901).

necessary for carving the more natural representation of the body. The characteristics of archaic art are not due to incapacity. In Egypt, at the time when the monumental sculpture showed a stylification as great as any we find in archaic art, the domestic art of the period exhibited a most astonishing realism. In pure technical ability, in mastery of raw material, the Egyptians have never been surpassed. It is quite obvious that what they did was intentional.[1]

We are forced back on the idea, then, that geometrical art differs from our own because the creators of that art had in view an object entirely different from that of the creators of more naturalistic art. . . .

Take first the art which is most natural to us. What tendency is behind this, what need is it designed to satisfy?

This art as contrasted with geometrical art can be broadly described as naturalism or realism—using these words in their widest sense and entirely excluding the mere imitation of nature. The source of the pleasure felt by the spectator before the products of art of this kind is a feeling of increased vitality, a process which German writers on aesthetics call empathy (*Einfühlung*). . . . Any work of art we find beautiful is an objectification of our own pleasure in activity and our own vitality. The worth of a line or form consists in the value of the life which it contains for us. Putting the matter more simply we may say that in this art there is always a feeling of liking for, and pleasure in, the forms and movements to be found in nature. It is obvious therefore that this art can only occur in a people whose relation to outside nature is such that it admits of this feeling of pleasure and[2] its contemplation.[3]

Turn now to geometrical life.[4] It most obviously exhibits no delight in nature and no striving after vitality.

[1] I understand Professor Gleadowe to suggest (Slade Lecture at Oxford, November 1930) that the 'intention' of some ancient, as of some modern, monumental works was to satisfy the conventionality of wealthy patrons, but that 'domestic' works were more sincere.

[2] ? in.   [3] Cf. Hegel on Classical Art, p. 169.   [4] ? art *or* line.

Its forms are always what can be described as stiff and lifeless. . . . This is what Worringer[1] calls the *tendency to abstraction*. What is the nature of this tendency? What is the condition of mind of the people whose art is governed by it?

It can be described most generally as a feeling of separation in the face of outside nature.

While a naturalistic art is the result of a happy pantheistic relation between man and the outside world, the tendency to abstraction, on the contrary, occurs in races whose attitude to the outside world is the exact contrary of this. This feeling of separation naturally takes different forms at different levels of culture.

Take first the case of more primitive people. They live in a world whose lack of order and seeming arbitrariness must inspire them with a certain fear. . . . In art this state of mind results in a desire to create a certain abstract geometrical shape,[2] which, being durable and permanent, shall be a refuge from the flux and impermanence of outside nature. . . .

In the case of the orientals the feeling of separation from the world could not be dispelled by knowledge. Their sense of the unfathomable existence was greater than that of the Greeks. A satisfaction with appearances[3] is limited to Europe. It is only there that the superhuman abstract idea of the divine has been expressed by banal representation. No knowledge could damp down the Indian inborn fear of the world, since it stands, not as in the case of primitive man before knowledge, but above it. Their art consequently remains geometrical. . . .

However strong the desire for abstraction, it cannot be satisfied with the reproduction of merely inorganic forms. A perfect cube looks stable in comparison with the flux of appearance, but one might be pardoned if one felt no particular interest in the eternity of a cube;[4] but if you

---

[1] *Abstraktion und Einfühlung* (1907). Cf. H. Wölfflin, *Kunstgeschichtliche Grundbegriffe* (1919).   [2] Cf. Hegel on symbolic art, p. 168.
[3] Cf. Nietzsche, p. 185.   [4] Cf. Bell, p. 264, and Fry, p. 267.

can put man into some geometrical shape which lifts him out of the intransience [1] of the organic, then the matter is different. In pursuing such an aim you inevitably, of course, sacrifice the pleasure that comes from reproduction of the natural.

Humanism. The disgust with the trivial and accidental characteristics of living shapes, the searching after an austerity, a *perfection* and rigidity which vital things can never have, lead here [in Byzantine art] to the use of forms which can almost be called geometrical. Man is subordinate to certain absolute values: there is no delight in the human form, leading to its *natural* reproduction; it is always distorted to fit into more abstract forms which convey an intense religious emotion.

These two arts thus correspond exactly to the thought of their respective periods: Byzantine art to the ideology which looks on man and all existing things as imperfect and sinful in comparison with certain abstract values and *perfections*. The other art corresponds to the humanist ideology, which looks on man and life as good. . . . We place *Perfection* where it should not be—on this human plane. As we are painfully aware that nothing *actual* can be *perfect*, we imagine the perfection to be not where we are, but some distance along one of the roads. This is the essence of all Romanticism. [2] Most frequently, in literature, at any rate, we imagine an impossible perfection along the road of sex; but any one can name the other roads for himself.

C. K. OGDEN, I. A. RICHARDS, AND JAMES WOOD

The Foundations of Aesthetics (1922)

xii. What we refer to by 'the common peculiar quality' [of beautiful things] is something different from the character of the effect we notice [in ourselves].

---

[1] ? transience *or* impermanence.   [2] Cf. Hegel on romantic art, p. 170.

xiv. We are aware of certain shapes and colours. These when more closely studied usually reveal themselves as in three dimensions, or, as artists say, in forms. These forms must in some cases, but in others may not, be identified as this or that physical object. Throughout this process, impulses are aroused and sustained, which gradually increase in variety and degree of systematization. To these systems in their early stages will correspond the emotions such as joy, horror, melancholy, anger, and mirth; or attitudes, such as love, veneration, sentimentality. . . .

Not all impulses, it is plain, as usually excited, are naturally harmonious, for conflict is possible and common. A complete systematization must take the form of such an adjustment as will preserve free play to every impulse, with entire avoidance of frustration. In any equilibrium of this kind, however momentary, we are experiencing beauty. . . . As we realize beauty we become more fully ourselves the more our impulses are engaged. . . . The reason why equilibrium is a justification for the preference of one experience before another, is the fact that it brings into play all our faculties. . . . Through no other experience can the full richness and complexity of our environment be realized. The ultimate value of equilibrium is that it is better to be fully than partially alive.

IVOR ARMSTRONG RICHARDS
1893–

Principles of Literary Criticism (1924)

ii. All modern aesthetics rest upon an assumption which has been strangely little discussed, the assumption that there is a distinct *kind* of mental activity present in what are called aesthetic experiences. . . . It may be held that there is some unique kind of mental element which enters into aesthetic experiences and into no others. Thus Mr. Clive Bell[1] used to maintain the existence of an unique

---

[1] Cf. p. 264 and Bergson, p. 207, Bradley, p. 210, Gentile, p. 322.

emotion 'aesthetic emotion' as the *differentia*. . . . Alternatively, the aesthetic experience may contain no unique constituent and may be of the usual stuff but with a special form. . . . While admitting that such experiences can be distinguished, I shall be at pains to show that they are closely similar to many other experiences, that they differ chiefly in the connexions between their constituents, and that they are only a further development,[1] a finer organization, of ordinary experiences, and not in the least a new and different kind of thing.[2] . . . We are accustomed to say that a picture is beautiful, instead of saying that it causes an experience in us that is valuable in certain ways. . . .

vii. Anything is valuable which satisfies an appetency. . . Any one *will actually prefer* to satisfy a greater number of equal appetencies rather than a less. . . . The importance of an impulse can be defined for our purposes as *the extent of the disturbance of other impulses in the individual's activities which the thwarting of the impulse involves.*

viii. The most valuable states of mind, then, are those which involve the widest and most comprehensive co-ordination of activities and the least curtailment, conflict, starvation, and restriction. . . . [The artist's] work is the ordering of what in most minds is disordered. . . . [Tragedy] is still the form under which the mind may most clearly and freely contemplate the human situation, its issues unclouded, its possibilities revealed.

x. The world of poetry . . . is made up of experiences of exactly the same kinds[3] as those that come to us in other ways. Every poem is, however, a strictly limited piece of experience, a piece which breaks up more or less easily if alien elements intrude. . . . We must keep the poem undisturbed by these or we fail to read it and have some other experience instead. For these reasons we establish a severance, we draw a boundary between the poem and what is not the poem in our experience. But this is no severance between different things but between different

[1] Cf. p. 283.   [2] Cf. Wordsworth, p. 129.   [3] Cf. p. 283.

systems of the same activities.[1] . . . We cannot e.g. read Shelley adequately while believing that all his views are moonshine.[2] . . . Into an adequate reading of the greater kinds of poetry, everything not private and peculiar to the individual reader must come in. The reader must be required to wear no blinkers, to overlook nothing which is relevant, to shut off no part of himself from participation.

xiii. Persons with exceptional colour-sense apparently judge most accurately whether two colours are the same, for example, or whether they have some or have not some definite harmonic relation to one another, not by attentive optical comparison or examination, but by the general emotional or organic reaction which the colours evoke when simply glanced at.[3] . . . This kind of intervention of organic sensation in perception plays a part in all the arts. . . . It is not a mode of gaining knowledge which differs in any essential way from other modes.

xvi. Emotions are primarily signs of attitudes and owe their great prominence in the theory of art to this. For it is the attitudes evoked which are the all-important part of any experience. Upon the texture and form of the attitudes involved its value depends. It is not the intensity of the conscious experience, its thrill, its pleasure, or its poignancy which gives it value, but the organization of its impulses for freedom and fulness of life. . . .

xviii. What matters to the musician is not the physical connexions between notes but the compatibilities and incompatibilities in the responses of emotion and attitude which they excite. . .

It may be freely granted that there are great pictures in which nothing is represented, and great pictures in which what is represented is trivial and may be disregarded. It is equally certain that there are great pictures in which the contribution to the whole response made through representation is not less than that made more directly through form and colour.[4] . . . There is no reason why

---

[1] Cf. Croce, p. 238.   [2] Cf. p. 283.
[3] Cf. Plotinus, ii. iii, 18, p. 47; Dewey, p. 308.   [4] Cf. Bell, p. 264.

representative and formal factors should conflict, but much reason why they should co-operate. . . . The psychology of 'unique aesthetic emotions' and 'pure art values' upon which the contrary view relies is merely a caprice of the fancy. . . . Representation in painting corresponds to thought in poetry. . . . The views recently so fashionable that representation has no place in art and that treatment, not subject, is what matters in poetry spring ultimately from the same mistakes as to the relation of thinking to feeling, from an inadequate psychology that would set up one as inimical to the other.

xix. What we transport from Egypt to London is merely a set of signs, from which a suitable interpreter, setting about it rightly, can produce a certain state of mind. . . . That we interpret a picture or poem is obvious upon very little reflection. . . . The historical accident that speculation upon Beauty largely developed in connexion with sculpture is responsible in great degree for the fixity of the opinion that Beauty is something inherent in physical objects. . . .

xx. We do well to beware of empty speculations upon 'necessary and inevitable relations' as the source of the effect. Of course in a given case a certain relation, a certain arrangement, may be necessary, in the sense that the elements, if differently disposed, would have a quite different combined effect. But this is not the sense in which necessity is usually claimed. . . . The value lies not in the apprehension, conscious or subconscious, of the rightness of the relations,[1] but in the total mental effect which, since they are right (i.e. since they work), they produce.

xxii. The greatest difference between the artist or poet and the ordinary person is . . . in the range, delicacy, and freedom of the connexions he is able to make out between different elements of his experience.[2] . . . In order to keep any steadiness and clarity in his attitudes the ordinary man is under the necessity on most occasions of sup-

[1] Cf. Kant, § 58, p. 123.   [2] Cf. Croce, p. 240, and Collingwood, p. 293.

pressing the greater part of the impulses which the situation might arouse. He is incapable of organizing them; therefore they have to be left out. In the same situation the artist is able to admit far more without confusion.

xxiv. Given some impulses active, others are thereby aroused in the absence of what would otherwise be their necessary stimuli. Such impulses I call imaginative, whether images occur or not; . . . which other impulses are brought in is in part determined by which were cooperative together originally. . . . In so far as this factor comes in, the imagination may be said to be *repetitive*. The imagination we are concerned with may be called *formative* by way of distinction (Coleridge's distinction between *imagination* and *fancy* was in part the same as this). For present circumstances are at least as important. Remember in a changed mood a scene which took place under a strong emotion. How altered is its every aspect! . . . If the artist's organization is such as to allow him a fuller life than the average, with less unnecessary interference between its component influences, then plainly we should do well to be more like him, *if we can*.[1]

xxx. Let us mean by *Westminster Bridge* not the actual experience which led Wordsworth on a certain morning about a century ago to write what he did, but the class composed of all actual experiences, occasioned by the words, which do not differ within certain limits from that experience. Then any one who has had one of the experiences comprised in the class can be said to have read the poem. The permissible ranges of variation in the class need (of course) very careful scrutiny. . . .

xxxi. In ordinary life a thousand considerations prohibit for most of us any complete working out of our response. . . . As a chemist's balance to a grocer's scales, so is the mind in the imaginative moment to the mind engaged in ordinary intercourse or practical affairs.

xxxii. Impulses which commonly interfere with one

[1] Cf. Lipps, p. 257.

another and are conflicting, independent, and mutually distractive, (in the artist) combine into a stable poise. . . . But these impulses active in the artist become mutually modified and thereby ordered to an extent which only occurs in the ordinary man at rare moments, under the shock of, for example, a great bereavement or an un-dreamt-of happiness. . . . Pity, the impulse to approach, and Terror, the impulse to retreat, are brought in Tragedy to a reconciliation which they find nowhere else.[1] . . . Suppressions and sublimations alike are devices by which we endeavour to avoid issues that might bewilder us. The essence of Tragedy is that it forces us to live for a moment without them. When we succeed we find, as usual, that there is no difficulty; the difficulty came from the suppressions and sublimations. The joy which is so strangely the heart of the experience is not an indication that 'all's right with the world' or that 'somewhere, somehow, there is Justice'; it is an indication that all is right here and now with the nervous system. . . . Tragedy is perhaps the most general, all-accepting, all-ordering experience known. . . . This balanced poise, stable through its power of inclusion, not through the force of its exclusions,[2] is not peculiar to Tragedy. . . . It can be given by a carpet or a pot or by a gesture. . . . The balance is not in the structure of the stimulating object, it is in the response. . . . A balance sustains one state of mind, but a conflict two alternating states. . . . Since more of our personality is engaged, the independence and individuality of other things becomes greater.[3] We seem to see them as they really are, . . . because we are freed from the bewilder-ment which our own maladjustment brings with it.

xxxiii. A statement may be used for the sake of the *reference* [=scientific or historical judgement], true or false, which it causes. This is the *scientific* use of language.

---

[1] Cf. Aristotle, p. 33; Goethe rendered κάθαρσις by *Ausgleichung* (*Nachlese zu Aristoteles Poetik*).

[2] Cf. Ruskin on Imagination, p. 177, Santayana, p. 202.

[3] Cf. Bridges, p. 331.

But it may be also used for the sake of the effects in emotion and attitude produced by the references it occasions. . . . Many arrangements of words evoke attitudes without any references being required *en route*. They operate like musical phrases. But usually references are involved *as conditions for*, or *stages in*, the ensuing development of attitudes, yet it is still the attitudes not the references which are important.[1] It matters not at all in such cases whether the references are true or false.[1] . . . Further . . . for emotive[2] purposes logical arrangement is not necessary, it may be and often is an obstacle.

xxxv. Many attitudes, which arise without dependence upon any reference . . . can be momentarily encouraged by suitable beliefs held as scientific beliefs are held. . . . Wordsworth puts forward his Pantheism. . . . The effect is twofold: an appearance of security and stability is given to the attitude, which thus seems to be justified; and at the same time it is no longer so necessary to sustain this attitude by the more difficult means peculiar to the arts, or to pay full attention to form. The reader can be relied upon to do more than his share.[3] That neither effect is desirable is easily seen. . . . Remove the belief, once it has affected the attitude; the attitude collapses. . . .

The bulk of the beliefs involved in the arts are . . . provisional acceptances made for the sake of the 'imaginative experience' which they make possible. The difference between these emotive[4] beliefs and scientific beliefs is not one of degree but of kind.[5] . . .

We can now take this feeling of a revealed significance for what it is—the conscious accompaniment of our successful adjustment to life. But it is, we must admit, no certain sign by itself that our adjustment is adequate or admirable.

[1] Cf. p. 278.   [2] i.e. emotional (purposes of arousing emotion).
[3] Cf. Wordsworth, p. 130.
[4] i.e. emotional (beliefs feigned in order to arouse emotion).
[5] Cf. pp. 278-9.

PHILIP LEON

1895–

Aesthetic Knowledge

Read to the London Aristotelian Society on April 6th, 1925

To experience colour, sound, taste, a new thrill, to appreciate and enjoy the light or movement of life, to gauge its seriousness, savour its joy, and penetrate its gloom is, I take it, to have knowledge, and the object of this knowledge is constitutive of the world.[1] We shall scarcely deny this if we consider what kind of knowledge and what sort of a world we should be left with if we removed from them the experience of the so-called secondary and tertiary qualities; if we were left only with the comfortless company of the dreary formulae of mathematics, the sciences, and philosophy. The above experience may be distinguished as knowledge of quality: its objects are the entities to which the term qualities secondary or tertiary are applied, in it alone do we know what anything is like, *quale sit*, all other knowledge being knowledge only *about* a thing, knowledge of its relations.[2]

Aesthetic or imaginative knowledge, the experience we have with the help of works of art, both in their creation and their appreciation which is re-creation, is knowledge of quality. Through works of art we know serenity, majesty, mysteriousness, pathos, tragedy, the gorgeous gloom and splendour which is the *Agamemnon* of Aeschylus, the serene and tranquil horror which is the *Oedipus Tyrannus* of Sophocles, the bright speed of Homer, the brooding pathos of Virgil. Be it well understood that any of these words and phrases is general and consequently inadequate; for the full realization of a unique quality it is necessary to have a whole work of art, the *Agamemnon* or the *Oedipus Tyrannus*, which is both the full description of the quality and the quality itself. The essence of a work of art, whatever its subsidiary aspects,

[1] Cf. Mitchell, p. 260.   [2] Cf. Schopenhauer, p. 138.

such as those of representation or imitation and of theory or doctrine, is that it is a synthesis which is the revelation of a new quality such as we should have if we could suddenly become aware of the colour of ultra-violet rays. The converse, I think, can also be maintained, namely, that all knowledge of quality, when adequate and complete, is art, the awareness of a bare secondary quality being a limiting case or an abstraction from a richer experience. . . .

The first characteristic of aesthetic knowledge is the oneness in it of subject and object, of the knowing and the known.[1] Even if as idealists we hold that that is the real mark of all knowledge, we must admit that in other knowledge the separation between subject and object, even though ultimately erroneous, does arise, whereas in aesthetic knowledge it is not present and cannot be present. Aesthetic knowledge is essentially a living through. Its object, quality, can be indifferently called the quality of the world or of our minds or souls. We may therefore speak of the aesthetic experience, meaning to indicate by experience the oneness of the knower, the knowing, and the known.

Secondly, the aesthetic experience is knowledge in which there is not present the distinction or separation between subject and predicate. It is all subject or all predicate, and there is no assertion or predication.[1] A poem or a piece of music may be considered as an adjectival texture, as quality enjoyed, realized, contemplated, but not predicated of anything. It is never 'about' anything. True, a literary work of art is made up of propositions, but that these are not real assertions or judgements can be seen when we reflect that the import of a work of art would be epitomized in a descriptive phrase, a description of a quality, rather than in a proposition or judgement, as would be the case, say, with a book of science, history, or philosophy. A poem can be merely exclamatory, and in its real import always is a mere exclamation, which you

[1] Cf. Croce, p. 238.

cannot meet with 'Yes' or 'No,' or with argument, as you can a judgement.

As there is no assertion, so neither is there the distinction between truth and error, appearance and reality. The aesthetic object, the aesthetic experience, is essentially appearance and essentially real. There can be no argument about its reality, just as there can be no argument about the reality of any apprehended colour. Argument in such a case, I take it, can only arise when we start attributing the colour and attributing it to one thing rather than to another. But the aesthetic experience as such is merely apprehension of quality, free from every act of attribution. Being non-assertive, it in itself does not contain the assertion of the reality or unreality of its object or of itself. But looking at that object and experience from a point of view other than the aesthetic, say as philosophers, I do not see how we can ever deny reality to it. A work of art either helps us to apprehend something or it fails to do so. But what we apprehend must be real, it being the same as the apprehension. It is imaginary because grasped by the imagination, but nothing is added or taken away from its status by saying that it is merely imaginary.[1] That holds true if we remember that what a work of art really gives us is what I have called a quality and not anything else. I do not mean that Centaurs are to be found in the animal kingdom because some one has painted them, or that the exploration of the skies or of Mount Olympus will reveal to us gods leading a riotous and immoral life because we read of them in Homer.

The aesthetic object *qua* aesthetic object, is, and is always apprehended as, essentially one, free internally from relations. It is an immediate unity or unity of quality, and is thus distinguished from other unities, e.g. the unity of a thing, a system, a universal, teleological unity. All these latter can only be apprehended by thought and their apprehension is the apprehension of relations. A work of art when not enjoyed as a work of art, when con-

[1] Cf. Collingwood, pp. 293-4.

sequently it is not an aesthetic object, can, of course, be analysed into parts and their relations to each other: a tragedy is divided into acts and scenes and sentences, a picture into different figures and colours uniting in a harmony, a temple into innumerable parts. But in the moment of aesthetic enjoyment there are not parts seen or rather thought in their relations.[1] The relations denoted by balance, harmony, proportions, contrast, form, are relations apprehended in immediacy, i.e. such that both the relations and the relata are all one quality. I mean that in spite of all diversity discoverable by analysis, in spite of its being somehow dependent on the apprehension of diversity and on different acts of apprehension, the enjoyment of the *Agamemnon* is essentially the apprehension of one quality, 'gorgeous gloom,' or whatever we may call it, and that we have here essentially the same unity as there is in the apprehension of a flash of light,[2] though physical analysis reveals the multeity of billions of vibrations, or in the apprehension of 'glittering sharpness' analysable psychologically into visual sensations and tactile images, or in that of genial light, warmth, and freshness, analysable into organic, kinaesthetic, and many other sensations and images.

Free in this sense from relations internally, the aesthetic object is also free from relations externally, from relations to another. It is complete, self-sufficient, isolated, a universe,[3] and a true individual. It is this which gives the aesthetic activity its repose and perfection. Any aesthetic object must obey the law which Aristotle lays down for a tragedy: it must have a proper beginning and a proper end; nothing outside it leads to it and it leads on to nothing outside itself. There is nothing else which is an 'it', or is called an individual, that possesses this individuality and self-subsistence. Everything else exists in an infinite environment and has its being in its relations and interactions with this environment, never completely

---

[1] Cf. Herbart, *Practical Philosophy, Introduction*, § 100, pp. 153, 155.
[2] Cf. Plotinus, p. 44.   [3] Cf. Collingwood, p. 293.

within itself. Consequently, no other knowledge has the completeness and satisfactoriness of the aesthetic experience. It is this which chiefly gives it its claim to being absolute or typical of the absolute.[1] That claim has by some been made for history. But history, it has to be admitted, is knowledge of an infinite whole whose parts are infinitely inexhaustible or unknowable, i.e. it is a knowledge which can never be complete or proper knowledge. All knowledge other than the aesthetic experience suffers from this infinity. Whether it be a single judgement, a whole book, or department of science, it is never self-subsistent. It is predicational: it attaches a predicate to a subject, the nature of which is apprehended in part at least elsewhere, outside the judgement or book or system. A judgement or system of judgements consequently always refers us outwards, to other apprehension: it forms part of a larger context to which both its beginning and its end point; in fact it has not properly either a beginning or an end. Its interests depend upon questions asked and answers given elsewhere; the dwelling in it is a continual excursion from it, and such excursion, such questioning, and endless reference and discursiveness is what constitutes the apprehension, the understanding, the knowing.

But it is not so with the aesthetic experience; the latter is an absorption; it is complete and self-contained; it is marked by repose and finality. It has these characteristics because its object is a complete self-subsistent universe. We do not come to a poem with questions, and its interest does not depend on answers given elsewhere; the asking of any questions does not constitute the aesthetic apprehension, but on the contrary, like any reference to anything outside the poem, song, or picture, it is fatal to the aesthetic attitude. Of course, the aesthetic object can, when we are not appreciating it as such, be related to others. We can give the sources of a drama, compare it to others, and make it the subject of an infinite series of

[1] Cf. Plato, *Phaedrus*, p. 16, Plotinus, p. 45, Gentile, p. 322.

judgements. But the point is that such knowledge does not constitute the act of apprehending the drama *qua* drama, i.e. seeing it acted and enjoying it, but is, on the contrary, incompatible with it and impossible till after the aesthetic apprehension proper is over.

I have emphasized the unity of the aesthetic object, but it is a unity which covers a rich variety or multiplicity, discoverable by analysis though not aesthetically apprehended as a many. This manyness in one is most obviously realized as a synthesis of the senses. Art is said to be sensuous, to appeal primarily through one of our senses, through hearing or sight. But then we must say that one of the senses does the work of all the rest, and all in one act. So in music we can be said to hear wetness, hear colour, a perfume, a taste. In a picture, we see warmth, we see loudness, sweetness and freshness, sharpness, &c. Hence it is that critics tend to speak of music in terms of colour and of painting in terms of music.

But the elements which enter into the aesthetic synthesis are not merely sensuous. It is all experience that may enter into it. . . . Such synthesis points to some experience where all the past, all experience, is resumed and preserved all in one in an immediate unity. That experience cannot be anything other than the Absolute, but its type and the approximation to it is to be found in the aesthetic experience only.[1]

The aesthetic experience presupposes perception:[2] to appreciate an aesthetic object we must perceive a picture, hear a poem, &c., to create an aesthetic object we must have lived through at least ordinary perceptual experience. While not itself conceptual, it presupposes the concept and, indeed, it contains it, though not explicitly in the form of argument or doctrine, but in an implicit immediate form[3] as a philosophy may be contained in a drama of Aeschylus. It is not in itself ethical, and its value is not ethical, but it presupposes the ethical exper-

[1] Cf. St. Thomas, p. 50.　　[2] Cf. Collingwood, p. 293.
[3] Cf. Croce, p. 238, Stace, p. 304.

ience in the sense that no art—at any rate, no great art and
least of all great poetry—can be produced or appreciated
except by men who are sensitive to good and evil. Like
the absolute, though in itself neither true nor false, since
it is not judgement or assertion, the aesthetic experience
contains both truth and error. The doctrines or judgements which we may extract from a poem, and which we
say are contained in it implicitly, may be either true or
false without affecting its own value, which is beauty.
For error we must find a place in the universe, since it is
a fact. . . . Aesthetic experience alone does not possess the
unsatisfactoriness of all other knowledge, i.e. knowledge
which is judgement or predicational, and therefore it alone
reveals reality satisfactorily. Beauty is the highest category and alone applicable to the Absolute, i.e. to the
unity of all experience or all experience in a unity.
Actual aesthetic objects are only types of this absolute or
partial revelations of it.

Suggestions from Aesthetics for the Metaphysic of Quality (II)

From *Mind*, vol. xxxiii, N.S., No. 129

What we have been dealing with, it may be objected, are
not qualities at all but feelings or emotions. Art expresses,
objectifies, externalizes, or embodies our feelings or
emotions or states of mind. In the aesthetic activity, we
project our feelings into an object, we experience them
in it. . . .

There is one use of the word feeling, so wide that it can
scarcely be misleading. When a work of art or an object
is said to 'express' bright speed, white simplicity, a light
aerial elegance, or majesty and stateliness, if I say that
the work or object gives me the feeling of bright speed,
white simplicity, or that I feel the light aerial elegance or
the mountain's majesty and stateliness, feeling here can
only mean *apprehending*. It can only have the sense it
would have if I said I felt the greenness or the hardness or

the sweetness of a thing. There can be no objection to the word, if it be realized that in all these cases we have knowledge, though it be knowledge of quality, and knowledge which is not judgement. It must also be realized that just as I do not mean, in the above cases, that I feel or am green or hard or sweet, so I cannot or must not mean that I feel or that I am majestic and stately, brightly speedy, whitely simple, or lightly and aerially elegant.[1] . . .

My feeling or state of mind when I am contemplating a mountain differs from my state of mind when I am contemplating a plain only because the mountain is different from the plain. It is the world, then, in this case the mountain or the plain, that invests feeling with character and not feeling which characterizes the world. The mountain is not solemn and awful because I have a feeling of solemnity and awe which I project or externalize into it; my feeling or state of mind may be said to be of awe and solemnity because I apprehend these qualities in the mountain. . . .

Once make a division, and place on one side a world stripped of many qualities, and on the other a mind, and no amount of externalizing or projecting of feeling or anything else will clothe it. . . . Now according to us, the aesthetic apprehension is essentially the pure apprehension of pure quality, i.e. of quality not attached to this or that particular thing. But before we come to developed aesthetic apprehension in art, this apprehension of unattached quality is probably not to be met with elsewhere than in emotion. For sensations, unless it be some vague organic sensations, we probably do not have except in perception; and in perception qualities are attached to particular things. Consequently the aesthetic apprehension in art may be considered as more particularly the development of one aspect or element of the psychological situation which is an emotion. . . . The aesthetics of feeling emphasize the fact that a world which contains qualities like weirdness, calm, mysteriousness, splendour, majesty,

---

[1] Cf. Lipps, pp. 252–8, Mitchell, p. 260.

must contain the 'things' of which psychology treats as well as those with which physical science deals. That is, of course, a fact. But it is not obvious on the surface nor necessarily implied in the mere act of attributing these qualities. When I say the mountain is stately or majestic, I am performing the same act of attribution as when I say the leaf is green. Neither in the one case nor in the other am I implying, reflecting, or stating that my feeling or my state of mind affects the thing, or that the thing affects my state of mind.

ROBIN GEORGE COLLINGWOOD
1889–

Outlines of a Philosophy of Art (1925)

2. Art is to mean the special activity by which we apprehend beauty. This implies that there are various activities of which we have experience, and that art has certain features in common with them all and others peculiar to itself. . . . For instance, religion is described as giving knowledge of ultimate reality, which is precisely what artists claim for art, scientists for science, and philosophers for philosophy; or as giving a sense of victory over our lower nature, of peace, of security, which are feelings involved in any activity whatever, provided it is pursued earnestly and successfully. . . . In every field of activity there is a theoretical element, in virtue of which the mind is aware of something; there is a practical element in virtue of which the mind is bringing about a change in itself and in its world; and there is an element of feeling. . . . 3. But the subject's activity, the object's nature, and the character of the relation between them have certain peculiarities which distinguish the case of art from other cases. What the subject does is to imagine: the object is an imaginary object,[1] and the relation between them is that the individual or empirical act of

[1] Cf. Moore, § 115, p. 246.

imagining creates the object. . . .To imagine an object is not to commit oneself in thought to its unreality; it is to be wholly indifferent to its reality. An imaginary object, therefore, is not an unreal object but an object about which we do not trouble to ask whether it is real or unreal.[1] . . . 4. Art is not based upon a previous perception of real objects. We do not first ascertain what the object really is and then modify it by allowing our imagination to play upon it. We first imagine.[2] . . . The child does not struggle to reach the imaginative point of view; he lives habitually in it; but the educated man cannot achieve it except by a struggle. . . . 5. To imagine is not simply to allow a train of images to drift idly across the mind, it is to make an effort to imagine, to work at imagination. . . . That which art is the attempt to achieve is beauty. . . . All ugliness, so far as it does actually exist, is not the ugliness of an object imagined, but the ugliness of an object not imagined: not imagined, that is, in the strict sense. . . . It is confused imagining, an imagining that slips over from one imagination to another, without imagining out any one thing to the end. . . . The mere act of imagination, by being itself, by being this act and not a different act, generates in its object that unity which is beauty.

6. Every work of art is a monad, a windowless and self-contained world which mirrors the universe from its own unique point of view, and, indeed, is nothing but a vision or perspective of the universe, and of a universe which is first itself.[3] . . . But whereas the artist regards it as expressive simply of itself, the historian [of his art] regards it as expressive of the experiences, now forgotten, which have paved the way for its creation.

9. Sublimity is beauty which forces itself upon our mind, beauty which strikes us as it were against our will and in spite of ourselves. . . . 10. The power which we attribute to the object is really our own; it is our own aesthetic activity. The shock of sublimity is the shock of an uprush of imaginative energy within ourselves. . . .

[1] Cf. Leon, p. 286.   [2] Cf. Lipps, p. 258, Leon, p. 289.   [3] Cf. Leon, p. 287.

The shock with which we discover a beauty dies away; we become familiar with the object, and familiarity breeds a feeling that the beauty which we saw in it was our own work and not due to any real power in the object.[1] The object no longer overawes or impresses us with its beauty, and this release from awe, uprush of positive self-feeling, or, as Hobbes called it, 'sudden glory',[2] is what we express by laughter.

11. Real beauty is neither 'objective' nor 'subjective' in any sense that excludes the other. . . . The experience of beauty is an experience of utter union with the object; every barrier is broken down, and the beholder feels that his own soul is living in the object, and that the object is unfolding its life in his own heart. . . . But that is a merely psychological description of the experience.[3] The feeling which we thus describe has a ground, and this ground can be made explicit by reflection on the feeling. The aesthetic activity is an act of imagination; and imagination creates its own object.

12. If to imagine an object is to find it beautiful, there is no difficulty in the fact that we find real objects, whether natural objects or works of art, beautiful; for it is just as possible to look imaginatively at these as it is to look imaginatively at objects which exist solely in our own imagination.

Both the natural object and the work of art present themselves to the artist himself as real and not merely imaginary: their reality enters into his aesthetic experience as a constituent element, giving it a quality of its own, and their different origin further differentiates this quality.

13. It may be doubted whether we ever imagine without also thinking. . . . There seems to be no case in which we make no judgement whatever as to whether we are imagining or not; in other words, whether the immediate object of our consciousness is a merely imaginary object or a real object. . . . Yet though the thinking self controls

---

[1] Cf. Kant's doctrine that beauty is more properly ascribed to objects, sublimity to our minds, p. 118.   [2] Cf. p. 57.   [3] Cf. Lipps, p. 253.

the imagining self, the artist does not know this is so, for he is only conscious that he is imagining, not that he is thinking; and therefore he knows that something is controlling his imaginative activity—something other than that activity itself—but he does not know that this something is his own thought. . . . 14. If, in so far as he thinks, he recognizes that his imagination is controlled by an activity higher than itself, this recognition must leave its mark on his imagination in the form of a feeling of 'givenness' which characterizes its awareness of its object. . . . As, in perceiving, we feel everything that we perceive to be a natural object, and as, in thinking, the scientist feels every object of his thought to be a part of nature, so, in imagining, the artist *feels* every object of his imagination to be nature.[1] . . . In general this sense of givenness is the finite mind aware of its own finiteness. . . . Hence the feeling of givenness in virtue of which the object of imagination is felt as real, as nature, is, properly considered, not an illusion at all, but the imaginative awareness of a profound truth. . . . If there could be a mind purely imaginative and devoid of all intellectual faculties, such a mind would be an artist, but its artistic experience would be altogether innocent of the feeling that its object was no mere fiction but a symbol of truth. . . . The object and our awareness of it are felt to be in perfect harmony with each other; but within this harmony there is a distinction between feeling that the object is presented to the aesthetic activity, and feeling that the aesthetic activity, whether in myself or another, has created the object; this is the distinction between the enjoyment of natural beauty and the enjoyment of the beauty of art.

16. The essence of the picturesque is the spectator's sense of a gulf between the object and his own habitual surroundings and activities, and at the same time the word is applied indifferently to natural objects and to the life and works of man.

[1] Cf. Mitchell, p. 261.

Speculum Mentis *or The Map of Knowledge* (1924)

iii. 2. The aesthetic experience is thus, in its concrete actuality, the creation or apprehension of works of art. The terms creation and apprehension are here synonymous, for the essence of art is that nothing is asserted and everything imagined, so that the question whether the work of art has or has not an existence independent of the apprehension of it is a question which has, for the aesthetic consciousness, no meaning whatever. From the point of view of that consciousness, every work of art is real just so far as it is imagined and no further. . . . Now this process of imagining a whole, or creating a work of art, is, as we have seen, no mere rudderless drifting of images across the mind; it is a process of unification in which the mind strives to see its world as a whole, the 'world' being just the work of art which for the time being absorbs the whole gaze of the mind. The various feelings, emotions, sensations, or by whatever other name we call the subsidiary imaginations, are modified and adapted so as to fall into such an imaginable totality.[1] . . . The whole is not first held in the mind as a whole and then filled out in detail; for, if it were ever held in the mind (that is, imagined as a whole), the work would already be complete. . . . Beauty means structure, organization, seen from the aesthetic point of view, that is, imagined and not conceived. This is the solution of the old difficulty arising out of the fact that when people try to describe the beauty of a thing they always either describe its shape, colour, and so forth, which are not beauty, or else describe its emotional effect on them, which is not beauty either. The first alternative leads to all the formalistic and intellectualistic theories of beauty, the theories of the serpentine line, of symmetry and proportion, of unity in diversity, of natural form or allegorical meaning; the latter to all the emotionalist and hedonistic theories. . . . An artist paints with one motive only: that he may help

[1] Cf. Ruskin on Imagination, p. 177.   [2] Cf. Hogarth, p. 88.

himself to see, and to see in the sense of to imagine. His picture, when it is painted, has done that, and he is not further interested in it. . . . 3. Any desire to communicate or seek an audience for his thoughts is subsequent and alien to the experience itself. . . .

There is a real difference between works of art in what we call their scale or size: and it argues a more powerful mind, a more highly developed art, to work on a large scale than on a small. Scale, in this sense, is not mere space and time; excellence in art is not bulk or duration; it is relative to the difficulty of the problem which the artist sets himself and the extent to which his whole being and all his resources are called into play in order to solve it. . . .

Every fresh aesthetic act creates a new work of art . . . the number of such works is therefore of necessity infinite, nor is it possible to delimit and define their kinds. . . .

6. Art makes for itself two claims. First, that it is the activity of pure imagination; secondly, that it somehow reveals the truth concerning the ultimate nature of the real world. Now for pure imagination there is no real world; there is only the imaginary world. Consequently we are tempted to revise the second claim and make it run 'reveals the truth concerning the ultimate nature of the *imaginary* world.' But then the second claim simply repeats the first, and adds nothing to it. This false reduction of the second claim to the first is, unless I am mistaken, the motive of Croce's famous identification of intuition and expression.[1] . . . Intuition and expression have not been reconciled. . . .

The meaning itself, the expressed concept, exists in the work only intuitively, under the form of beauty. . . . But this is a contradiction in terms. A concept can only be conceived, not intuited. . . . Kant was stating this fact when he said that beauty was purposiveness without purpose;[2] the beautiful, he meant, had the air of carrying out some purpose, of meaning or intending something,

[1] Cf. Leon, p. 291.   [2] p. 114.

and when you came to ask *what* it intended, you could never say. . . . When we discover what our meaning is, the aesthetic stage in the history of that thought is over and done with. Art must perish as knowledge grows. But it perishes like the phoenix, to rise again from the very ashes of its own body. . . .

7. The presupposition of the birth of a work of art is the purely abstract concept of relevance as such: aesthetic structure in general. . . . Art is thus an alternation between concentration on the abstract concept of relevance (the 'fundamental brain-work' of which Rossetti spoke) and flight to the abstract intuition of beauty.

RALPH BARTON PERRY

1876–

General Theory of Value (1926)

255. *De gustibus non disputandum est.* We have first to distinguish a difference between two judgements of comparative value from a difference of preference. The former case is represented by my judgement that '*b* is better than *a*', as opposed to your judgement that '*a* is better than *b*'. This is a difference of opinion, which assumes a common meaning for the predicate 'better'. . . . Preference would here enter into the discussion only so far as it was agreed to construe 'better' as 'preferred', there being a difference of opinion as to what was in fact preferred. This possible confusion being avoided, we may ask in what sense differences of taste are debatable, when these are construed as *differences of preference.*

In the first place, in so far as they are mediated by contrary judgement of fact. If you prefer a Raphael Madonna to a newspaper cartoon because you believe its composition to be superior, and I prefer the cartoon on the same ground, we can fall to debating the question of their composition, provided this in turn is not a matter of preference but of design. Or we may hold different views of the conception and intent of the artist, on the assumption that these actually occurred and are somehow ascertainable. In both cases we virtually appeal to the same set of facts to arbitrate our disagreement, and in so far as the difference of taste is really grounded on this difference of opinion it will be resolved by the correction of the opinion. . . . So far, in other words, as differences of preference are due to differences of opinion they may be discussed with the justifiable hope of being resolved. In the second place, differences of preference may properly be discussed when they are due in any degree to the relative ignorance of one party. If my preference of *b* to all other eligible objects is due to the fact that I am ignorant of *c*, you may properly make me cognizant of *c* and of its claims; or if my preference of *b* to *a* is due to the meagreness of my knowledge of either or both objects, you may present them to me more vividly, or represent them more adequately, or by demonstration enable me to compare them more fully or with a more refined discrimination. You may present the Raphael Madonna to me in a new light, and persuade me to look at it more closely, while at the same time keeping my interest alive by the contagious effect of your own admiration. . . . Or, thirdly, a comparison of taste may take the form of a mere comparison of preferences, in which a common object is measured by both of us, each according to his own interest. . . . When, in other words, all cognitive differences have been eliminated or discounted, and two preferences still conflict, we are confronted with two undebatable facts both of which have to be accepted by both parties, the facts, namely, that whereas in the last analysis I prefer *b* to *a*, you prefer *a* to *b*. Such a conflict of preference, like conflict of interest, is a datum of value and an instance of its ultimate and irreducible relativity.[1]

[1] Cf. Ross, p. 317–18.

JOHN LAIRD

1887–

The Idea of Value (1929)

vii. 3. If colour, sound, and similar properties really do belong to physical things, it seems unnecessary to deny that beauty also may exist in the things themselves. If so, many, though not all, beauties (not, for instance, most of the beauties of poetry) would be 'objective' in the sense of being non-mental. And beauties, we say, are values. It might, however, be contended, and perhaps with justice, that such beauties are not values unless and until they appeal to a mind.

If, on the other hand, these sensible shows cannot literally be found in physical things, but are caused in part by the play of our minds upon the things, it follows that the shows are in part mentally conditioned.[1] Since the shows could not exist apart from any mind, their beauty also could not so exist. On the other hand, if this statement were taken to mean, quite simply, that these sensible shows are, in part, *produced* by our minds, such products, though they have mental causes, need not contain any mental constituents or properties. Even if smells and colours are partially manufactured by our minds, we do not commonly think that minds have the properties of odours or of colours, i.e. that *minds* are red, or mauve, or fragrant.

According to this alternative hypothesis, therefore (interpreted as above), we ought to hold that the beauty of such sensible shows resides neither in minds nor in physical objects, but in a certain joint-product of both (which itself is neither mental nor physical). The second alternative, therefore, would not, any more than the first, properly suggest that beauty resides in the mind of the beholder. And the inference concerning the value of such beauty would be the same on either alternative. . . .

[1] Cf. Ross, p. 316.

It is at least highly disputable whether certain beauties may not be strictly non-mental. If so, a possible, although not a necessary inference is that their values may be non-mental also.

WALTER TERENCE STACE
1886–

The Meaning of Beauty (1929)

ii. 23. The apprehension of beauty is a cognition. It will therefore be either a pure act of conception, or a pure act of perception, or a combination of both, or, as another possibility, it may be some less well-recognized form of cognition such as intuition. We must examine the alternatives.

The first alternative, that the apprehension of beauty is a pure act of conception, is ruled out at once by the consideration that the beautiful object is never a pure abstraction or concept.

The next alternative is that the awareness of beauty is a pure act of perception. . . . This may be called the theory of naive realism. As far as I can understand, Mr. John Laird[1] advocates this view. . . . Artistic taste would depend solely upon the possession of acute physical senses. . . . It seems obvious that the beauty of a rose is not something that can be seen and pointed out in the same sense that its colour can be. . . .

There are two remaining alternatives. Either the apprehension of beauty depends upon a combination of concept and percept; or it depends upon some less well-recognized form of cognition such as intuition. . . .

[1] *A Study in Realism*, pp. 129–34. Beauty, in fact, is something that is judged, not something that is merely felt. . . . At the same time it is possible to argue that nothing is beautiful save our delight itself, and that we call things beautiful just because they cause beautiful delights. . . . Our delights are really valuable, some delights are really better than others; and that is the sum of the matter. . . . A perceiving and comprehending delight is no mere feeling. We may conclude, then, that delight enters into the recognition of all beauty, even if we have no right to maintain that things can be beautiful apart from a mind.

Bergson [1] argues that the artist is a man who, by some chance of nature, sees reality as it is, unveiled and unfalsified by concepts. . . . This view is, in my opinion, unacceptable for two reasons. Firstly . . . if concepts falsify reality, then all science and all philosophy, *including Bergson's philosophy*, are false. . . . Secondly, the application of this view to aesthetics in the manner indicated above renders impossible any distinction between beautiful and unbeautiful objects. Any object, any reality, must be beautiful if truly seen in its reality, stripped of concepts. [2] . . .

Croce postulates an intuition which is wholly free from any admixture of concepts or from any intellectual element. Such an intuition is an impossible abstraction for precisely the same reason as bare sensation is an impossible abstraction. His intuition might exist as an element in consciousness. But it could not stand alone. And the assertion of his aesthetic is precisely that, in the pure artistic consciousness, it does stand alone. [3]

My second objection is that, even if Croce's intuition is conceived merely as an element of consciousness, it cannot be rationally comprehended. For the endeavour to distinguish it from pure sensation is a failure. . . .

Any hypothesis as to the nature of beauty, to hold water, must first of all provide a satisfactory basis for the claim of the aesthetic judgement to universal validity. [4] . . . That which alone can explain and justify this validity is, in one way or another, the concept. [5] . . . The conceptless intuition —whether as conceived by Bergson, Croce, or any other philosopher—cannot be made the basis of a satisfactory theory of aesthetic. . . . The apprehension of beauty is not a pure act of conception, nor is it a pure act of perception, nor is it a pure intuition. The remaining alternative is that it is a combination of the concept and the percept. . . . The concept must be fused in the percept in a special way and disappear in it. . . .

[1] p. 205.   [2] Cf. Schopenhauer, p. 145.   [3] p. 258 ; cf. Gentile.
      [4] Cf. Ross, p. 317.   [5] Cf. Kant, § 6, p. 112.

Although Kant explicitly denied that concepts are involved in the experience of the beautiful, yet for him beauty is a meeting-point of intellect and sensation. And for him, as for Hegel, the beautiful is a reconciliation of matter and sensation on the one side with intellect and spirit on the other.

iii. *Beauty is the fusion of an intellectual content, consisting of empirical non-perceptual concepts, with a perceptual field, in such manner that the intellectual content and the perceptual field are indistinguishable from one another; and in such manner as to constitute the revelation of an aspect of reality.* . . . The perceptual, for us, includes both external and internal perception. . . . There may be beautiful characters, emotions, or ideas. . . .

Concepts fall into three classes. Those concepts which are most universal and most abstract are called *categories*. Categories are those concepts which universally and necessarily apply to *all* objects of experience. Such are unity, existence, quality. . . . At the other end of the scale, in respect of universality, are what I propose to call *perceptual concepts*. Examples of perceptual concepts are the abstract ideas of house, man, star, redness, sound, roughness, jealousy, hitting, fighting, in, outside, to the left of, before, circularity, three. . . . What distinguishes perceptual concepts from all other kinds of concept is that *percepts directly correspond to them*. They are simply the concepts, or abstract ideas, *of* percepts. . . . Between these two extremes lies the realm of what I wish to call *empirical non-perceptual concepts*, which form the content of the beautiful. Such concepts are empirical because they are derived from experience, and are not the conditions of experience as categories are. . . . [They] are, on the other side, called non-perceptual because, although they are derived from concrete experience, there yet correspond to them no immediate percepts.[1] . . . They thus occupy an intermediate position as regards universality. They are more universal than perceptual concepts because they

[1] Cf. Kant, § 57, p. 121.

consist, not of abstractions of particular entities, but of abstractions from areas of human experience so large that they cannot be grasped together in any single act of perception. Examples of empirical non-perceptual concepts are evolution, progress, harmony, goodness, civilization, law, order, peace, gravitation, spirituality. No single percept corresponds to any of these concepts. . . .

Without the categories and perceptual concepts we could have no perception, but only a confused, chaotic blur of sensations. In perception, therefore, perceptual concepts and categories are already fused with the sensory elements of experience. . . . The intermediate class of empirical non-perceptual concepts alone are impalpable abstractions, free concepts, which hover over the field of concrete experience but never find any resting-place within it. The theory embodied in our definition of beauty means that the fusion of these concepts with a perceptual field, though it does not take place in our ordinary perceptive or cognitive acts, takes place in the experience of the beautiful and constitutes the nature of beauty. When perceptual concepts and categories are fused with sensations, the result is perception. When empirical non-perceptual concepts are fused with perceptions, the result is beauty. . . . They must not appear as separate and distinguishable elements in our consciousness. . . . This is to be compared with the disappearance of perceptual concepts and categories in ordinary perception. They too are completely fused with sensory elements. . . .

Empirical non-perceptual concepts have not, as perceptual concepts and categories have, existed primordially and naturally as fused elements in all our ordinary acts of perception. We have seen houses, trees, stars. But no man has seen evolution, progress, civilization, spirituality, or the moral law. . . . Hence it happens that, when by an act of genius (as in art) such a concept at last finds a lodgment in concrete experience, is fused with percepts, is actually perceived for the first time as an existing thing before our eyes, we feel a sense of pleasure. . . .

. . . v. Distinctions between the kinds of beauty belong to popular discourse, to psychology, or to art criticism. . . . They are due, according to our theory, to the varieties of feeling-value which are connected with the intellectual content prior to its fusion with a perceptual field. . . . An intellectual content which is unpleasant and repulsive will, when fused with percepts, give rise to the aesthetic experience of the ugly. The sublime and the terrible are due to the fusion of concepts with which are connected certain shades of fear or the feeling of powerlessness. Concepts which are more or less indifferent as regards feeling-value will give rise to some shade of cold and purely contemplative beauty. . .

vii. This fusion may be less or more complete, and the resulting beauty will be less or more perfect. . . .

This fusion certainly takes place only within the human mind. . . . To this extent, therefore, beauty is certainly subjective. . . . As to the nature of the objective element in beauty, we can only affirm generally that some objects, by virtue of these purely physical qualities, lend themselves to the process of fusion with human concepts, while others do not. . . . It is precisely here, if anywhere, that the element of truth in what has been called associationist aesthetics is to be found. . . .

viii. The greater the wealth and profundity of the intellectual content, the greater will be the value of the aesthetic experience. . . .

ix. The intellectual content consists in the total intellectual reaction of the artist upon the world as exhibited in the work of art. . . . In a very general and approximate way we sum up a man's view of the world as pessimistic, optimistic, hedonistic, resigned, gay, sullen, cynical, joyful, tolerant, and so forth.

x. As soon as the concept became known as entirely false it would be seen that the supposed work of art was a sham and was not truly beautiful, and, further, that it never had been beautiful even when its content was believed to be true. . . . Wholly false attitudes to life do not exist except in pathological cases. . . .

Any empirical non-perceptual concept can be made the content of aesthetic experience. But art chooses those which are vital and profound and important to human life, because upon the worth of the intellectual content depends the degree of beauty.

JOHN DEWEY
1859–

Experience and Nature (1929)

ix. There are substantially but two alternatives. Either art is a continuation, by means of intelligent selection and arrangement, of natural tendencies of natural events, or art is a peculiar addition to nature springing from something dwelling exclusively within the breast of man, whatever name be given the latter. In the former case delightfully enhanced perception or esthetic appreciation . . . is the outcome of a skilled and intelligent art of dealing with natural things for the sake of intensifying, purifying, prolonging, and deepening the satisfactions which they naturally afford.[1] . . . But if fine art has nothing to do with other activities and products, then of course it has nothing inherently to do with the objects, physical and social, experienced in other situations. It has an occult source and an esoteric character. . . . Consider some of the terms which are in more or less current use among the critics who carry the isolation of art and the esthetic to its limit. It is sometimes said that art is the expression of the emotions;[2] with the implica-

[1] Cf. Croce, p. 234, Richards, p. 282.

[2] The following criticism is clearly not directed against Croce, who certainly does not hold that unexpressed emotion is aesthetic, nor that the character of the expressive *object* is irrelevant to the expression. He does hold that the character of the unexpressed emotion, so far as we can guess it from the expression, is aesthetically irrelevant.

tion that, because of this fact, subject-matter[1] is of no significance except as a material through which emotion is expressed. Hence art becomes unique. For in works of science, utility, and morals the character of the *objects forming their subject-matter*[2] is all-important. But by this definition, subject-matter is stripped of all its own inherent characters in art in the degree in which it is genuine art, since a truly artistic work is manifest in the reduction of subject-matter to a mere medium of expression of emotion.

In such a statement emotion either has no significance at all, and it is mere accident that this particular combination of letters is employed; or else, if by emotion is meant the same sort of thing that is called emotion in daily life, the statement is demonstrably false. For emotion in its ordinary sense is something called out *by* objects physical and personal; it is response *to* an objective situation.[3] It is not something existing somewhere by itself which then employs material through which to express itself. Emotion is an indication of intimate participation, in a more or less excited way, in some scene of nature or life; it is, so to speak, an attitude or disposition which is a function of objective things. . . . The origin of the art-process lay in emotional responses spontaneously called out by a situation occuring without any reference to art, and without 'esthetic' quality save in the sense in which all immediate enjoyment and suffering is esthetic. . . .

The same sort of remark is to be made concerning 'significant form'[4] as a definition of an esthetic object. . . . 'Art' does not create the forms; it is their selection and organization in such ways as to enhance, prolong, and purify the perceptual experience. It is not by accident[5] that some objects and situations afford mankind perceptual satisfactions; they do so because of their structural

---

[1] This evidently does not mean the emotion nor yet the physical medium used. Perhaps it means the natural *objects* represented in some arts. It is not quite clear to me what it would mean in music. But cf. Bradley.

[2] My italics. [3] Cf. Leon, p. 289. [4] Cf. Bell, p. 264. [5] Cf. Hegel, p. 165.

properties and relations. An artist may work with a minimum of analytic recognition of these structures or 'forms'; he may select them chiefly by a kind of sympathetic vibration.[1] But they may also be discriminatively ascertained; and an artist may utilize his deliberate awareness of them to create works of art that are more formal and abstract than those to which the public is accustomed. Tendency to composition in terms of the formal characters marks much contemporary art, in poetry, painting, music, even sculpture and architecture. At their worst, these products are 'scientific' rather than artistic: technical exercises, sterile, and of a new kind of pedantry. At their best, they assist in ushering in new modes of art. . . . The creators of such works of art are entitled, when successful, to the gratitude that we give to inventors of microscopes and microphones; in the end they open new objects to be observed and enjoyed. This is a genuine service; but only an age of combined confusion and conceit will arrogate to works that perform this special utility the exclusive name of fine art.

DAVID WIGHT PRALL
1886–

Aesthetic Judgement (1929)

ii. 1. It is characteristic of aesthetic apprehension that the surface fully present to sense is the total object of apprehension. . . . In our apprehending beauty or in beauty's being manifested to us, the character of the transaction depends as clearly on the apprehending process as upon the other main term in the transaction, that is, the object; and while the object may remain the same, persons differ greatly by nature and training with respect to this apprehending activity. . . . There is even ground for supposing that beauty is constituted in the very transaction that is this pleasurable apprehension, and that it is therefore properly called a tertiary quality. . . . We

[1] Cf. Plotinus, iv. iii. 18, p. 47, Richards, p. 279.

attribute beauty to all that there is present to consciousness in the case, namely, the so-called external object
entering into this elaborate transaction. . . .

ii. 2. Since such functioning is actually necessary to any
beauty at all, just as necessary as the relatively permanent
properties of the prospect, it also seems reasonable to say
that the same object perceived by the same person may
at one time be beautiful and at another time not.[1] . . .

iv. 1. Primitive art gives us examples of the free expression in graphic forms of those inner images and
feelings and emotions that could be externalized in the
exciting and significant details of the represented objects
themselves. And primitive life offers a still purer form of
art, where the very ground of it ceases to be either useful
objects or acts or the familiar objects of experience lending
themselves as subjects of representation to express in
peace and at home the dangers and thrills of fighting
and hunting. For there appear to be spontaneous activities not explicitly useful or even consciously directed,
such as the production of sounds by the human throat
and movements of the human body in general, which are
still natural, and which in themselves give relief or pleasure and express emotions for their own sake. . . . In
primitive art we find that active aesthetic experience in
its genuine and simple actuality is first of all expressive.

iv. 3. If certain qualities of sound are, so far as psychology knows, among the very few genuinely natural
sources of fear, this may remind us that those sounds
simply carry fearfulness as their felt nature to any ears
and minds that belong to bodies developed through long
ages to be human beings.

vi. 1. Colour is, of course, expressive too; but while, for
example, red is vaguely warm, and green is cool and thin,
sharp, high-pitched tones are directly exciting and rolling
low ones directly ominous.[2] . . .

x. 1. It is only as works of art give specification—not
linguistic names or any other sort of symbol merely, but

[1] Cf. Xenophon, p. 2, Ross, p. 318.   [2] Cf. Aristotle, p. 35, Leon, p. 291.

actual present determination for direct sense-perception —to human feelings, emotions, desires, and satisfactions, embodied in the sensuous surface and felt upon it as being its character and quality—only so do they share in the nature of actual concrete works of art.

x. 3. It is obviously in music proper that a completely satisfactory aesthetic auditory surface is perfect art. But this is not at all the case with poetry. Not even the beauty of poetry is mainly auditory; for poetry, being intelligible language after all, intends to function as all language functions, not merely to produce an aesthetically satisfying surface for the ear, subtle and important as that sounding-surface is in heightening its value and even in defining it as verse, and absorbing as this surface is to some artists, whose practice tries to make patterned syllables the whole content of poetic art.[1] If it is sweet syllables that poetry discourses, poetry is still symbolic linguistic discourse; its syllables carry meaning and reference. Between these extremes lie the other arts. It has become fashionable in modern discussion and criticism to discount entirely from the value of drawings and paintings and sculpture their representative intent.[2] . . . Even when the most enlightened artist, working for purely aesthetic effect, in terms of sensuous and formal beauty of surface, uses familiar natural forms, no matter how modified or even distorted, as in the manner of so-called primitivism, these forms are those given in nature and necessarily recognized as such by any innocent eyes that see them. . . . What, after all, either of sensuous elements or structural forms, is to be found even in the imagination of a genius that has not been given him through nature? Not that he merely copies what faces him—a flat impossibility in any full literal sense—but that all the form and content at his disposal has been offered him in the life, and on nature's surface. . . . To attempt to free art of some of its delight, in order to keep it purely aesthetic, is a new kind of fanatical asceticism

---

[1] Cf. Bradley, p. 226.   [2] Cf. Bell, p. 264.

no more to be respected as reasonable or sane than more ancient or familiar kinds. . . . There is no reason in the nature of things why subjects before a camera may not have expended upon them the whole power and skill of a great artist, or why, for the preservation of his vision of them, a camera of sufficient delicacy and contrivance might not be the best means. . . .

x. 5. A work of art may have a lovely sensuous aesthetic surface as form and structure for direct intuition, and reveal in this structure the technical nature of the processes that have produced it; but, if it is a work of the human spirit, a work of art functions also in expressing that spirit's feelings and emotions of desire and satisfaction. The beauty of poetry is clearly dependent for its depth and power on this function that it performs. But this expressive functioning does not take place through linguistic symbolism alone, which is common to verse and the least artistic prose discourse, but also through its whole artistic character, including its strictly aesthetic surface, which by means of sounds and rhythms is a verbal and auditory specification of the exact emotional effect that it embodies and thus expresses. And the vitality and life of art and of its aesthetic surface depend almost wholly upon this expressiveness. If the 'significant form' of modern critics has any meaning, this is it.[1] . . . And of all the arts, perhaps music is in the matter of emotional expressiveness the deepest and richest, of the widest range and greatest power, as well as the most flexible and most delicately precise. . . . If a composer has no emotions to express, no vital feelings to externalize in sound, the best that he can do is to repeat more or less conventional or banal patterns.[2] . . .

xi. 5. If one had to define lonely grandeur, or bizarre opulence, or studious quiet,[3] in anything but other phrases, if one had finally to point to data in perception upon the surface of which such characters or qualities are

---

[1] Cf. Bell, p. 264.   [2] Cf. Herbart, p. 156, and Hanslick, p. 180.
[3] Cf. Leon, p. 284.

discernible, one could hardly find better or more precise specifications of them than works of architecture[1] or particular features of such works.

CURT JOHN DUCASSE
1881–

The Philosophy of Art (1929)

viii. 9. *Aesthetic*, in these pages, is used to mean, *having to do with feelings obtained through contemplation.* . . . Any object is to be called beautiful when, or in so far as, the feelings which one obtains in the aesthetic contemplation of it are pleasurable feelings. . . .

On the other hand, a work of aesthetic art, being simply the consciously achieved objectification of a feeling, will not be beautiful unless the feeling objectified in it, and reflected by it in contemplation, is a pleasurable feeling.

xi. 5. An *aesthetic symbol* of anger, i.e. an aesthetic object embodying anger, would be, among the sorts of things which are evidences of anger, any situation allowing, or still better, inviting aesthetic contemplation, and such as to yield through it to us the 'taste' of anger,—not the mere intellectual information . . . *that* some one is angry. Such a situation might consist merely in the *representation* of behaviour 'empathically' evidencing anger (rather than in the actual *presentation* of such behaviour, which might make impossible the contemplative attitude); for instance, it might consist in the representation of a scowling face, or of the speeches of an angry man, such as those of Achilles in his quarrel with Agamemnon. . . .

6. Associations, of course, affect the feeling experienced, and are variable. But associations are *internal to the aesthetic object*, not external; and this means that when the associations of some entity change, the aesthetic object (consisting as it does of the entity *and* its associations) itself has changed.[2] . . .

xii. 2. Feeling is aesthetic feeling whenever its status is

[1] Cf. Herbart, *Encyclopaedia*, 72, p. 156.   [2] Cf. Moore, p. 247.

neither that of a mere incitement to or accompaniment or result of practical activity, nor that of an accessory or by-product of cognition, but is, on the contrary, the status of something being sought or entertained for itself, and simply 'tasted'. The aesthetic feelings are not qualitatively different from the non-aesthetic, and this involves that there is no sort of feeling which may not on occasion acquire the aesthetic status, or which art may not attempt to objectify.

xiii. 1. Although form and content are inseparable in fact, our attention may focus on one of the two and relegate the other to the margin of consciousness, thereby subordinating that other to a condition sometimes approaching that of non-existence. The possibility of thus 'giving the centre of the stage' to the form-aspect of the object, and of the apprehending in contemplation its import of aesthetic feeling, is well recognized by the formalists. But they overlook the fact that in a precisely similar way the *content*, instead of the form, may be made to occupy the focus of attention and be contemplated; and that it, too, is then found to have a definite feeling-import of its own. Normally, however, the attention tends to take in both form and content rather than to centre upon one to the virtual exclusion of the other.[1] . . .

xv. 3. The most common form of criticism of works of art is criticism in terms of beauty and ugliness. The terms beautiful and ugly, however, have no meaning whatever in terms of the creating artist's point of view, but only in terms of the spectator or 'consumer', whether he be the artist himself later contemplating and evaluating his creation, or some one else. That which is evaluated in terms of beauty and ugliness is therefore not at all the work of art as such, viz. as product of the artist's endeavour to give his feeling embodiment in an object, but only the object itself that the spectator contemplates, and wholly without reference to the question whether that object is a product of art or of nature.[2]

[1] Cf. Bradley, p. 221.   [2] Cf. Tolstoy, p. 193, Santayana, p. 204.

On the other hand, criticism of a work of art, considered as such, would be concerned solely with the measure of success or failure of the art, i.e. of the artist's attempt consciously to objectify his feeling. It is obvious, however, that no one but the artist himself is in a position to say whether, or how far, he has succeeded in creating an object adequately embodying his feeling. The test of the success of his attempt at objectification, as we have seen, is whether the object created does, in contemplation, mirror back the feeling which he attempted to express. What that feeling was, however, is something which is known to no one but himself; and therefore he alone is in a position to perform the test. If the artist is able to say: 'Yes, this exactly reflects back to me the feeling I had', then the last word has been said *as to that*, i.e. as to the success of his attempt at objective expression of his feeling. It may quite properly be insisted, however, that success of that sort is something which is of interest to no one but himself, or, possibly, his mother or his wife. Conscious objectification of feeling, as defined by that test, may therefore be termed *private or individual objectification*, as distinguished from *social objectification*, the test of which would be the object's capacity to impart in contemplation the artist's feeling not merely back to himself, but on to others also. Criticism in terms of this test will be considered presently.

As already noted, however, the artist's *final* criticism at least, of his own work, is likely to be based not so much on the question whether the feeling which he finds he has objectified is exactly that which he attempted to objectify, as on the question whether, after thoroughly 'tasting' (through contemplation of his work) the feeling he has actually objectified, he finds it to be one that he is *willing to own*, i.e. to acknowledge as being really a part or aspect of his emotional self at the time. In other words, the question is whether the work he has created is one which he honestly feels he can sign.[1]

[1] Cf. Lipps, p. 257.

It is obvious that, again, no one but the artist himself is in a position to criticize his own work on that basis. Criticism of this sort would normally accompany criticism of the kind first mentioned, which passes on[1] the question of the sameness of the feeling actually objectified, and of the feeling which was to be objectified.

As pointed out earlier, this sameness obviously cannot be sameness in every respect, but only *qualitative* sameness. Such qualitative identity of the two feelings, however, leaves room for gain in clearness and vividness of the given quality of feeling, as a result of the process of objectification.[2] Such a gain in clearness and vividness beyond question occurs, but it is the only respect in which the feeling need become different through the process of objectification. Indeed, the qualitative identity of the feeling before and after objectification is an absolute prerequisite, if one is to be able to say that it is *that* feeling which has been clarified. That the feeling should be clear, however (in the sense in which it is possible for a feeling to become so), is in turn a prerequisite of criticism of one's work in terms of the second question mentioned above, namely, the question whether it constitutes objectification of an emotional self *truly one's own*.

It is perhaps unnecessary to point out in this connexion that approving on this basis the object that one has created is quite a different thing from finding it beautiful.[3] The pleasure which such approval does express is pleasure found, *not in the feeling* objectified by the work (which would be what would constitute the work of art beautiful), but *in the success* of one's attempt to objectify an aspect of one's emotional self; and this latter pleasure remains, whether the feeling objectified be a pleasurable or a painful one, i.e. whether the object created be beautiful or ugly. The difference is analogous to that between the pleasure of having succeeded in stating accurately some thought that one had, and the pleasure

---

[1] i.e. judges.   [2] cf. Nettleship, p. 188.
[3] cf. Santayana, p. 204.

(or displeasure) of finding true (or false), on reflection, the statement that one has made.

Criticism of a work of art (and equally of a natural object) on the basis of the question whether one is willing to *own* the feeling which it objectifies, is possible to others than the artist himself. The only difference is this. When the artist answers that question in the negative, he then proceeds to alter the object he has created until he finds himself able to say: 'Yes, the feeling which this now objectifies is truly a part of myself.'[1] But when the critic, on this basis, is some one else than the artist, that critic is then not trying to objectify his feeling himself, nor therefore is he called upon to make alterations in the object before him. His problem is simply to decide whether or not the thing before him objectifies a feeling that was his, or one that perhaps he had not yet experienced but that he is able and willing to call his. And, once more, this decision is one quite distinct from the question whether or not the feeling objectified is pleasant and the object therefore beautiful.

WILLIAM DAVID ROSS
1877–

The Right and the Good (1930)[2]

iii. Beauty is not a form of intrinsic value, but only the power in an object of evoking something that has value, the aesthetic experience.

iv. If we are right in holding that beauty is bound up with what is sensuous and that what is sensuous is at any rate partly dependent on a mind, can any account of beauty be given which will do justice to this fact and at the same time avoid the fatal objections which we have seen to arise against a purely subjective account of beauty,

[1] Cf. Lipps, p. 257.

[2] The Provost of Oriel introduces this discussion of beauty by reference to Professor Moore's argument in *Principia Ethica* and to Professor Perry's *General Theory of Value*. Cf. also Laird, p. 300, and Herbart, pp. 153-4.

i.e. one which identifies 'this is beautiful' with 'this arouses some particular feeling or opinion in some mind or minds'? The view to which I find myself driven, in the attempt to avoid the difficulties that beset both a purely objective and a purely subjective view, is one which identifies beauty with the *power* of producing a certain sort of experience in minds, the sort of experience which we are familiar with under such names as aesthetic enjoyment or aesthetic thrill. Does such a theory really escape the objections to a purely subjective theory? We shall see the position of affairs if we suppose first two people maintaining respectively that a certain object is beautiful and that it is not beautiful; and secondly two people maintaining respectively that an object is beautiful and that it is ugly. (1) When a man thinks an object to be beautiful, either he is holding an independent personal opinion, or he is judging the object to be beautiful out of deference to the opinion of some other person or persons. For brevity's sake I will omit the latter or conventional type of opinion, which raises no special difficulty, and concentrate on the former. Every independent opinion that an object is beautiful has for antecedent, it will be agreed, a feeling of enjoyment which either is, or is taken to be, aesthetic; there is no other basis for thinking an object beautiful than such an experience. Yet what the judger is judging is not that he has this experience. For (a) the judgement is a judgement about the object, not about the judger's state of mind. And (b) though we cannot judge an object to be beautiful till we think we have been aesthetically thrilled by it, we judge that it was beautiful before we were thrilled by it, and will be beautiful when we have ceased to be thrilled by it. The judgement, while it is not a judgement about the judger's state of mind, is one in which, on the strength of his knowledge of (or opinion about) his state of mind, he ascribes an attribute to an object. And if we ask ourselves what is the common attribute belonging to all beautiful objects, we can, I believe, find none other than the power of producing the kind of enjoyment known as aesthetic.[1]

Now observe the difference between this view and that which identifies 'this is beautiful' with 'this produces a certain feeling in me'. The latter view is open to the fatal objection that it leaves no real point at issue between the man who says 'this is beautiful' and the man who says 'no, it is not'; for it may well be true *both* that the object produces aesthetic enjoyment in one man *and* that it does not produce it in the other. But if one is in effect saying 'the object has it in it to produce aesthetic enjoyment in any one sufficiently capable of feeling such', there is a question really at issue between him and one who says 'no, it has not'.

That this is no unnatural account of the question at issue between them may be seen by considering separately the two cases in which the person who asserts the object to be beautiful is right, and is wrong, respectively. (*a*) When he is right, he is actually having or has had genuine aesthetic enjoyment of the object; the other has had no such enjoyment and is inferring from this that the object has no power of producing such enjoyment in any one. But the actual occurrence of the enjoyment depends on conditions in the experient as well as on conditions in the object. While his own lack of susceptibility or of aesthetic education is at fault, he is supposing that the conditions in the *object* are not those required for aesthetic enjoyment.

(*b*) When the man who pronounces the object beautiful is wrong, what is happening is that he is receiving *some* kind of pleasurable thrill from the object, confusing this with aesthetic enjoyment, and on the strength of this

---

[1] I think, however, that it must be admitted (and this is, for what it is worth, an objection to the view suggested) that we do not *mean* by 'beautiful' an attribute having even this sort of reference to a mind, but something entirely resident in the object, apart from relation to a mind. What I am suggesting is that we are deceived in thinking that beautiful things have any such common attribute over and above the power of producing aesthetic enjoyment. [W. D. R.]

mistake wrongly attributing to the object the power of producing the aesthetic thrill.

(2) When one person pronounces an object beautiful and another pronounces it *ugly*, there are, I think it must be admitted, four possibilities. The first person alone may be right, or the second alone be right, while the other is mistaking some other emotion for aesthetic repulsion or enjoyment, or making a conventional judgement based on his opinion that some one else thinks the object ugly or beautiful. Thirdly, both may be wrong, both making the sort of mistake that in the first two cases one of them has made. But fourthly, it appears that both may conceivably be right. For when we consider how beauty is bound up with sense-perception, and how dependent sense-perception is on our equipment of sense-organs, it seems not improbable that owing to differences in the sense-organs of different individuals, or of different races, the same object may produce (or minister to) genuine aesthetic enjoyment in one individual or race and genuine aesthetic repulsion in another. And if so, the same object will be both beautiful and ugly; whether we think this probable or not, it seems clear that it cannot be ruled out as impossible. And to this extent our ordinary ideas about beauty and ugliness require revision; for we certainly in general mean by 'beautiful' and 'ugly' attributes which cannot belong to the same thing[1] (i.e. to the same thing taken as a whole; we well know that some *elements* in a thing may be beautiful and others ugly).

In a sense, then, beauty is perfectly objective. An object may be beautiful though no one has ever felt or will ever feel its beauty, provided that there is some mind which if confronted with it would get aesthetic enjoyment from it, or could be so educated as to get such enjoyment. The further question may be asked, whether there could be beauty in a world in which there were no minds at all. If it is possible for a mind to *come into being* in such a world (a question on which I offer no opinion), there too there

[1] Cf. Xenophon, p. 2.

might be beauty; for an object in a mindless universe might be such as to produce aesthetic enjoyment in some mind which might come into existence.[1] So far the theory is purely objective; but in so far as it holds beauty to be indefinable except by reference to a possible effect on a mind, and to involve a certain relation between the nature of the object and that of mind (or of some mind), our theory might be called subjective. And its objectivity in the one sense seems to be quite compatible with its subjectivity in the other.

Finally we may ask whether beauty is an intrinsic value. Apparently we must say that it is not. For even if it be held that beauty might exist in a mindless universe, there is no reason for regarding the beautiful things in such a universe as having any value in themselves. Their value would be solely instrumental to the production of aesthetic enjoyment in such minds as might later come into being. Aesthetic enjoyment is good in itself, and beauty is valuable simply as productive of it; in any assignment of intrinsic value to a mindless universe or to anything in it there is a surreptitious introduction of a subjective factor, namely of oneself imagined as contemplating such a universe or the things in it.[2]

GIOVANNI GENTILE
1875–
The Philosophy of Art (1931)

GENTILE claims that his philosophy is the only true idealism, and it is certainly uncompromising. It allows of no object (God, Absolute, History, Nature, or Minds) transcending the actual thinking activity (*pensiero pensante*) which alone is real and which is development. The life or being of this reality consists in the activity by which it distinguishes or creates within itself a subject or self and an object (God, Nature, History, other Minds). The results of this distinction or creation, taken to exist (as they do not) outside the thinking activity which generates or distinguishes them are 'dead thought' (*pensiero*

[1] Cf. Hutcheson, p. 72.   [2] Cf. Moore, p. 251.

pensato). They are then forms of error. But error is only error for the thinking act which distinguishes it as error. Consequently beauty cannot be anything presented to thought from outside; nor can it be any 'expression' other than thinking itself; nor can what is expressed or thought be feeling or any subject matter other than thought itself. So the problem of aesthetics for this philosophy of immanence is to justify or explain our distinction between the aesthetic and scientific or philosophic experiences. Beauty is the identical form of subjective feeling given to any thought.

Introduction ii. 4. Men have excluded from the creative activity of the human mind all those logical and ethical values with which is welded together the whole fabric of civilization: they have thought that without the aid of some higher power, however it might be conceived, mortals could not find in themselves the source from which might flow the truths and values which are the light and warmth of their life. And yet in every age men have believed that they must be conceded a certain power to create a world, not indeed firm and solid as reality itself, but yet able to reflect that reality: a power to create men and things not identically like the men and things of nature created by God, but worthy to be compared with them. These were works of art.[1]

iii. 1. One of the first prejudices from which philosophy has to free us is that there are, within the mansion of the spirit, different apartments or storeys, accessible no doubt from one another for the agile, but separate and distinct, each with its own place. This is a materialistic prejudice. . . . The mistake of this kind made by Vico[2] is well known; he was a zealous champion of 'pure reason' against the materialized thought embodied in imagination; he was never weary of warning us against the dangers of fancy.

i. i. 6. The difference between historical facts and a work of art is that for any historical fact, properly so called, it is always possible in actual thought to assign a perspective, giving it its chronological place and such other determina-

---

[1] Cf. Cicero, p. 36, Bacon, p. 55.   [2] Cf. p. 73.

tions, according to its nature, as belong to its individuality. But for the work of art such a perspective is rendered impossible by the peculiar fusion and identification of the subject knowing with the object known. And this peculiar form results from the essential nature of the work of art.

A poem is a single word; a whole, infinite and absolute. It is neither a part of a greater whole, nor has it parts of its own.[1] Whence it follows that, if we succeed in entering into it, or, to speak more simply, in *reading* it, we may indeed break off and go on to other poems and other thoughts (for we still may know that in the depths of our hearts other interests are active than that which led us to read this poem); but this breaking off cannot be a continuous progress like that from one verse to another within the poem, or from one chapter or volume to another of the same treatise, or even from one treatise to another on the same subject. . . .

Here we begin to notice a strange resemblance of art, which is an activity of the spirit when it is most awake and most clear-sighted, to dreaming, which is the unguided free play of sleeping thought. Art, it is well known, has often been compared with dreaming; not, as has been asserted by recent writers, because in both alike the spirit rests rapt in pure contemplation without asking, still less deciding, whether or not the world it contemplates is real; but simply because there is no continuity between our dreaming and waking experience. Otherwise, indeed, the two experiences are identical.[2] In our judgements during the alleged aesthetic contemplation of dreaming we find the same activity of assertion as in those from which we construct the reality and the facts of our waking experience. . . .

9. If a dream could be written down it would be poetry; and many poets, from Dante onwards, have found no better way of describing the ideal character of their poetry than by calling it a dream or vision. Yet this same unreality or ideality, when contemplated in the

---

[1] Cf. Leon, p. 288.　　　　　[2] Cf. Richards, p. 277.

light of imagination, is a living, present reality. . . . Art for the artist, while he remains an artist, is life itself, and therefore not art; just as the dream is no dream to the sleeper. In short, as the dream would not be a dream but for a higher form of experience which contains it, and by rising above it judges it, so we can only speak of art in a judgement about it which is not art. The canvas of art can only be seen enclosed in a frame, and it is the canvas not the frame which is art. . . .

10. The artistic element of a work of art does not exhaust all that the work contains, but only covers so much as remains when we have made abstraction of the elements of criticism, reflection, and, in general, of conscious thought. Yet this residuum is only ideally distinguishable, in fact it cannot be separated from the entire body of the work.

ii. 1. Art is indeed in the spirit and in the living spirit (in the spirit therefore of the man who is reading a poem, when it is being read, and not in that of the author who wrote it[1]); but within this whole we must strip off from the spirit its living form, which is that of thought, reflection, judgement, in order to discover ideally the true and peculiar essence of pure art.

3. The form of art, which every man recognizes from his own experience, or to speak more exactly, the form of certain products or experiences of the spirit which have artistic value, is the form of the Ego as pure subject. But if we tried to lay our hands on this form as a concrete existence, it would be proved, as we have said, to be a vain shadow. Yet it reveals itself in experience in the medium of the whole creative act of thought, which besides being pure subjectivity, is also pure objectivity. . . .

We all know the famous saying of Kant[2] that intuitions without conceptions are blind and thoughts without content empty; and consequently we all know that, according to him, we do not find in experience intuitions on the one hand and conceptions on the other, but that

---

[1] Cf. p. 330, and Bradley, p. 209. [2] *Critique of Pure Reason* (2nd ed.), 75.

all experience is a synthesis *a priori* of these two terms, as we find it in the judgement. And since we have mentioned Kant we may also mention Baumgarten[1] and his *scientia cognitionis sensitivae*, which he was the first to call *Aesthetic*, and which he contrasted with logic, the science of intellectual cognition;—as if it were possible to have a sensuous cognition without intellectual elements....

5. In the first place it is false to distinguish art and scientific knowledge as having different objects, namely, the particular (or individual) and the universal. Aristotle[2] in the *Poetics* already recognized that we always attribute to poetry a certain universality denied to historical narrative. In fact there is no artistic representation, however particular it may be, even a portrait, which does not lift the mind above that mortal world to which all particular things and men belong, by giving us a vision of something immortal, infinite and divine. And even the most abstract thoughts have often the power to move our souls by the profound feeling with which they have been thought and expressed. . . .

Secondly it is equally false to distinguish *imagination* and *understanding* as spiritual faculties or functions which answer to two different kinds of object or product of the spirit. . . . Imagination is neither a faculty nor a special function of that inner activity which is always thought, though different aspects may be distinguished in its development. . . . It is false to distinguish imagination and understanding as if the first were the thought of something non-existent, freely created by the spirit, and the second were the thought of the true or existent which binds the mind and confines it within objective limits. . . . It is false to distinguish the objects of imagination and those of pure thought as if the first were sensuous bodies and capable of being represented in space while the latter were not. . . . The only body which can be thought, as that round which and with which every other body forms a single physical system, is *our own*, which is a body

---

[1] Cf. p. 84. [2] Cf. p. 32.

just so far as it is felt, not felt because it is a body. And its bodily nature is nothing but that spontaneous and fundamental feeling through which the Ego constructs and affirms itself—the bodily nature of the Ego, which must therefore always be present, since the Ego is always present. The violence with which a thought is affirmed —what we call excitement or emotion—is proportionate not to the connexion of that thought with bodies supposed to operate on our souls through the senses, but to the amount of self, so to speak, which the Ego puts into the thought. . . . The objects of imagination are indeed 'bodily'; not in that absurd sense which opposes one body to another and would separate the spirit from things and even from other spirits, but with the intimate and fundamental bodily nature of the Ego, which extends from so-called sensations (which are thoughts directed towards spatial and temporal things) to the purest ideas of things infinite and eternal.

6. That then which has been called the *material* or *subject-matter* of art is something outside the world of art[1] though inseparably joined to it. It is in fact thought— thought of anything whatever, representation and re-flection united, as all thought is—image and judgement in one. And poetry or art consists wholly in the form which this material takes on. . . .

7. The form of art is not identical with the form of thinking, for art, as we have seen, is not thought but prior to thought. Art is the soul of thought, not the body: that pure soul which we distinguish as being the *principle* of life, out of which the living thing draws its whole being and makes itself an actual body: the principle in which and by which we really live. This soul in itself, prior to the body which it animates, is the unique form in which art consists.

8. Natural beauty has been and is spoken of in two senses, in both of which the attempt is made to escape a contradiction in terms and to avoid the absurdity of

[1] Cf. Bradley, p. 214.

assigning value to mechanical products. Either we attribute to nature an internal purpose[1] which spiritualizes
it as if it were a rudimentary form of spirit—and then
natural beauty turns out to be the work of a mighty art
which achieves its triumphs before the appearance of
spirit proper, the human spirit. Or else nature is regarded
as a mirror in which we think we read human feelings[2]—
and then beauty belongs not to unconscious nature but
to the man who sees in a landscape the reflection or
expression of his own state of mind. . . . Both meanings
are inadmissible, because of their philosophical presuppositions. We can justify neither the notion of a
nature which, though not itself spirit, is yet guided by
an internal purpose; nor yet that kind of dualism in
which the spirit is opposed to an external nature that
limits it, a dualism which can thus think of accidental
coincidences and correspondences between the two kinds
of reality.[3]

iv. 1. If we are to use popular language, this pure subjective form of every thought, in which art consists, can
only be *feeling*. Yet it is feeling not in the ordinary
psychological sense but in one strictly philosophical.

v. 1. Art then is shown by our inquiry to be not, as some
have said,[4] the expression or intuition of feeling but
feeling itself. The well-known doctrine which defined art
in the former way struggled long and vainly for a theory
by which art should be distinguished from philosophy and
yet share with it in the nature of the theoretic spirit. But
it never succeeded in exchanging that doctrine of aesthetic subject-matter from which it had started for that
doctrine of aesthetic form at which it aimed. It began in
distinguishing the theoretical activity of art from the
theoretical activity of philosophy by distinguishing their

---

[1] Cf. Kant, *Critique of Judgement*, Part II, and p. 122 above.

[2] Cf. Ruskin, p. 179; Croce, p. 244.

[3] Cf. II. i. 10 'Wherever thought rests and gathers up in its synthesis the
vibration of the soul, that soul invades the thought itself with the force, the
energy, the life of soul itself. And there is beauty.'

[4] Cf. Croce, p. 243.

subject-matters as particular and universal. It ends in differentiating the intuitive form of knowledge, supposed to be peculiar to art, by allotting it a special subject-matter called feeling, from which the lyrical character of art could be derived. But such a difference of subject-matter cannot be resolved into a difference of form. For the author of this doctrine gave to feeling an existence of its own, independent of its function as material of art. Feeling was, for him, in its vague obscurity, that practical activity of spirit which he held to be as real as its theoretical activity. So art came to be conceived dualistically. It was verbally defined as a synthesis, but it was impossible to see such a synthesis as creative *a priori*. It was a mere result of adding the intuitive form to the subject-matter of feeling. First there was the feeling and then the vision of this feeling; as if such immediate vision could be possible, or indeed any spiritual activity could be directed upon an object already existent.

2. What is called a work of art (poem, symphony, picture, statue), just so far as it is a work of art, is closed within itself, incomparable with any other. For its artistic character is to be found in the feeling that animates it, in the soul that governs it and that makes us feel something inwardly alive, for which our hearts beat with that secret passion which is the very passion of life. This feeling, which underlies every distinction, is indistinguishably one and without parts. Yet at the same time it is the whole. Nothing is outside it, and all that comes to light in the life of the spirit must be born of it and be its offspring. . . .[1]

7. Thus we attain a clearer idea of beauty as a property of feeling or of the self. For we love all that is beautiful, and what we love is properly that intimate nature of the self which is called feeling. We love art and all works of art; we love all products or productive activities of spirit, because there is no such activity but thought. And there is no concrete thought, that is to say no thought

[1] Cf. Plotinus, p. 49, Croce, p. 243.

which any one thinks, which is not the thought of a feeling. It is like a body which is only alive because it contains a soul that feels and makes itself felt (if we are not too obtuse) in every part of the body. And we attain a clearer idea of art as the activity which creates beauty, for it is now clear that this is the very same activity in which thought consists. . . .

Within the synthesis of thought we shall necessarily always find the three elements: the subject, the object, and their relation. Thought consists in the relation, but within the relation there is the object and first of all the subject. Of this subject the relation must be born, it does not descend from heaven. Thus every man is a man; that is, he is thought; but first of all he is an artist, which is as much as to say that he has a soul and exhibits it in thinking. Within the synthesis of thought, as within every other, we can analyse. But analysis, we must always remember, is the analysis of a synthesis. . . . As a result of this analysis we can see all the history of the spirit, in its singularity, completeness, and indivisibility (that fragment of history, ever capable of extension, to which our horizon is limited) from the point of view of the pure subject. We can see in every work of the spirit a work of art, and in the total work of the spirit also, which is history itself, a work of art. . . . Art is the whole spirit from the point of view of art.

10. The author[1] who has recently identified aesthetic with the science of language was led to do so by his dualistic doctrine, already described, of a form understood as the expression of a subject-matter immediately given and so preceding the expressive activity. . . .

II. i. 1. To look for feeling (in accent, tone, expression, and the like) outside the elements in which the feeling is realized would be to grasp at a shadow. We should reach at last that pure feeling, prior to thought, which is in fact nothing. Accent is in discourse and is the accent of discourse. . . . Therefore we hold that language is feeling

[1] Croce.

and is also thought; the one in so far only as it is the other.

8. Feeling differentiates itself concretely by thought. But when we consider, and so far as we have occasion to consider, the creation of the spirit as a work of art, we see that it seems always the same feeling, always the same soul. Whatever be the subject on which one of our friends talks to us, he is always himself, recognizable in the tone of his voice.

ii. 1. The world of the thinker and of the man of action is a laborious construction. But the world of the poet is the soul that underlies any such construction: that feeling which is identical in every man, on the royal throne and in the meanest hovel, in the mind of the erudite theologian and in the heart of the pious lady, in the learned universities and the embrace of lovers, in joy and in pain. No matter if, to get back to this soul and fundamental feeling of mankind, we may have to read books and understand them and, for that purpose, to study with learning and with diligence, and, in short, to undertake after all the labour of thinking; . . . art does not *consist* in thought, but in that moment when the mind returns to the thrill of simple feeling . . . and we find that in the end we are all of us men.[1]

7. The artist, like the critic, must rise above his subject-matter and come into confident possession of his technique, so that, when he sings or paints, he simply translates into objective representations (in self-consciousness) nothing else but his own feeling, in which all the rest is united and fused. When he has succeeded in dissolving the world in his pure subjectivity, that is to say in feeling it, then only can he express it, drawing from himself what has flowed into him, and analysing in the light of consciousness the dim and formless matter within him, the mere feeling. . . .

9. Everything is art so far as everything is feeling. . . . But pure or abstract art, mere ideal subjectivity has no existence. . . . Art is the form of a subject-matter; it is the

[1] Cf. Tolstoy, p. 193.

feeling which has a definite being of its own as the subject experiencing a certain world; it is the feeling of a personality which, as body and thought, includes everything within itself.

iv. 9. The ugly can be nothing but the expression of feelings into which a man has not put the whole of himself; that is to say, superficial feelings not profoundly felt. For that lack of seriousness (seriousness which is as necessary to art as to morality), that frivolity and giddiness which give birth to whimsical, extravagant, sentimental, rhetorical, or erotic art, arise simply from want of feeling. Where there is feeling there is everything; it is as universal and infinite as the soul whose essence it is.[1] And this universality and infinity of feeling is the humanity of true art, which, in expressing the most secret heart of every individual, turns out to be what is most intimate to the hearts of all men, without limit of time or place. Thus it makes all men brothers by uniting them in a single soul.[2]

v. 3. In a work of art the feeling is everything. For the feeling is the form in which the subject-matter is fused and transfigured . . . When the poet said 'The gods die, but our hymns to them live', what he said was not strictly true. . . . The poet's hymn lives only while we sing it, when by appreciation we overcome its subject-matter and reach its form. But to reach this goal we must pass through the subject-matter. And it forbids our passage if we put into the words which formulate its message for us a thought different from the poet's thought, from his conception of the world, from his religious faith or, in short, from that complex idiosyncrasy which made up his concrete feeling. . . .[3] The critic who still distinguishes a subject-matter, with a value of its own, from the form with which it is identified, and from which alone it gets form and actuality, is still upon the threshold of art and has not the key to unlock the door. The truth is that if the hymns live, the gods live too: they live in the hymns.

[1] Cf. Croce, p. 244.   [2] Cf. Tolstoy, p. 193.   [3] Cf. p. 323.

ROBERT BRIDGES

1844–1930

The Testament of Beauty (1929)

ii. 842–7.

Beauty is the highest of all these occult influences,
the quality of appearances that thru' the sense
wakeneth spiritual emotion in the mind of man:
And Art, as it createth new forms of beauty,
awakeneth new ideas that advance the spirit
in the life of Reason to the wisdom of God.

·　　·　　·　　·　　·　　·

iv. 1439–41.

God is seen as the very self-essence of love,
Creator and mover of all as activ Lover of all,
self-express'd in not-self, without which no self were.

INDEX

[Where a subject is treated continuously on consecutive pages the first only is given. 'Beauty 'in the subject-entries is abbreviated as B.]